Baseball in
Territorial Arizona

Baseball in Territorial Arizona
A History, 1863–1912

JOHN DARRIN TENNEY

McFarland & Company, Inc., Publishers
Jefferson, North Carolina

LIBRARY OF CONGRESS CATALOGUING-IN-PUBLICATION DATA

Names: Tenney, John Darrin, author.
Title: Baseball in territorial Arizona : a history, 1863–1912 / John Darrin Tenney.
Description: Jefferson, North Carolina : McFarland & Company, Inc., Publishers. | Includes bibliographical references and index.
Identifiers: LCCN 2016007848 | ISBN 9780786496105 (softcover : acid free paper) ∞
Subjects: LCSH: Baseball—Arizona—History. | Arizona—History—To 1912.
Classification: LCC GV863.A72 T46 2016 | DDC 796.35709791—dc23
LC record available at http://lccn.loc.gov/2016007848

BRITISH LIBRARY CATALOGUING DATA ARE AVAILABLE

**ISBN (print) 978-0-7864-9610-5
ISBN (ebook) 978-1-4766-2144-9**

© 2016 John D. Tenney. All rights reserved

No part of this book may be reproduced or transmitted in any form or by any means, electronic or mechanical, including photocopying or recording, or by any information storage and retrieval system, without permission in writing from the publisher.

On the cover: 4th Cavalry baseball club of Fort Huachuca at Fort Lowell on December 3, 1887 (Arizona Historical Society)

Printed in the United States of America

*McFarland & Company, Inc., Publishers
Box 611, Jefferson, North Carolina 28640
www.mcfarlandpub.com*

Table of Contents

Preface	1
Introduction and Acknowledgments	3
1. Uncle Sam Brings the Game Westward	9
2. The Red Stockings Are Here! (Or Were They?)	37
3. Town Rivalries Take Shape	52
4. Women and Minorities on the Diamond	99
5. The Company Nine	125
6. The Barnstormers	153
7. Summary	171
Appendix A. List of Active Arizona Territorial Newspapers, 1863 to 1912	177
Appendix B. Chronological List of Base Ball Clubs During the Territorial Period	178
Chapter Notes	180
Bibliography	184
Index	186

Preface

This book presents the history of baseball in the Arizona Territory between 1863 and 1912. I became interested in researching this topic after reading through the *Mining Towns to Major Leagues: A History of Arizona Baseball*, published by the Society for American Baseball Research (SABR) in conjunction with its 1999 annual convention, held in Scottsdale.

I am proudly a member of the Flame Delhi Chapter of SABR, made up of members from throughout Arizona. Upon glancing through this publication, I noticed it was merely a collection of articles, with each one being less than five pages long. The first article, "Baseball in the Arizona Territory, 1863–1912," was written by historian Jeb Stuart Rosebrook. After reading its four pages with much interest, I came away with more questions than the article had answered. I was determined to expand on the material presented, in a way that would broaden a reader's understanding of the subject matter but in an entertaining way. Eventually I decided to write a book.

As a starting point, I consulted broad topical resources such as the *Historical Atlas of Arizona,* second edition, written by Henry P. Walker and Don Bufkin, to draw necessary clues as to the early towns and military posts of Arizona. With this beginning, I turned to the historic newspapers of the territory on microfilm, held by the Arizona State Library and Archives, Arizona Historical Society and Arizona State University, to get a more detailed picture of the development of baseball in Arizona's formative years. I also searched through these institutions for other documents such as photographs, letters and personal journal writings of early Arizonans in an attempt to understand who they were, what their chief concerns and motivations were during this time period, and what life was like for them in and around baseball. I have taken what has been written, with the aim of expanding the scope of research to include all the early towns and military posts in the state. Hopefully, this work represents the next step in bringing the story of early Arizonans to life in a way that paints a different picture. Arizona was more than the stereotypical "gunfight at the O.K. corral" image that has been in place in the minds of many for so long.

I have looked at special, historical games in Arizona that exist only in photographs to paint a vivid picture of the earliest days of the territory as told through baseball. Taking this approach to explore the details of the photos, I have aimed to expand our understanding of what was going on besides the game.

The Arizona Territory was a growing place, much more than what we've grown up knowing about the gunfights and Indian raids. The people who moved to the territory were very much like we are now, minus the widespread technology. I hope this book will serve as a reminder that baseball was and still is a favored pastime in the Grand Canyon State.

Introduction and Acknowledgments

   This is the story of the national game of baseball as it was played by the soldiers, miners, farmers, ranch hands, pioneers, students, newspaper men and other settlers of the Arizona Territories from 1863 to 1912. I will attempt to tell their story and weave the fabric of a tale that deserves to be told in a true and accurate light—or as close as I can get to recounting the past faithfully and correctly. The national game of baseball, originally spelled as two words until the early 20th century, was the vehicle used by communities to bring themselves together during holidays, celebrations and any other time a good ball game was sought between two opposing ball clubs by the locals, or cranks, who followed them. This book is also a candid tale about how the game was brought west by the United States Army, the integration of the game into local schools and communities, and crossing boundaries of race, creed, religion and gender.

   While I have tried to make the narrative complete as possible, the whole story may never be told. Much of the history and records that marked the players, places and games that were played between the settlers of the Arizona Territories have been either lost, destroyed or remain hidden and therefore shrouded in mystery. Sadly, there are no living persons available to draw even second- or third-hand eyewitness accounts from through direct interviews. There will no doubt be many conclusions and inevitable gaps left to be filled in the narrative that is their story—and, in a unique way, our own as benefactors over the succeeding generations.

   What has been unearthed represents a unique view of Arizona's past. The most rewarding thing about doing this research has been looking back into the pages of history in an honest attempt to understand how the early pioneers of the Arizona Territories lived their lives. I have included plenty of photographs, newspaper excerpts, and journal/diary entries that mark a faithful representation of the diverse people and places in baseball's history in this exceptional place I am proud to call home.

I would like to start by expressing a sincere word of thanks to a few people who have inspired me, as well as to those who have lent their time and expertise. Those people are many, but in the event that I forget any of you in the forthcoming pages—it is not my intent in doing so. First, I would like to thank the library staff of the Arizona Historical Society at Papago Park, namely Rebekah Tabah, Susan Irwin and Linda Whitaker. Their kind efforts in helping me locate documents and other types of source materials were the starting point of a long journey of research. Their assistance and sincere friendship has been remarkable. Secondly, I would like to thank the staff of the Special Collections and Archives of the Hayden Library at Arizona State University. Third, I thank the members of the Flame Delhi Chapter of the Society for American Baseball Research. SABR has been an invaluable resource and has provided much-needed advice, support and avenues of research that I would not have access to otherwise.

Of the many museums and libraries I had the fortune to visit, and the correspondence with the curators and archivists that staff them, there are none finer than the Museum Technician of the Fort Huachuca Museum—Mr. Stephen C. Gregory. He has been a constant source of support, and without him the history behind the soldiers who served at Fort Huachuca would not be where it is now. I sincerely thank him for his efforts and passion for this history.

I would also like to thank the many ballists and other persons who make up the Arizona Territories Vintage Base Ball League. The ATVBBL has been a great joy to participate in, as well as watch grow and prosper, as both a ballist and arbiter. I have made many lasting and genuine friendships with fellow 19th Century baseball enthusiasts within this special organization that thrives in Arizona and in other clubs and similar leagues nationwide. Among them, Herb Clark has been a big source of inspiration and assistance. Without his guidance, the league would not be where it is today. My former club-mate and friend, Mike Dietrich, has been a great source of knowledge and constructive criticism about the manuscript and research. His understanding of the history of the game in its entirety, as well as the evolution of equipment, is nothing short of colossal. His comprehension, and the willingness he has shown to share that knowledge, has been a great resource to rely upon, especially when identifying equipment used in photographs and the appropriate decades that the photos might be from. I am truly in his debt for such a wonderful friendship, one I sincerely hope will continue for many, many years.

Certainly not to be forgotten are Lance and Shelby Busch. They have done so much for the league and the advancement of education in baseball history across Arizona and have been a source of constant support, friendship and, at times, valuable research assistance. I would also like to thank my friends Tom Hansen, Bert Hunt and Dave Marli, all of whom have taken the time to listen to my many rants, raves and theories regarding the contents of this book and how I went about writing it. In my own close circle of friends, there is no one else who has the passion for baseball that matches my own besides Mike Anderson of Bisbee, Arizona. His dedication to the preservation of the Historic Warren Ballpark in Bisbee is both humbling and awe-inspiring. I marvel at his devotion and the energy he displays both in writing and talking about this special landmark. Mike has been a very good friend and mentor throughout this whole project. I am, and always will be, eternally grateful for his continued friendship.

My friends Melanie Tighe (a.k.a. Anna Questerly) and Thom Butcher deserve special recognition as fellow readers, authors and owners of a great book store—Dog Eared Pages in North Phoenix. They've helped me locate many books on 19th Century baseball to complete my own personal library on the subject while simultaneously offering a kind ear to listen to how this book has evolved into its final form. They're both some of the best people one could ever wish to know, and be friends with. I truly appreciate them and all the help that's been kindly offered.

Not to be forgotten is Jared Smith of the Tempe Museum of History. Jared has been a kind "sounding board" of sorts while doing research on local baseball clubs in the Salt River Valley area, as well as a good friend, making suggestions about the manuscript's direction and substance while lending a keen ear about the topics I have been researching. His assistance in locating documents has proven invaluable. Without him, there are parts of this book that simply would not exist. I am grateful for his friendship and dedication that have been pivotal to ensure this book sees the brilliant light of publication. He is a gem, a gentleman in the utmost sense of the word, and someone I am honored to call friend.

A special word of gratitude must be expressed to Shiela Stubler, manager of the Fort Verde State Historical Park. She has graciously helped locate additional documents, roster information and other biographical material that relates to the original Fort Verde Excelsiors baseball club of 1879. She has been instrumental in organizing vintage baseball matches as a part of the annual Fort Verde Days celebrations and History of the

Soldier events that have become an integral part of the history of the fort and local community of Camp Verde, Arizona. Her efforts have turned an event that was once looked upon as an oddity into a staple attraction for Northern Arizona in October and April of each year.

    I would also like to thank fellow author and historian Edward Achorn. Ed inspired me to tackle this work in a unique way, especially after reading his landmark book *59 in '84: Old Hoss Radbourn, Barehanded Baseball & The Greatest Season A Pitcher Ever Had.* Ed's representation of baseball history and engaging narrative in describing the people, places and matches that occurred during that epochal season have served as a true measure of what I've aimed for this work to become or even, in some ways, surpass. Ed has been so kind in offering support and advice about research and writing techniques.

    I'd like to offer a heartfelt thanks to the 13 wonderful friends who came forward to donate the funds necessary for photograph permission fees through a crowd-funding project launched through Facebook. I sincerely thank each and every one of them, and although not specifically named in this passage, they know who they are. Again, I thank and salute each and every one of you for the immense help. Without your kind donations, this work would not be what it is. I am honored to call each of you my extended family.

    Lastly, but certainly not forgotten, is my beloved wife and fellow baseball zealot, Julia. She has been a constant source of strength and patience through the duration of this project. She has been my cheering section and provides strength to continue the fight through the arduous and sometimes daunting periods of discouragement and frustration such a work naturally carries with it. She has patiently listened to the often wild and crazy tangents of seemingly unending angst and irritation while offering kind words of support and reassurance which proved to be the underlying strength needed to finish this book. Without her, this work would not exist let alone be where it is now. She's been a calm, soothing voice when at times I felt like scrapping the whole project out of sheer frustration. She has helped review research and in her own eclectic way has helped conduct some of the newspaper microfilm searches that compose a majority of this body of work. She has been a joy to travel with, talk to and watch Red Sox & Diamondbacks games with. I couldn't have asked for a better partner through this process. I look forward to many more seasons of baseball with her at my side, ready to talk about our beloved national pastime while opening packs of Topps baseball cards.

    In closing, a last but special dedication—I write this book in special memory of my father, who passed away after a brief battle with pancreatic cancer in April 2009. It was through his patient and loving hands that I received the passion and gift for playing, watching, and understanding the finer points of this beloved pastime we call baseball. The love I have for him is forever expressed through the many memories that will never fade through the passing of time, which ultimately transformed into the development of a deep love for baseball. It is to him, and his memory, that I dedicate this work. Any errors, omissions or other mistakes found in the following pages remain entirely my own.

I truly hope that you, my cherished reader, enjoy this excursion through time to relive the glorious past of the Arizona Territory as told on the many rudimentary baseball diamonds scattered throughout every part of the land. Enjoy what's to come.

Chapter 1

Uncle Sam Brings the Game Westward

Arizona is known for many things, among them citrus, copper, cattle, cotton and of course climate. Every spring thousands of baseball fans flock from around Arizona and from all corners of the United States to take in the various spring training games offered in February and March in the Cactus League, taking advantage of ideal pre-spring weather for watching baseball. The Detroit Tigers would first set up camp in Phoenix for spring training in 1929, well before the formation of the Cactus League in 1947, when both the Cleveland Indians and New York Giants established training camps in the Phoenix area. Long before that, however, baseball established itself as the state's first pastime amongst the many military posts and frontier towns of a young territory that was rapidly growing with mines, agriculture, transportation and commerce.

Military posts of the U.S. Army were firmly established in every corner of the Arizona Territory by 1870. A frontier soldier's life was not easy by any means. During the patrol duties and other assignments when in camp, boredom was a constant issue that confronted officers of any post. When soldiers were in camp, time weighed heavily upon their hands, as officers and enlisted men drilled, policed the grounds, and waited to be called upon to participate in various military actions across the territory. Officers, their wives, and their children created their own amusements to help pass the time. This would include cards, horseshoes, foot races, horse races, dances, banquets and other group activities. A new form of entertainment for these soldiers was baseball. Military authorities permitted this kind of recreation because it provided a positive form of recreation for young soldiers, removing them from the negative influences of alcohol abuse and gambling. The quickest way for an enlisted man to be relieved of duty was to show up drunk for his assigned post duties.

Simply put, military life on the frontier was one of discipline laced with confinement. To preserve and promote the health of the soldiers, the newly appointed U.S. Sanitary Commission of 1861 recommended that "whenever practicable, amusements, sports, and gymnastic exercises should be favored amongst the men."[1] Baseball was among those favored pastimes. Officers encouraged the sport to relieve the boredom of camp life among the enlisted men and keep young soldiers out of trouble. Organized matches between units became a source of motivation for training, helped foster group cohesion and loyalty, and promoted fitness and pride in their respective units. As late as 1884, *The Army and Navy Journal* supported and recommended athletics as a means to strengthen soldiers for active duty.

The Official United States Army Manual for 1872 specifically lists what types of goods and supplies were available for requisition through the Quarter-master. Unfortunately, baseball equipment was not available or furnished through proper channels of the U.S. Army. Even though the policy of caring for soldiers' health became an instituted policy, there is no record of the U.S. Army ever supplying any kind of baseball equipment to units stationed on the early frontier posts across the Arizona Territory. This would have forced the soldiers to rely on their own resourcefulness and ingenuity along with help from any interested officers of their respective units, to devise a way to get or make equipment and find a place to play. Normally, a soldier's pay would be handed out by the paymaster, with two deductions. One would be for the cleaning and repair of his uniforms by laundresses on post. The second withholding came as a part of a general "welfare fund" that was held by the unit or post's First Sergeant. Often those funds were used to purchase books and magazines for the post library and baseball equipment. In 1890, as a noted exception, at the Benicia Barracks in California, the on-base Post Exchange would expend $75 for sports equipment, including a dozen baseballs and bats.[2] Eventually, uniforms would be available to military teams through mercantile and sporting goods stores like Brooklyn's Kiffe Sporting Goods Store, which ran an advertisement in 1890 within the pages of *The Army and Navy Journal*. In the ad, the uniforms offered through Kiffe's came in various grades, with prices ranging from $3 to $9 each, and athletic shoes, also in various grades, ranging from $1 to $9.50 a pair. But until then, the earliest days of baseball played by the officers and enlisted soldiers on the frontier were done so with home-made equipment on makeshift diamonds, wherever a flat and wide space of ground could be found. If they wore uniforms, they were tailored by a seamstress on post. Most often, soldiers played in their standard-issue uniforms.

The largest newspapers in the Arizona Territory during the period were the *Arizona Miner* and the *Arizona Journal Miner*. The *Miner* reported on all business within the new territory, including affairs with the newly established House of Representatives, mining laws/claims, Indian troubles—which in turn prompted the urgent call for more troops—civic issues of the day, new towns and settlements that were establishing themselves, poems and other diversions, and news of desertions from the local army posts. A regular single issue of the *Arizona Miner* cost ten cents, with a special edition covering the events of the new Territorial Legislature costing 25 cents, and a subscription for a year was $2.50. The *Miner* was printed and distributed in the territorial capitol of the day, which until 1881 was the small, burgeoning town of Prescott.

On April 27, 1872, the *Miner* related that the spring-time weather was enough to induce the local residents to venture outdoors. The good spring weather no doubt helped bring cheer to soldiers and officers stationed at both Fort Whipple and Camp Hualpai, thus making them "in need of exercise and employment of some sort, & organize a Base Ball Club, and on Tuesday Last, a portion of the members of said club repaired to the plaza and went through several base notions with balls and bats."[3] This article notes that as soon as the newly formed club became experts at the game, no doubt that challenges for baseball games would be accepted. This was followed by a printed challenge, advertising the formation of the Independent Base Ball Club, comprised of the soldiers of K Troop of the 5th Cavalry stationed at Camp Hualpai, as openly challenging any military or civilian club to play a single match game in Prescott for either prize money or amusement, with the bat and ball being provided. This is the first known baseball club/organization in Arizona's history.

From there nothing more is known about any matches played by the newly formed Independent Base Ball Club, any other units from Fort Whipple or citizens of Prescott for several years. Even though no further events were reported in the *Arizona Miner*, it is easy to imagine groups of young men from Prescott and the local Army posts of Fort Whipple and Camp Hualpai gathering on the Plaza for a spirited match of baseball, with interested citizens as spectators, gleefully cheering on their favorites during the match.

The first known baseball match in the Arizona Territories was played on December 26, 1872, at Camp Grant, as related in a letter to the *Arizona Miner* signed under the auspicious moniker of "ARNO." This correspondence, printed on January 11, 1873, read: "In the forenoon, an exciting game of base ball took place. This occupied the attention, both of combatants and non-combatants, until one o'clock, when the welcome call to dinner was wafted to our ears and readily responded to."[4] The letter adds that I Troop of Fort Grant had "spent the afternoon in a variety of ways, and the day wound up by a game of 'base bawl' not on the program." This suggests that the second match contested that afternoon was indeed an impromptu pick-up game between soldiers in the I Troop of the 23rd Infantry and perhaps troops of either the L or W troops of the 5th Cavalry, after dinner had been enjoyed by all. The general sentiment in correspondence to the editor of the *Arizona Miner*, and in previous articles, suggested a keen interest in the game amongst the military and civilian residents of the territory. The soldiers of both Camp Grant and Camp Hualpai relished these games in an effort to promote an outlet for pent-up energies and emotions while encouraging company and unit pride.

How the soldiers from Camp Grant and Camp Hualpai learned about baseball is a mystery. However, two likely sources of discovering the game present themselves. First, other soldiers being transferred to the Arizona frontier from posts in the Midwestern and Eastern states would have brought their own knowledge and experience of playing the game with them, and perhaps rudimentary equipment such as a bat and ball. The game might have been introduced to the army posts in the Arizona Territories through the pages of newspapers and periodicals available to the soldiers at that time. Most posts in the territory stocked a few hundred books and assorted periodicals like *Wilkes' Spirit of the Times, Harper's Monthly, Century Magazine* and *The Army and Navy Journal*. A fine selection of newspapers from across the country was also available for reading, including the *Daily Alta California, San Francisco Chronicle, New York Herald, Baltimore Sun*, and *Chicago Daily Times*,[5] in addition to the territory's own leading newspaper, the *Arizona Miner/Journal Miner*. All of those may have printed articles about baseball at one time or another, as well as printed advertisements for equipment and rule books available for sale. It does make one wonder if the introduction of baseball into the territorial posts of Arizona was a mix of these two sources, or if one was more predominant than the other. Unfortunately, until further sources are discovered, this question will probably remain a mystery to us.

Most likely, this match was played on the parade ground located in the center of camp. This would have been the most logical place to conduct a baseball game, and as indicated in the text of *Letter from Camp Grant*, the ballists would have been within ear-shot of the mess hall so as to hear the dinner bell easily. The field measured an estimated 750 feet to right field, 650 feet to center field and 750 to left field. Both left and right field lines would have been open, with considerable gaps between buildings that lined the perimeter.

Distances of the base paths would have been set at the standard 90 feet, with the hurler's box set 50 feet from home plate while measuring four feet wide by six feet long. Logically, home plate might have been placed in the Southeast corner near the Company Quarters and adjacent the Company Mess buildings, otherwise known as the Quartermaster's office and Common House. It's also noteworthy to mention that there would have been a flag pole, as well—placed in the middle of left-center field! One can imagine that this would have made playing "center garden" or "second sack" an interesting experience. The field of play was a rough, uneven and rocky parade ground frequently used as a training ground for cavalry units stationed at Fort Grant. Other posts across the territory were very similar in layout and design.

The slightly larger lemon-peel ball may have still been used on the frontier despite the change to the modern two-piece "figure eight" ball adopted the same year by the National Association of Base Ball Players (NABBP), the professional clubs of the East. Fielding the lemon-peel ball would have been a challenge indeed! The ball, measuring 9 1/2 inches in circumference, put into play on the rocks, ruts and uneven ground in the middle of camp, would have made each play an adventure. The ground itself would most certainly deflect and re-direct the path of a well-struck ball. One could imagine the soldiers, striking and fielding the ball in their blue uniform pants and shirtsleeves, being cheered on by fellow soldiers, the few wives and children of officers and a small number of civilian staff that lived on post.

The pitching would most likely have been either a swift or slow, loping underhand delivery, with the striker swinging at each pitch using home-made bats manufactured from local woods or unused wagon tongues. The soldiers would have played the game without any kind of glove or mitt, as the baseball glove wouldn't be invented until 1886 by the legendary Arthur "Foxy" Irwin of .the Providence Grays club. Although there is no reported final tally of this match, and no box score or list of ballists who competed, this article demonstrates the excitement and immediate attraction to the game of baseball generated by the soldiers of the U.S. Army stationed at camps like Fort Grant, Fort Whipple and Camp Hualpai.

While these holiday matches set an example of sorts, playing on Thanksgiving and other holidays began to assert itself amongst holiday traditions on the military posts across Arizona. As revealed in correspondence from Camp Bowie to the Department of Arizona Headquarters in Prescott, the post was not as isolated as would be suspected from "all pleasures as the manner in which our late general Thanksgiving-day was spent can testify."[6] In 1873 the soldiers from Fort Bowie challenged their comrades from Fort Grant to a baseball match over the Thanksgiving holiday. Prior to the match, the correspondent writing to department headquarters noted that the units of the 5th Cavalry and 23rd Infantry had played a few games on post "with varying success," mentioning that considerable interest in baseball was present at Fort Bowie. The letter also noted that the games were not solely contested by enlisted men, but by the officers as well. Here we see that baseball had brought together men of differing ranks, backgrounds and education levels. The two clubs that would compete that afternoon were the Sumner B.B.C., representing Fort Grant, and the Neversink B.B.C. that would host the match. According to the rudimentary box score included in the letter sent to headquarters in Prescott, the game was an interesting one that captured the attention of everyone on the post. At the end of a two hour and 50-minute contest, the tally stood 39 to 24, a victory by the home club. Later that evening, a celebratory ball was held and widely attended. It even attracted the warrior chief Cochise and a few of his tribesmen, who looked upon the revelry celebrating the Neversink B.B.C. victory with amazement that a game could inspire such a festive atmosphere. Cochise's attendance at the celebratory ball represented a new feeling of goodwill between the Chiricahua Indians and the U.S. Government, which had recently negotiated peace to halt hostilities in the ongoing Indian Wars that would plague the Arizona Territory until 1890. Interestingly, a recent search through the *Arizona Weekly Citizen* and the *Arizona Journal Miner* for 1873 and 1874 reveals that neither the game nor the accompanying festivities with Cochise in attendance was mentioned in either newspaper.

The trend of reporting matches to newspapers like the *Arizona Miner* would grow over the coming years, as baseball spread throughout the various military forts, camps, and towns of the territory. The reports made one thing clear—baseball was gaining serious interest amongst the people in the Arizona Territories.

By 1876, the soldiers of Fort Whipple had formed the Whipple Base Ball Club. They would play games against other Forts in the area, such as Fort Verde and Camp Hualpai. The Whipple Base Ball Club would also take part in the first Territorial Championship against the Champion Base Ball Club of Prescott, as discussed in greater detail in the following chapter.

1. Uncle Sam Brings the Game Westward

Meanwhile, on the far western boundaries of the young territory, baseball was making a transition from casual pick-up matches to serious competition between the town of Yuma and the soldiers of Fort Yuma, California. The first matches of baseball were reported on the streets of the frontier town in the early spring months of 1876. The soldiers of Company C of the 12th Infantry had organized themselves into their own baseball club and competed in the first known match with a loosely organized club from Yuma sometime in January, winning the contest that was played on the flat below Fort Yuma. The following week the two clubs met for another match, as reported in the *Arizona Sentinel* on February 5, 1876, and drew quite a crowd from town.[7] The paper added that another match between the two clubs would take place at a later date.

A few weeks later, the *Sentinel* reported that the soldiers from Fort Yuma had renamed their baseball club the "C. A. Earnest B. B. Club." C. A. Earnest was a post trader who had garnered plenty of respect amongst the troops, and perhaps introduced or supported the new game of baseball enough to encourage them to use his name for their club. Their local adversaries, the boys from Yuma proper, would be known as the "Yuma Club."[8] This article points out that both the military post and the town of Yuma now had an official baseball club, and that future games would require the visitors to travel across the Lower Colorado River, which at the time was no easy task. Forging the Lower Colorado River was dangerous and often deadly to the ferry's operators, their passengers and cargo that were being shuttled across the unpredictable waters. The games between the two nines were well contested, with both clubs about equal in strength in the areas of fielding and striking. The *Sentinel* writer noted that "it is a fine game, leading to develop the muscle of young men" but also a bit rough and dangerous, adding that injuries were not an unusual event.

In the weeks between the matches featuring the soldiers and the citizens of Yuma, the Yuma club—then called the "Red Shirts" instead of the "Yuma Club" by the *Sentinel*—had selected a "Scrub" nine to play in practice games so that they could sharpen their fielding and striking skills. In a practice match on March 25, 1876, between the Red Shirts and the Scrub nine of Yuma, the Scrub nine forfeited the match due to age and injury. No score was reported.[9]

As spring passed, both the C. A. Earnest Club and the Red Shirts of Yuma had been practicing for the last match of the season, which took place on April 22, 1876, on the flat below Fort Yuma. The weather was warm, making for an unpleasant affair for both clubs, who took the field clad in heavy wool uniforms. Undaunted by the warm weather, both clubs were eager to play the match for bragging rights until the following spring season in 1877. It was a close match, with the C. A. Earnest Club scoring in the bottom half of the first frame, leading one ace to nothing. In the top of the second frame, however, the Red Shirts broke things open, scoring nine aces of their own, then recorded a white-wash to lead the soldiers 9–1 at the end of the second inning. The third inning would see the home club score seven aces to get back into the match, while the visitors would tally two more aces to make it an 11–8 affair heading into the middle frames. The fifth inning saw the clubs score four aces each, keeping the Red Shirts' lead at three aces. The sixth inning was a wild affair, with heavy hitting and errors contributing to ten runs by the C. A. Earnest Club and a colossal 18 runs by the visiting Red Shirts. From there the visitors wouldn't look back, securing the victory with a final tally of 40 aces to 35 and thus securing the final match of the season between the two clubs. There would be no baseball played at the post for many years afterwards. The post would be abandoned in 1883 and move across the river to California. From the new location of Fort Yuma, the soldiers would re-organize their baseball efforts and begin competition anew with the surrounding communities which would last well into the coming decades.

The earliest mention of baseball near Tucson came on March 18, 1876, when the *Arizona Citizen* reported on the celebration held by the soldiers of Fort Lowell and their guests. Among the festivities listed in a neatly printed event program were foot races, sack races, dancing jigs, and a greased pig chase in the morning of St. Patrick's Day of 1876. Later that afternoon, in addition to horse racing, a baseball game took place on post. Unfortunately, the article does not clearly detail whether the baseball match was a pick-up game between two nines comprised of soldiers from the various units on post or if there was a visiting club. The date of March 1876 suggests that the game would have indeed been a pick-up game between units stationed at the fort, simply because the first newspaper account given of a civilian team playing in the nearby town of Tucson wouldn't appear until 1877. According to the *Citizen*, the program of festivities was a smashing success.

A year later, in an effort not to be outdone by happenings in the northern and western parts of the territory, the units of the 2nd, 4th, 5th, and 6th Cavalry and men of the 1st, 8th and 12th Infantry Regiments of Camp Lowell organized themselves into the Worth Base Ball Club. Situated on the Gila River, Fort Lowell would serve as a supply base for other posts in the area as well as a source of protection for citizens of Tucson against Apache Indian attacks. The soldiers stationed at Fort Lowell were also assigned duty as guards to overland supply trains, thus manning picket posts to further protect settlers in the Southwest.

To counteract the boredom of this duty, the baseball club was organized and matches amongst other soldiers at the fort soon began. In subsequent years they primarily played a club from Tucson known in 1877 as the Lone Star Base Ball Club. As related in the *Arizona Weekly Star* on November 29, 1877, "The members of the Lone Star Base Ball Club respectfully invite the public to attend the game of base ball between the said club and the Worth B.B.C. of Camp Lowell."[10] The match would be played on the grounds in front of the public school building at 1:30 p.m. on Sunday, December 2, 1877. It is unknown how many soldiers from the military post and citizens from town attended the match, or what the final score was. It seems that baseball had arrived early in the history of the Old Pueblo. Almost a decade later, in April 1887, the Lowells would travel north to compete with the Phoenix Base Ball Club for the Territorial Championship of 1887. Fort Lowell would lose the first match by a score of 9–7. The following day's match, held at the original Territory Fair grounds, would see the Lowells go down in defeat, 14–7, losing two straight matches and the championship to a superior Phoenix Base Ball Club. The *Arizona Gazette* reported that an undisclosed amount of money had been collected in order to show the soldiers from Fort Lowell a good time while they were in town for the championship matches. From 1887 to 1891, the soldiers on post would be busy performing transfers, supply movements and other military activities that would make it difficult for them to field a competitive nine. The soldiers that did form a club to represent the post would offer no real competition to the Tucson Base Ball Club, and would serve as a "practice squad" to the boys from town as they prepared for Territorial Championship and Territorial Fair matches against opponents from across Arizona. The post would eventually be abandoned in 1891. The grounds now serve as a museum and, like Fort Verde, a state park that welcomes visitors year-round.

Following the example of the Whipple Base Ball Club, the soldiers of both Troop B of the 12th Infantry and Troop K of the 6th Cavalry, stationed at Fort Verde, on the Verde River approximately 50 miles east of the first territorial capitol of Prescott, decided to organize a formal baseball club, following the example of Fort Whipple and Camp Hualpai to the north. The Fort Verde Excelsiors made their first competitive appearances on the makeshift diamonds of the Arizona Territories between 1879 and 1881. The roster of the Fort Verde Excelsiors in 1879 was as follows:

Pearce, first base; Wipperman, second base; Snyder, third base; Church, right field; Pheifer, left field; Smith, center field; Broman, short stop; Egan, catcher; and Covy, acting as the club's hurler. At this time there is little evidence of the Fort Verde Excelsiors in action other than that list of names from the 1879 roster.

The first reported match featuring the nine from Fort Verde was played against the Prescott Base Ball Club on May 19, 1881. The match started a few minutes after one o'clock in the afternoon, played on the grounds of West Prescott. The Verde Nine were first to strike, tallying three aces. The Prescott nine responded by scoring two aces of their own. In the top of the next frame, the boys from Fort Verde unleashed a torrent of offense, tallying an amazing 21 aces due in part to heavy striking, as well as mismanagement, errors and general carelessness by their opponents.[11] At the time the paper went to press, a reporter for the *Weekly Arizona Miner* returned from watching the early innings of the match and was understandably reluctant to relate, to the editor of the paper, news which didn't favor the home nine. From there, the pace would remain the same, with the Fort Verde Nine in complete control of the match until the end. The *Weekly Arizona Miner* did not report the names of the Fort Verde Nine, except for noting that the catcher, Murray, had "his finger badly torn in the third inning, which necessitated his retirement." The paper noted that three ballists from Prescott had exhibited excellent play. Among them were gentlemen named McAbee, Dake and a soldier nicknamed "Toughee"—perhaps for his overall toughness and rugged demeanor. The paper suggested that the Prescott Nine were in dire need of a skilled catcher and recommended more practice and training so that the next time the two clubs met on the diamond, they could give the Verde club a "strong rattle." Unfortunately this is the last known record of any games played by the club from Fort Verde, as much of the records other than a list of names have been lost to history. The Fort was abandoned on April 10, 1890, and subsequently sold to a private individual for the amazing price of just one dollar. In later years, the town of Camp Verde purchased the site and began restoration, and the military post still stands and serves as a museum and state park.

Located on the banks of the Rio Verde, Camp McDowell was established in 1865 by the California Volunteers to combat the surrounding Indian tribes. Later named Fort McDowell, the post would serve as an early base for troops brought in to protect the settlers, miners and travelers, and as a launching point to the Indian wars. In a personal letter, an officer's wife named Evy Alexander wrote home to her mother, describing the environment on the post as having the river in the foreground, surrounded by cottonwood trees, with the fort in the foreground featuring tents among adobe housing, similar to a photo of Fort Grant that she had sent to her father, remarking that "is a perfect representation of Ft. McDowell."[12] It seems that in continuation of an obvious theme, the baseball clubs of Fort McDowell would play where they could, namely the parade grounds in the middle of the post, much like the soldiers at Fort Grant did a few years earlier.

In 1875, while the territorial legislature was busy with governing the land, notably passing a bill creating Pinal County, and the citizens of Prescott were passing a town-wide petition calling for better mail service between their hometown and Santa Fe, baseball was picking up interest among the military posts in the territory. There were two clubs from Fort McDowell, the Light-Foot Club of the 8th Infantry and the Shamrock Club of the 5th Cavalry. Both nines got together for the first known match at Camp McDowell, on New Year's Day, 1875. The final tally, as reported by the *Weekly Arizona Miner*, stood at 14 aces to ten in favor of the Light-Foots.[13]

Over the next few years, little mention of baseball activity at Camp or Fort McDowell appeared in the few territorial newspapers. At the turn of the next decade, two new clubs representing the post would emerge to take on surrounding competition. First was the Chaffee Club, led by Captain Chafee and Lieutenant Charles E. Dravo, who acted as the club President. The first match played by the Chaffee Base Ball Club (B.B.C), was against the Phoenix B.B.C. on January 3, 1880, on the grounds of Fort McDowell, with the losing club to "forfeit a ball."[14] The challenge suggested a return match on January 8, again at Fort McDowell. The match on January 3 ended in defeat for the Chaffee club, with the final tally 34–29 in favor of the Phoenix B.B.C. The Phoenix ballists would travel back to Fort McDowell for a return game, as originally requested in the challenge issued by the Chaffee B.B.C. After the match was over, with different results from before, the *Phoenix Herald* commented that "Our boys were badly beaten by the McDowell club in the game at Fort McDowell." Apparently the margin of defeat was so great that when the returning ballists reached the outskirts of Phoenix, they separated in the "most quiet manner possible"[15] from the celebratory committee, who showed up armed with all kinds of horns, cymbals and other noise-making instruments, along with a decorated wagon, in anticipation of victory. The news of the defeat spread quickly through town, resulting in the whistle at the flour mill being blown and the flag at the center of Phoenix being lowered to half-staff. The *Phoenix Herald* correspondent who covered the return match declined to give the final score. Interestingly enough, in the same edition of the *Herald*, a column-long piece titled "The Book of Baseball" was printed, giving a history of the Phoenix B.B.C. and the two matches played against the Chaffee B.B.C., written in biblical prose. Near the end of the column a score of 54–17 is given for the return match, obviously in favor of the Chaffee B.B.C. It contrasted the accompanying account of the return match by another writer or editor of the *Herald*. Perhaps the terrible loss suffered by the Phoenicians was caused by the solar eclipse witnessed on the previous Sunday afternoon by townsfolk who viewed the celestial event through panes of smoked glass. Afterwards, the *Herald* printed a letter in which the president, Samuel E. Patton, and secretary, James Fitzgerald, of the Phoenix B.B.C. thanked the ladies and gentlemen of the Chaffee Base Ball Club for their hospitality, conceded defeat, and complimented the victorious club by writing, "It is a pleasure to be vanquished in a civic game by manly and magnanimous victors and that our club will not forget that hospitality which was so freely given, and accepted by us, and further hope that it may be only the forerunner of many like enjoyable occasions wherein we may be joined, both at Phoenix and McDowell."[16]

The other baseball organization to represent Fort McDowell was the Norvall, sometimes misspelled as "Norvell" by the *Arizona Weekly Republican* and the *Phoenix Herald*, Base Ball Club, comprised of soldiers and officers of Troop I of the 6th Cavalry and Company G of the 12th Infantry. With Lieutenant James Fitzgerald acting as the club's secretary, it issued the first challenge to the winner of the Chaffee Base Ball Club versus the Phoenix Base Ball Club match to be contested on January 3, 1881. The secretary of the Phoenix B.B.C., James E. Fitzgerald (not the same person) responded in kind, accepting the challenge through the pages of the *Phoenix Herald*, but suggested that the match take place on February 23, 1881, and that the losing club pay the winners $25.[17]

The earliest recorded game played by the Norvall Club of Fort McDowell was on Christmas Day, 1880, reported in the *Arizona Weekly Herald* on January 3, 1881. The *Phoenix Weekly Herald*, in anticipation of the match, reported that the game would be of great interest to the citizens of Phoenix, noting that both clubs were in fine form and anticipating a closely played match, "and we think our boys will have a sharp tussle to get away with them."[18] Among the preparations made to the field for the upcoming match between the Phoenicians and soldiers from Fort McDowell, seats were prepared for any ladies that wished to attend the game. The match between the two clubs, reported by the *Herald* on December 31,

1880, was described as "well played by both clubs, and was witnessed by a large audience, many of whom were ladies."[19] The match was officiated by Mr. Charles McNeil, with Mr. William Andrews and Mr. Harry Wharton acting as tally keepers. The action seemed to be one-sided, as up until the fourth inning the Phoenix Base Ball club dominated the match, scoring nine unanswered aces. The Norvall B.B.C. answered in kind, scoring one run in the fifth inning and three runs in both the sixth and seventh innings. But it was too late and proved not enough to win the day. The Phoenicians proved to be too much that afternoon, with the final tally 13–9. The *Arizona Weekly Herald* added that "many fine plays were made by members of both clubs, and such never failed to elicit the hearty applause from the crowd assembled." The popularity of baseball had definitely taken a foothold in the Arizona Territories by this time. It is unclear where this match was played, Fort McDowell or Phoenix. From the excerpts of the article about a large crowd, with most being ladies, the match was probably played in Phoenix. Most likely, it was played at the Territorial Fairgrounds, located a few miles south of town on Central Avenue north of the Salt River.

The Norvall Club would play another match two weeks later on January 17, 1881, against the same opponents faced on the previous Christmas Day, the Phoenix Base Ball Club. The result of the second match, played at Fort McDowell, would have a different outcome. Once again, the *Arizona Weekly Gazette* reported a close battle through nine frames of play. It was a spirited match with "fine playing being the order of the day."[20] The article mentions the battery of F. Widmer and Hellmich specifically, noting that Hellmich pitched a superb match, allowing only three base hits while suffering a couple of unfortunate experiences at the plate in which he broke two bats. Spirited pitching indeed! The final tally for this return match was 17 to 16 in favor of the Norvall Base Ball Club. These baseball fraternities would see many more contests between them in the years to come, with both clubs recruiting some very talented ballists.

Further south, at Fort Huachuca, the soldiers and officers of Troops B and M of the 6th Cavalry, who were most likely the first units to establish the post, would have played each other in a similar fashion to the pickup games previously reported at Fort Grant in December of 1872. As the post grew in size with more companies/troops added to its muster rolls, more games would have been played between the soldiers themselves as well as the surrounding towns, including Tucson and, in later years, the mining towns of Bisbee and Tombstone. It is also likely by this time that clubs formed at the respective forts in the Territories would have been issuing

Fort Huachuca Nine of 1884. Standing, rear left, is Sergeant "Diamond" Emil H. Pauly, first base, Troop I, 4th Cavalry. Rear, third from left, Burlingame, rear right, Collins, center field. Kneeling on right, Johnson, third base. (Fort Huachuca Museum)

and accepting challenges for baseball games, either for an agreed-on purse or bragging rights.

The first known uniformed Arizona club to be photographed was from Fort Huachuca. The club posed for a photograph, displaying uniforms and equipment of the day, sometime in 1884. Only a few players in this photograph are identified: Standing in the rear, third from the left, was a soldier named Burlingame; in the left rear corner stood Sergeant Emil H. Pauly of Troop I, 4th Cavalry, who played "first sack," in the far right stood Collins, who played "center gardener" for the Fort Huachuca club. Kneeling in front, on the right side, is Edward Johnson, listed as a civilian employee of the Fort, as of March 1883 the blacksmith contracted to work for the post's quartermaster, drawing $100 salary for the month. As described in the photo, he played "third sack" for the club. Until further records are found, it remains unknown who the other six soldiers were who comprised the baseball club, as well as the identity of the well-dressed, mustachioed man sitting in the center of this photo.

1. Uncle Sam Brings the Game Westward

Two years later, the clubs from Tombstone and Fort Huchuca met for a match at the race track near Tombstone. The match was announced in *The Tombstone* newspaper, listing the names of the Tombstone Club playing as well as mentioning that horse races, games and other attractions would be offered at the event.[21] Noted frontier figure George W. Parsons, who served as Tombstone's first librarian, recorded the baseball match in the pages of his journal, commenting that the "ball match this afternoon attracted the whole town pretty nearly. Huachuca Soldier Boys plated the Tombstone boys and beat them. Score: 18 to 25. Many Ladies out." The bases and bats used for this contest were home-made, with the only expense being the ball, and perhaps uniforms purchased through a Spalding Sporting Goods retailer or by mail order through outlets in Denver or Los Angeles. Balls were the most expensive part of a club's expenses as they had to be purchased, ranging in price from 50 cents to over two dollars each. Replacing them was so costly due to the initial price and the time it took to receive them through the mail. Thus retrieval of a lost ball due to a long hit was very important. On the national baseball scene, National League umpires were officially required to wait a full five minutes when a ball was lost to resume play, with the idea of using just two baseballs per game being proposed by the Boston Union club in 1884. Even the professional nines, who were well funded, regarded preservation of a ball in the highest regard.

The 1886 baseball season would witness the 4th Cavalry that comprised the Fort Huachuca Nine defeat the club from Fort Grant on their home grounds for the second "Championship of Arizona" by a score of 21–11—earning them a handsome $200 prize for the match and the well-deserved title as Champions of the Territory. The game must have been hard-fought on both sides as it was reported that Sergeant R. Mannion, Troop E of the 4th Cavalry, was seen in Tombstone nursing several broken fingers.[22]

Over the years, the baseball club of the 4th Cavalry would continually prove that they would indeed travel anywhere for a ball game. The earliest recorded game between the soldiers of Fort Lowell and the club from Fort Huachuca was in December of 1887. For the lads from Fort Lowell, there wasn't much local competition, as the Tucson Base Ball Club had at one point either disbanded or was in disarray and would rarely play, much less at their former level of competitive glory. In the *Arizona Weekly Citizen*, the staff reporter would write that the locals had scratched together a nine and traveled to Fort Lowell to take on the "soldier nine" on the grounds at the post. After relating a lopsided tally of 19–8 for the match, the writer quipped, "It is a shame that Tucson has not got a regularly organized base ball club." In getting a victory over their local civilian competitors, the Lowells—perhaps feeling pretty confident in their skills on the diamond—published challenges in other newspapers such as the *Tombstone Epitaph* or *Arizona Weekly Star*, inviting any other club in the area to come to their home grounds for a match. It would be the 4th Cavalry nine, comprised of members of the E Troop, that would answer that challenge, and make the arduous journey northward to meet their challengers and give them a good showing.

There isn't any record of the nine from Fort Huachuca practicing for this match or not. However, on December 3, 1887, the match between both military clubs did commence on the grounds at Fort Lowell. From the after-match report in the *Citizen*, it appears that the 4th Cavalry club, led by Lieutenant James Brailsford Erwin, took the game seriously. In the photo of the Fort Huachuca club, Lieutenant Erwin is seated in the center, wearing a white pill-box style cap while the rest of his club-mates wore dark-colored caps. This photograph was taken looking east between the infantry barracks on the left and the post hospital on the right, just beyond the picket fence on the Fort Lowell grounds. The game was well played on both sides, with many fine points displayed both in the field and at the

Fourth Cavalry Club of Fort Huachuca at Fort Lowell, December 3, 1887. Seated in the center is Lt. James Brailsford Erwin. (Arizona Historical Society)

Tombstone and Fort Huachuca Base Ball Clubs of 1890. Photograph taken at baseball grounds near Tombstone. (Bisbee Mining & Historical Museum)

bat. The 4th Cavalry, Company E club from Fort Huachuca took the game a little more seriously than their counterparts, or perhaps were simply more skilled, as the final tally was 20–5 in favor of the Huachuca nine.

Memorial Day, formerly known as Decoration Day within the territory, was celebrated by a baseball match between the Fort Huachuca and Tombstone clubs, set for May 30, 1893. There was much anticipation on behalf of the Tombstone club, as they were putting together quite an impressive record against rival nines from neighboring towns. The Tombstone club arrived on the grounds of Fort Huachuca expecting to play against a "colored nine" from one of the four companies of the 24th Infantry. While waiting for the match to begin, the Pioneer club of Tombstone was missing one ballist who was supposed to bring his girlfriend to the match but never materialized. The idea was presented to pick a substitute from the other club on post. This idea was immediately rejected, perhaps because the 24th Infantry nine didn't want to hand the Pioneers from Tombstone any advantages by having a rival player provide advice on how to defeat them. The game fell through, much to the disappointment of all in attendance. Fortunately, the members of the 2nd Cavalry baseball club accepted an impromptu challenge and the game was formally

Fort Huachuca versus Tombstone game on parade ground in front of barracks at Fort Huachuca, 1890. (Fort Huachuca Museum)

called at one o'clock. Being out of practice, the Pioneers walked away with the laurels of victory by a score of 12 to 8.[23]

The 2nd Cavalry would be active against Tombstone the same season, filling in for the newly organized Bisbee Base Ball Club as arrangements were being planned for them to face the Tombstones for the Fourth of July match in 1893. Late word was sent that the Bisbee nine could not make the match, so the club from the 2nd Cavalry took their place for the afternoon match on July 4 in Tombstone. The post club took to active practices in order to avenge their loss on Decoration Day to the Pioneers. Both clubs were in fine trim that afternoon, with splendid plays performed on both sides. The soldiers were not able to walk away with victory, however, falling to the Tombstone lads, 14–8.

Over the next decade or so, from 1894 through 1905, the soldiers from Fort Huachuca kept the same role as a long-time rival to nearby towns such as Bisbee, Douglas, Tombstone, Tucson and Nogales. On occasion they would make appearances in Phoenix, mostly keeping their competitive efforts closer to home. Most of their baseball activity remained on post between units stationed there, and as always the frequency of games was subject to their duty schedule as full-time soldiers of the United States Army. The photograph below, taken sometime between 1904 to

1907 featured the 5th Cavalry baseball club. The nine from Fort Huachuca emerged successful through the 1904–1905 campaign, largely due to their activity on post doing various maneuvers while playing in quite a few competitive matches with the clubs from Douglas, Bisbee, and Cananea, Mexico. Normally, Tombstone would be included with the town ball clubs that the post would compete against, but for some reason the club from Tombstone had stopped competitive play altogether and had allowed their home ball grounds to fall into such disarray that it warranted mention in the April 1, 1906, edition of the *Bisbee Daily Review.*

Lying down on the far left of the 1904 photo of the 5th Cavalry, Troop B photo is First Sergeant Ward C. R. Hoover. Seated in the middle is Captain Pritchard, the unit commanding officer and quite possibly the baseball club's manager. Hoover enlisted at Fort Huachuca on February 21, 1904, and left service with the U.S. Army less than three years later in January 1907. In his official military files, his "excellent service, honest and faithful" was noted during his time with the 5th Cavalry. Over the duration of his

B Troop, 5th Cavalry Base Ball Club of 1904. Lying left is Lt. Ward C. R. Hoover. (Fort Huachuca Museum)

military career, Sgt. Hoover played second base for the post team. After being honorably discharged from military service in January 1907, Ward Hoover would wind up in Nogales, Arizona, where he would be instrumental in the revival of baseball in the area. His re-organization of a local club known as the "Diamond N Boys" was reported in the *Border Vidette* and a competing publication, *The Oasis*. Hoover was identified by the local paper as the club's captain, but in scouring newspapers from the formation of the new club on May 4 through the July 4 festivities in nearby Patagonia, there is no indication if he ever took the field as an active ballist for the Diamond N Club. One thing is certain: the club did get off to a rousing start, including holding two fundraising events and even getting Mr. Nathan Leeker, a member of another local nine called "La Barata," to donate a set of uniforms for the new club.[24] When the team even stepped onto the diamond for competition, the *Border Vidette* noted, they would use the talents of former Diamond N players and athletes from around Nogales, specifically a power hurler named J. F. Brady. Hoover had done his homework while organizing the club, utilizing his experience while playing for the 5th Cavalry post team out of Fort Huachuca. Over the next few weeks, the Diamond N Club would compete in a series of exhibition games against the Nogales Base Ball Club and the La Barata nine. Their record would stand at 0–2 against a very good Nogales club before finally getting a win from a scratched-together baseball club from Patagonia on July 4. Hoover had a big influence in organizing the club and getting games going again in the area for the foreseeable future in southern Arizona.

In the eastern part of the territory, soldiers from Camp San Carlos began formal play in competitive games against their civilian counterparts from the mining town of Globe. Beginning in April of 1884, the *Arizona Silver Belt* announced that "The San Carlos base ball club have accepted the challenge of the Globe club, and the game has been set for Sunday, the 20th inst."[25] The paper also noted the names of the delegates chosen to represent Gila County in the upcoming Republican Convention in Phoenix. Two weeks later, on April 26, 1884, the *Arizona Silver Belt* reported the first series match between the two baseball nines. Contested on Sunday, April 20 at one o'clock on the grounds of "the agency," it was described as being "a close and exciting contest, resulting in a tie at the end of the ninth inning." The match opened with the lads from Globe being white-washed in the first frame, while their hosts tallied three runs. By the ninth inning, fortunes had reversed and it was the gentlemen from Globe who were ahead by a tally of 28 aces to 23. The soldiers rallied back, tallying five aces to tie the match at the end of the ninth inning. By this point, the *Silver Belt* related, "The contestants were pretty well tired out by this time, and the catchers disabled, so both sides were content to quit with honors easy." Apparently, both clubs agreed to call the game a tie. The reporter from the *Silver Belt* noted that the boys from San Carlos excelled at base running, and the Globes in batting. The hero of the day, a man named Jones who pitched for the Globe nine, was thrown from a buggy on the way to the match, sustaining injuries that made it difficult to hurl nine innings. He persevered and went on to pitch a complete game. It was also mentioned that a return match would be played in Globe in a week's time and that the strikers from Globe had recorded three home runs in the course of the four-hour match officiated by Mr. A. B. Simmons.

In September and October of 1884, the ball players from Globe were busy strengthening their nine in anticipation of future matches with the soldiers from Camp San Carlos. The writer covering the return match between the two clubs was reluctant to speculate on an outcome, noting both clubs "have been materially strengthened since the contest between them last spring." Not to be outdone by the soldiers from Camp San Carlos, the Globe club used intrasquad games as a form of practice. "Two nines have been chosen from our local base ball talent and a match game will be played tomorrow afternoon."[26] As reported in the *Arizona Silver Belt*, a letter was received by the club secretary/president of the Globe City Nine, Mr. W. W. Jones, containing a challenge from Captain Crawford and a proposed date of November 2 for a return match between the two clubs in Globe.[27] It was also mentioned that there were new players added to the ranks of the San Carlos club, and the forthcoming contest should be an interesting one.

In the landmark book *Baseball: The People's Game* by Harold Seymour, there is a similar story about when the soldiers soundly defeated the men from Globe in the fall of 1884 and "relieved them of their spare cash."[28] Naturally the citizens of the proud mining town demanded a return match to even the score and reclaim their pride. The story illustrates how perilous travel to matches was during the territorial years. The soldiers from Camp San Carlos, under the command of Lieutenant Britton Davis, headed out towards Globe for the agreed-upon return match, a 55-mile journey from the army post to town. It began to snow, and ten miles up into the Superstition Mountains, the soldiers quickly found themselves in deep snow, and by the next morning the weather had turned into blizzard conditions. To keep from freezing, the men dismounted and walked. To make matters worse, one of their pack mules slipped and fell into the freezing waters of the Black River, effectively soaking all of their bedding. When night came there was no doubt that all of the soldiers felt "done in" from struggling against the winter weather. Finally, the group made it through the mountains, built a bonfire to keep warm, and tried to rest before their match. The ball players from Globe showed no mercy on the field, as the misfortune of the soldiers continued. They lost the match badly, and the Globe ballists "got back their cash with compound interest." Apparently Lieutenant Davis refused to take responsibility for the loss, stubbornly commenting on the play of fellow club-mate Lieutenant Dugan by allegedly saying "a short-scout who puts his knees together and leaves his feet a foot apart doesn't throw much of a scare into the opposition, and more than his share of batted balls are likely to come his way."

Searching through articles from April–December 1884 in the *Arizona Silver Belt*, it appears that Lieutenant Britton Davis was part of the San Carlos Nine, playing First Sack in the first series match between the two clubs as well as in subsequent matches. However, it is unclear what role Lt. Davis had in command of the troops, as Captain Crawford was listed as officer in command of the post. In the same pages of the *Silver Belt*, he seemed to have an active role in supporting baseball matches between the army post and the town of Globe, even offering to guide their civilian guests who made the trip to Camp San Carlos to watch the matches.

The return match was played on November 1, 1884. As the paper had predicted, the match was indeed a more colorful and interesting experience. The boys from San Carlos appeared "in neat uniforms consisting of blue shirts, white caps and pants and red stockings."[29] The home club's uniforms, "which had been made specially for this occasion, were very handsome; they were composed of white flannel shirts and pants, white caps with blue trimmings, blue belts and dark blue stockings." With both clubs now clad in colorful uniforms, the match promptly began at 12:20 P.M. The clubs engaged in a few minutes of preliminary practice exercises, to warm up before the contest. After the toss, the San Carlos nine went to strike first, only to be retired in order. The Globe men scored three aces before the side was retired. By the end of the next frame, both clubs had five aces. In the third inning, the Globe club figured out how to hit the San Carlos hurler and recorded four more aces to secure a lead that was never relinquished. In the post-match analysis, the writer for the *Silver Belt* declared, "It was very evident that the San Carlos club had more practice and had been better coached on base running than their opponents." However, it was Globe's timely hitting, with right gardener Walker leading the way, that made the difference in securing a 15–12 victory.

In most frontier towns, the life of a baseball club was short. On average, a town nine or a club from a nearby military post was active for two, maybe three seasons. Then, due to economic distress, natural catastrophe such as flood or fire, or simply the rotation of infantry and cavalry units stationed at any one military post—baseball would disappear. Globe was no stranger to this phenomenon, as the club faded from the pages of the *Arizona Silver Belt* after the late 1880s. This was illustrated on March 21, 1891, when the *Arizona Silver Belt* reported that the soldiers of Troop E, 2nd Cavalry had been ordered to Fort Bowie, thus postponing any games with the Globe nine. A new club representing San Carlos would have to fit the bill as replacements, with the newspaper noting that "the playing strength has been pretty evenly divided." Before the 2nd Cavalry was relocated to another post and the Globe Base Ball Club had re-organized at the Champion Saloon & Billiard Hall on Main Street in town, a heavy deluge of rain flooded the area, causing widespread damage. Roads and bridges were washed out. A full mile and a half of telegraph line was knocked down, interrupting communications between Globe and San Carlos for several days, requiring costly repairs to restore service. The reorganization of the Globe nine would commence under caution, or as the newspaper would say, "weather permitting."[30]

Fort Thomas, a smaller military post to the east of Globe near the fledgling LDS settlements of Pima and Thatcher, was no stranger to baseball or forming a winning club that could take on any other in the territory and be victorious. The post was roughly 55 miles east of the Globe mining camp. Initially constructed in 1864, the original location was known as Camp Goodwin and would be abandoned in 1876 due to consistent outbreaks of malaria from contaminated water sources, and poor buildings which earned the dubious title of being the "Worst Fort in the Army." The new post was located closer to the Gila River and renamed to honor Civil War Major General George W. Thomas. The post didn't receive any direct funding from the Army until two years before the capture of Geronimo in 1886. After the post closed in 1892, the town was a railroad outpost infamous for prostitution, gambling and saloons, which ceased in 1895 when the native Apaches refused to let the Southern Pacific Railroad continue construction on a rail line that would divide the reservation. The immediate benefit of this refusal was the growth of the town, which included a Wells-Fargo station. Following the adage that to be successful, every town needed both "an Opera House and a Base Ball Club," the residents of Fort Thomas developed a championship caliber baseball club in the shadows of the old military post.

In the 1895 campaign, the Fort Thomas Base Ball Club would see action against town clubs from nearby Globe, Bisbee, Tucson and Phoenix. On September 10, the *Arizona Daily Star* reported the results of the Globe series, saying that a sound, 20 to 1 drubbing dealt to the Globe nine was "something never heard of before in base ball history." The writer for the *Daily Star* added that the victory had "swelled the heads of the Fort Thomas boys and without going to the top by degrees, they challenged Tucson." That left little doubt that pride was evident in the home town nine for Tucson, as perhaps this challenge to the Territorial Champions of 1894 for the prize was looked upon with a degree of contempt. The Tucson B.B.C. considered the sweeping victories by the Fort Thomas nine against Globe and Bisbee as a stroke of luck and viewed themselves as being undefeatable because of dominance throughout the territory over the past few years. To ensure success, the Tucson club met at the Drachman Cigar Store that evening to discuss the series and formulate a plan to defend their crown.

The games were scheduled to be held on September 15, 16 and 17 in Tucson. When the news of the sound thrashing that the boys from Fort Thomas handed to the mine-hardened ball club from Bisbee, the townsfolk in Tucson started to get nervous that the Territorial Championship for the 1895 campaign might slip away from them. The *Arizona Daily Star* admonished that more practice was needed and that the series would be a true challenge. With no delays, the series began in earnest on September 14, with the first pitch hurled at Union Park in Tucson at 2:30 P.M. The first contest was advertised as "Ladies Day," with all ladies in attendance admitted without a gate fee.

As feared by the locals, the lads from Fort Thomas went to work tallying aces in an all-out effort to win the day. Tucson was hammered to the point where Emmanuel "Manny" Drachman was tapped to replace Walter Zabriskie in the sixth inning as hurler for the Tucson nine. Fort Thomas was unafraid of the hot-tempered Drachman, who had a penchant for fighting with opposing players after the game was finished. The visiting club hit Drachman for "four or five runs"[31] before he could figure out the opposing strikers and settle in. Frustration must have been at a high level for Drachman, who chose to show his displeasure with the Fort Thomas nine by sending a curveball to the jaw of center fielder Harry Floyd at the start of the seventh inning. The injured Floyd spent the rest of the match being tended to on the sideline while the manager, J. L. Alexander, would finish the game in center field. The Tucson nine suffered a humiliating defeat by a score of 19 to 9. The writer from the *Daily Star* summed up the day's action by noting that the hometown club needed more practice and that errors were a contributing factor to the loss.

The next day's match drew just as large a crowd as the first game, the spectators anxious to see if the feat could be repeated. Pitching for Tucson was hot-tempered Emmanuel "Manny" Drachman, and behind the plate, catching his deliveries, was the sturdy Walter Zabriskie. Fort Thomas started the same battery as in game one of the series. Interestingly enough the *Daily Star* writer interjected that Tucson would still retain the championship of the territory regardless of the outcome of the games, citing that "the terms under which it becomes a stake were not complied with." It seems apparent that the heavy loss that the Tucson B.B.C. suffered the day prior had prompted the writer, cranks and club management to try to find some legal loophole that would exempt the club from losing the championship under such embarrassing terms. The second match started with the cranks that traveled with the Fort Thomas club laying down heavy bets. First wagers made were at 10 to 7 odds. At some point during the game they fluctuated, at first being 2 to 3, then at one point 2 to 1.

More errors by the Tucsonites would again prove their downfall in game two. The hometown nine seemed to make rapid improvement during this match. The score was tied 6–6 going into the ninth inning, when Tucson errors proved costly. Fort Thomas pushed across four aces in the top of the frame and held the home nine scoreless at the bottom half to secure a 10–6 victory. Normally this would have sealed the series, but not so in 19th century baseball. A series was played for all three games no matter the outcome of each match. The two contestants met once more the following afternoon, where an equally sizeable crowd gathered to see what effect the two losses had on their hometown heroes. Tucson changed their battery, perhaps in a desperate attempt to slow down the offense being put up by Fort Thomas. With Walter Zabriskie now hurling and his younger brother B. J. Zabriskie catching, the Tucson lads finally had the break they were looking for to redeem some lost pride from the two error-prone losses. The move proved successful as the change in positions on the diamond led to a 10–8 victory. With the series won by Fort Thomas, the victors boarded a train on the Maricopa Rail Road line and headed north to begin the next series against the Phoenix Base Ball Club. Before departing, an effort was made by the Tucson nine to secure another game, with the wager being an astonishing $1,000 per side, to be played in 30 days. The offer was declined with rumor swirling that the visitors wanted no more of a rapidly improving Tucson Base Ball Club.

The issue clouding the terms of the territorial championship was the use of "imported professionals." There was certainly talk, if not an indirect accusation being levied at the manager of the Fort Thomas nine about using a professional hurler and catcher, Jordan and Tomlin—the winners of games one and two of the series with Tucson. The *Daily Star* retold the story of how a local machinist used a simple ruse to get Jordan, whose real name was Dick Hathaway, to reveal his identity as a former catcher from the professional Indianapolis Hoosiers of the National League, who competed within the ranks of the American Association in 1884, then revived for competition in the National League for the 1887–1889 seasons. After thorough investigation of the rosters and active seasons for the Indianapolis Hoosiers, it appears that Dick Hathaway never played as a catcher professionally. It seems that rumor was enough to convince the people of Tucson that this man on the Fort Thomas nine was something else. It is possible he was playing under an assumed name, which happened frequently, but for far different reasons than covering up a professional baseball career.

The Fort Thomas nine departed from Tucson and made the trip northward via the Maricopa Rail Road to begin the next series with Phoenix. The *Arizona Republican* printed the names of the nine men selected to compete against them on September 18, 1895. Interestingly, a member of the Phoenix B.B.C, a young Chris Sigala, would be among the home town nine. Sigala would later go on to athletic glory competing for both the Tempe Normal School's new foot ball club and the historic Tempe Crimson Rims Base Ball Club. The series in Phoenix would be held at Eastlake Park, located on 16th Street and Washington Street and accessible by horse-drawn trolley car for a modest five-cent fare. Game one was a rousing success for the Fort Thomas nine. In addition to reporting the final tally of 18 to 9, the editor for the *Arizona Republican* issued an apology to his readers for the lack of a detailed game report, explaining that the reporter sent to cover the game was an avid baseball enthusiast and had joined the Phoenix cranks in rooting for the home nine, forgetting entirely about his assignment. The *Arizona Republican* offered a different viewpoint of the Fort Thomas club, declaring that they were the "Champions of Arizona,"[32] having won two games out of three against Tucson. The *Arizona Republican* tried to dispel the myth that the lads from Fort Thomas were soldiers, instead stating that they were "composed of merchants, clerks, school teachers, farmers and operators."

The boys from Phoenix gathered their composure and regrouped for the second game of the series. Attendance at East Lake Park increased for the match, with the visitors from Fort Thomas now being dubbed the

"Athletics" in the *Arizona Republican*. The Phoenix nine would receive much-needed help from three of its regular players who were absent from game one. Without any kind of detailed game report being offered, the hometown gents reclaimed their pride with a resounding 19–1 victory. The stage was set for a third game to decide the series and, in the minds of some, the Territorial Championship of 1895. The attendance at East Lake Park surged, and heavy wagers were placed on both clubs. The final game was called at 2:15 p.m., with clear skies and temperatures in the mid-90s. The early frames were slow going on both sides, until finally, in the sixth, Fort Thomas broke through for six runs to take a 7–2 lead. The next inning would see another seven aces come across for the visiting nine, with the home club being blanked. With such a one-sided score, the cranks began to leave the park in droves—who could blame them? The Phoenix club regrouped again, determined to make it close, and over the last few frames scored 11 unanswered runs to bring the score close. This valiant effort went largely unnoticed with the exception of a small group of dedicated, enthusiastic cranks who yelled for the home nine through the last frames, only to culminate in a 15–13 defeat. Fort Thomas quietly left town, returning home with heavier purses. Over the entire tour, they would play a dozen games, with ten wins and two losses. News of their

Fort Whipple B.B.C. of 1895. Back row, left to right: Billy Osterman; unknown; unknown; John Riley; center: Lew Kortman, second base; Francis (?); unknown. Front: John Reilly, first base; unknown; unknown. (Arizona State Library)

success was reported territory-wide, even making the local news in the pages of the *Coconino Weekly Sun* out of Flagstaff.

Further north on the Upper Colorado River was Fort Mohave. In operation from 1866 as Camp Colorado, it was later renamed Fort Mohave for its participation as a base of operations for the U.S. Army's action against the Mohave people. Unfortunately, there was no newspaper account of baseball ever being played at or near Fort Mohave. It's quite possible that the commanding officers of the post felt that the men's energies were best suited elsewhere, or they simply disliked the game altogether. We will never truly know as no indication has yet been discovered and may be lost to the annals of time.

There is no doubt that most of the early Arizona baseball matches took place on military posts. Often, soldiers played amongst themselves on holidays, using homemade equipment on makeshift diamonds wherever they could find a level piece of ground such as the parade ground in the middle of camp. However, as the years passed on and the surrounding towns grew in population, so did interest of the sport. Supported by local newspapers like the *Arizona Miner, Arizona Silver Belt, Arizona Republican, Daily Star, Tombstone Epitaph* and others, baseball gained a popular foothold in the minds and hearts of young men who populated the Territory during these early years. The matches contested between the various Army units and citizens of nearby towns were an important way to bring communities together. The military posts were such an integral part of each town's existence and survival during this period; ball clubs fostered pride while offering a way to grow the National Pastime. Notably, the correspondence from Fort Bowie to Department Headquarters in Prescott in December of 1873 illustrates that the beginnings of baseball in Arizona were frequent games at the posts between units stationed there. Occasionally games against other posts were arranged during the holidays. As the population of surrounding towns grew, so did interest in baseball outside the post. The competition was fierce, with more than civic pride on the line as the first known wagering on sporting events seems to have taken place on baseball games. This rivalry between the Army posts and the nearby towns would continue well into the future of the young territory. The townsfolk would not only learn the game of baseball, but as will be seen in future chapters, they would make it their own long after the posts of the Arizona Territory had been shut down. It is a humble, yet integral beginning to the spread of our National Game within Arizona's rich past.

Chapter 2

The Red Stockings Are Here! (Or Were They?)

Less than one month before the nation's telegraph wires would explode with the shocking news of General George Armstrong Custer and 261 of his loyal soldiers of the 7th Cavalry having been decimated on the battleground at Little Big Horn, a historic event took place in the small frontier town of Prescott, Arizona Territory. Tragically, many of the fallen soldiers that were lost with Custer were members of the legendary Benteen Base Ball Club. The men formed the athletic association of Company H, 7th Cavalry. It was named after Captain Frederick Benteen, who inspired loyalty amongst his men in the regiment. The "Benteens," as they were known, were a highly skilled group of baseball players who would take on clubs from other posts on the Great Plains with regularity and would be consistently victorious. The Benteens reportedly defeated another club from a nearby post by an overwhelming tally of 51 to 3. The tragic loss in battle followed a monumental series of baseball games in the Arizona territorial capitol of Prescott.

On May 19, 1876, the *Arizona Weekly Miner* proudly announced that on the following Sunday, May 21, there would be a "match game of base ball, for the Championship of the Territory, between the Champion Base Ball Club (B.B.C.) of Prescott, and the Whipple Base Ball Club of Fort Whipple at 2 o'clock on the Plaza." The *Miner* writer added that a good match between the two clubs, who were familiar with each other on the field of play, was expected, and that both were in fine condition for competition. On a previous Sunday, the two clubs had squared off for a match contested on the Plaza, located between Gurley Street and Montezuma Street in the middle of the growing "village" of Prescott. The match was briefly reported in the pages of the *Miner* on May 5, noting that the

First Territorial Championship of 1876, featuring the Whipple B.B.C. and the Champions B.B.C. of Prescott. (Sharlot Hall Museum, Prescott)

Whipple Base Ball Club (a.k.a. the Whipples) was primarily composed of soldiers from nearby Fort Whipple and perhaps Camp Hualpai, which was located a short distance north of the fort.

From the rudimentary box score that accompanied the article, we learn that the Whipple B.B.C. led off in the first inning, tallying three aces. The Champion B.B.C. responded in their half of the frame with four aces. Both clubs would score three aces in the second inning. In the third frame, the Champion B.B.C. held the soldiers from Fort Whipple scoreless, otherwise known as a "white wash," while tallying two aces of their own to take an 8–6 lead going to the fourth inning. If the Champions of Prescott thought they had turned the tables in their favor, they were sadly mistaken. In the top of the fourth inning, the soldiers from the Whipple B.B.C. stormed back and recorded 12 aces, while returning the favor and whitewashing the Champions to take a commanding 18–8 lead with four innings to go.

From this point onward, the Whipple B.B.C. was in firm control and would score an additional 29 aces. The final tally, as reported by the *Miner*, was 47–21 in stark favor of the Whipple Base Ball Club. Upon reporting

2. The Red Stockings Are Here! (Or Were They?) 39

the wide margin of loss suffered by the hometown Champion B.B.C., the *Miner* sarcastically quipped, "By which it will be seen that the Champions got badly beaten." This would mark the first known contest between the club from Fort Whipple and the local favorites, the Champions B.B.C. of Prescott.

In order to restore their honor, it is believed that the Champion B.B.C. had contacted the Boston Red Stockings, either by telegraph or post, to request some much-needed assistance for the upcoming championship match where they would, once again, face their territorial rivals from Fort Whipple. How the challenge was issued for the Territorial Championship remains unknown, as the tradition of the day was for the challenging club to write to a club chosen for a match, which was then accepted or denied. The challenged club could agree to the match under proposed conditions or suggest an alternate date, location or stakes for the match. Often this was done through a local newspaper, such as the *Arizona Weekly Miner*. Unfortunately, no such correspondence has been found, and no record of a challenge being issued between the Whipple B.B.C. and the Champion B.B.C. has been found in any printed letters, private journals and correspondence from that time. Looking back, we are simply left to wonder about the finer points of exactly how the match was proposed and arranged.

With the announcement made in the newspaper readily accepted by both clubs, the game was on. The results of the match were published a week later, on May 26, 1876. The article came directly from the scorer's record, noting that the prize at stake was a "fine Regulation Dead Base Ball, 9¼ inches, 5¼ ounces; etc. … and the Championship of the Territory."[1] Before relating the box score, the writer cautioned readers that the territory was "a large field, and it may be that some Club at a distance may be inclined to dispute the right of the Clubs as to thus dispose of the Championship."

The Champions B.B.C. was indeed excited about the club's success, and if any other club in the territory issued a challenge, the hometown club would meet their challengers halfway for a match. The confidence level of the Champions B.B.C. had recovered from taking such a beating a few weeks earlier at the hands of the soldiers from Fort Whipple. Perhaps their excitement sprang from the knowledge that the vaunted Red Stockings from Boston would be on the field to help them achieve victory. The box score, which appeared on the front page of the *Miner*, reads as follows:

Whipple B.B.C.

	Run	Out	F.Catch	H.Run
Pitcher—Smith	3	2	1	0
2d B.—O'Neil	3	4	0	0
Catcher—Reynolds*	1	0	0	0
" "—Thornhill**	0	2	0	0
L. F.—Cody	1	3	1	0
1st B.—Ochus	3	3	1	0
S.S.—Phillipson	1	5	0	0
3d. B.—Guylfoyl	5	1	1	0
Right F.—Murray	3	3	0	0
C.F.—Schoemaker	2	4	0	0

Captain—Reynolds.

*Quit the field on account of injuries.
**Took Reynolds' place.

Champion B.B.C.

	Run	Out	F.Catch	H.Run
Pitcher—Caton	7	1	2	2
L.F.—Miles*	5	3	1	0
1st B.—Wheeler	4	4	0	0
S.S.—Sivyer	5	4	1	0
2d B.—Pettibone	7	2	1	0
C.F.—Jennison	4	5	0	0
Catcher—Heenan*	4	5	0	0
3d. B.—Schroeder	7	1	1	0
Right F.—Pierce	6	2	0	0

Captain—Heenan.

*Good foul catch.

Innings:	1	2	3	4	5	6	7	8	9	Total
C.B.B.C.	2	12	2	8	4	6	10	4	1	49
W.B.B.C.	1	2	2	6	1	3	1	4	2	22

Time, 3½ hours   Parker, Umpire.

Analysis of the box score does reveal some of the action that took place during the match, but does not give a complete picture of the action that transpired. This printed account doesn't follow the method of recording a game score that was used by Eastern newspapers after being developed in 1867 by Henry Chadwick and subsequently published in *Haney's Base Ball Book of Reference*. Besides the lopsided score of 49–22 we can see that it was a high-scoring affair, with several good plays being recorded by the reporter from the *Miner*. The hurler for the Champions, Mr. Caton, hit two home runs while scoring seven aces, making two foul catches and making one out during numerous appearances at the plate. His club-mates

2. The Red Stockings Are Here! (Or Were They?)   41

fared nearly as well, with second baseman Pettibone also tallying seven aces while making one foul catch and recording two outs at bat. The rest of the hometown club also did very well, resulting in their being crowned as the new Territorial Champions. However, the gallant efforts of the Whipple Base Ball Club cannot be completely ignored. Although they posted only 22 aces, there was one ballist whose performance led the way for the soldiers. Playing third base, Mr. Guylfoyl tallied five aces while making one foul catch and recording one out at bat. Even though disappointing for the soldiers from the Fort and those cheering them onward, this match must have been something to see for the citizens of Prescott who attended the match on the Plaza that afternoon.

In an effort to commemorate the day's festivities, a photo was taken after the match. Ballists[2] from both sides, along with interested spectators, stood on the grounds used for the ball field that were directly in front of C. T. Rogers & Co., Prescott Market, and the proprietorship of T. W. Otis. C. T. Rogers & Co. doubled as government contractors with the military posts at Fort Whipple and Camp Verde. They would supply the town of Prescott and the military posts with freshly butchered meats, and as of 1876 were the largest meat merchants in Arizona, supplying over 1,500 persons daily with meats and other supplies. Next door to the Prescott Market of C. T. Rogers & Co. stood the shop of T. W. Otis, a general store for groceries, cigars, tobaccos, stationery, cutlery, garden seeds. Otis was also an agent or retailer for both Singer and Wheeler & Wilson Sewing Machines.[3] Both faced the north side of the plaza along the 100 West blocks of Cortez and Gurley Streets. Mr. Otis would also serve as the postmaster in Prescott, earning an additional $1,900 per year for his services.

The photograph clearly shows soldiers, most likely enlisted men, standing to the left of center. Other participants and townsfolk make up the center and the right side of the photo. Clearly, the ballists from Boston are visible, posing in the front, right-hand side of the photo. The frontier photographer who was present for the match, W. H. Williscraft, also managed to take the first "in-action" shot of a live baseball game in Arizona's sports history. As reported in the *Miner*, Williscraft had opened a "Flying Gallery" that had his own photography equipment and supplies placed on wheels so he could travel to the outskirts of Prescott to take pictures for interested patrons to "send away to friends to see how Prescott looks."[4] He was 31 years old when the photos were taken and would enjoy several other professions other than being a frontier photographer. For one thing he became a shoemaker, owning a shoe and boot shop located "on the street leading from Prescott to Fort Whipple."[5] He was married in 1879 to

Luella Rogers and would live in the Prescott area until sometime around 1900.

With a mobile photographer on the scene for the post-match pictures, two surviving photographs reveal quite a bit about the happenings that day and the atmosphere in which the game was contested. Quite a few townsfolk were present to cheer both clubs on during the match, and in one photograph there were quite a few ladies visible.

The weather could hardly be more idyllic for the athletes and spectators. Warm sunshine and perhaps a light breeze made the day all the more pleasant for watching this exposition of the American game. Gentlemen and ladies in attendance no doubt wore suitable day-wear apparel, though perhaps not in the same Victorian tradition that was the standard of the day in the Eastern United States. The after-match photograph, along with the mention of the Champion B.B.C. receiving help during this match in a previous article, does raise a few significant questions. First, were these players from Boston really the much-respected and vaunted Red Stockings? If they were indeed in Prescott, then who were the men that provided the assistance requested? And if they weren't the Red Stockings, then who exactly were these gentlemen photographed with a "B" on their chest and remarkably different uniforms?

The Boston Red Stockings, a charter club in the newly formed National League in 1876, had started their regular season of play on April 22, 1876,

First known action shot of a live baseball game in Arizona. The Whipple B.B.C. and the Champions B.B.C. of Prescott play on the Courthouse Plaza, Prescott, 1876. (Sharlot Hall Museum, Prescott)

facing the Philadelphia Athletics in front of a crowd of 3,000 at the Jefferson Street Grounds in Philadelphia. With Cincinnati joining the National League that year, it was decided that the club from Boston would be re-named the "Red Caps" to allow for the Cincinnati nine to regain their former club name in honor of the legendary and undefeated 1869 season that brought glory and honor to the Queen City of Ohio. With the 1877 season in mind, it is questionable that nine of the Boston Red Caps had the time to complete such an arduous journey from Boston across the plains to the Arizona territories for one match. However, problems still persisted in scheduling games, as the tradition of having future contests arranged by the individual clubs through their respective secretaries remained in place. This no doubt may have created a gap in the early goings of the 1876 campaign that may have allowed the Red Caps to travel westward to play alongside the Champion Base Ball Club of Prescott. The post-match photograph that was taken by frontier photographer W. H. Williscraft does provide some evidence that a club from Boston was there for the match. But which club was it? With the newspapers in New York, Boston and Cincinnati covering professional baseball that season and reporting that the Red Caps were in those respective cities for regular season games, was it really the Boston Red Caps? Or was it an elaborate ruse put on by the Champion Base Ball Club in order to gain a psychological edge over their opponents?

The Boston area was teeming with baseball clubs and games. Other than the Red Caps, the Boston Lowells were the other mainstay club and attraction for baseball action whose results regularly appeared in local newspapers. The Boston Lowells baseball club was originally formed in 1861 as a junior organization. The Lowells were one of only three New England teams to hold the much-coveted Silver Ball trophy that was hotly contested every season in the region. The other two were the Tri-Mountain Club and the Harvard Club. The trophy was commissioned by John A. Lowell, an engraver, who was once the president of the Boston Bowdoin Club and a respected umpire in Boston. The results of championship matches were engraved on the ball, and a total of 17 matches were recorded at the time of its destruction in 1868. The New England Association of National Base Ball Players elected to destroy the trophy due to the bad behavior the players exhibited while attempting to win it. The Silver Ball was melted down and sold for $19.46 in silver bullion. Such a trophy today would have been worth $423.04 in silver, adjusting for the current rate of inflation. The worth of the trophy to baseball collectors and historians today would be much higher, as similar items have been auctioned off by Sotheby's of London for thousands of dollars apiece.

The *Lowell Courier* reported that on May 19, 1876, the "Bostons" defeated the New York Mutuals, seven aces to four, and across town the Lowells defeated the Fall Rivers, 13–1. Published alongside the scores was a brief box score of the Lowells versus Fall Rivers match, with names from both clubs reported within its pages. Apparently, it was commonplace to call the baseball club that represented the suburb of Lowell, Massachusetts, as the "Bostons." This naturally re-raises the question whether it was the Red Caps themselves or the nine from Lowell that made the journey to play in Prescott alongside the Champions B.B.C. After comparing the names in the box score as well as the rosters from both encyclopedias, it is clear that the Lowells were not the men who were here for the championship on the plaza.

After careful and thorough research of the group photograph that was taken after the match, it is apparent that the Red Caps could have been involved in the match. After studying the same photograph of the players taken after the championship on the plaza the library and archives of the Atlanta Braves, who draw their history and heritage from the Red Caps Club that might have been present in Arizona, it is reasonable to conclude that the following players could have been present: Starting on the left with the first ballist in a "B" jersey, we find Jim "Orator" O'Rourke, Foghorn Bradley, Lew Brown, Harry Schafer, Andy Leonard, an unknown ballist, Jack Manning, Tim Murnane and "Honest" John Morrill. Each of these Boston ballists had his own storied life in and out of the game of baseball.

Jim "Orator" O'Rourke was born on September 1, 1850, to Irish immigrant parents in Bridgeport, Connecticut. Fiercely loyal to his Irish roots, he was once asked to drop the "O" from his last name before signing with Boston in 1873, but stubbornly refused, saying "I would rather die than give up my father's name. A million dollars would not tempt me."[6] He earned a Law degree from Yale University during his early playing years while stationed in left field for the Middleton Mansfields. His club-mates, no doubt spurred on by his educational background, intellect, and lengthy, ornate, on-field verbal inclinations, gladly gave him the nickname of "Orator." O'Rourke's major league career spanned 1872–1904 and he played 1,999 games, second only to Adrian "Cap" Anson, at the time of his retirement. In 1876, O'Rourke would be second in the National League with 15 walks while hitting .327 with two home runs for the Red Caps.[7] He had the distinct honor of recording the first hit in National League history, striking against the Philadelphia Athletics on April 22, 1876. Over his career, "Orator" O'Rourke would finish with a batting average of .310 with 2,639 hits and 1,729 runs scored. He would have a remarkable career, with his last major league appearance being in 1904 with the New York Giants at the age of 54. "Orator" O'Rourke remains the oldest player ever to hit safely in a major league game.

Standing next to "Orator" O'Rourke was George H. "Foghorn" Bradley. Born on July 1, 1855, in Medford, Massachusetts, Bradley would play only one partial season for the Boston Red Caps as a hurler. During that partial season of 1876, he started 21 of the Red Caps' last 22 games. He recorded nine wins and ten losses, with 16 complete games including one shutout. Bradley left the major leagues to sign a contract with a minor league club after suspecting that he would be replaced by promising hurler Tommy Bond for the 1877 season by the Boston manager, legendary George Wright. This was Bradley's only season as a major league player, but he would gain more fame as an umpire beginning in 1879. Bradley would umpire for six seasons, single-handedly as was the custom of the day. He had the honor of umpiring two historic games, first witnessing Lee Richmond of the Worcester Ruby Legs toss the first perfect game in major league history on June 12, 1880. On August 20, 1880, he was the umpire when future Hall of Fame hurler Pud Galvin tossed the fifth no-hitter in major league history, while wearing a Buffalo Bisons uniform.

Sitting to the left of "Foghorn" Bradley was 19-year-old rookie Lew Brown. Primarily playing catcher and first base. Brown played seven seasons and for seven clubs—the Boston Red Caps, Providence Grays, Chicago White Stockings, Detroit Wolverines, Boston Beaneaters, Louisville Eclipse and Boston Reds. Between stints with the Providence Grays in 1881 and the Boston Beaneaters/Louisville Eclipse in 1883, Brown missed the entire 1882 season due to being blacklisted for "confirmed dissipation and general insubordination." Apparently his antics weren't appreciated by the Providence Grays, and word spread throughout the rest of the National League, garnering him a one-year suspension that would send a message to the young ballist about his questionable behavior.

Standing to the left of the seated Lew Brown, with a bat partially resting in his right hand while he glares in the direction of the camera, was the veteran Harry Schafer. Schafer made his debut for the Red Stockings of the National Association on May 5, 1871, and would be a durable third baseman for Boston over eight seasons, with the club winning six championships. He was a durable player at his position and a solid hitter for a Boston club that would rise to dominate professional baseball through the early years of the National League. In 1876, he led the league in games played and hit .252.

Kneeling to the left of Harry Schafer was the legendary native-born Irishman, Andy Leonard. By the time Leonard played in the championship match on the plaza, he had been playing baseball since 1864, when he was a member of the Hudson River club of Newburgh, New York, within the amateur National Association of Base Ball Players (NABBP). He has the distinct honor of being commonly recognized as the first Irish-born major league baseball player. After playing five seasons with various clubs within the NABBP, Andy Leonard moved to Cincinnati, Ohio, to join the Buckeyes—at that time principal rivals of the mighty Red Stockings. He would compete in several hotly contested matches between the two rival clubs that represented a proud Queen City. Later in 1869, Leonard was one of five men hired by Harry Wright in order to complete the first openly paid professional club in baseball history. During that landmark season, Leonard was paid $800 as the regular left gardener for the Cincinnati nine and would also fill in as an infielder over the next ten seasons. After touring the nation in 1869 and 1870 with the mighty Red Stockings from the Queen City, Leonard signed with the Washington Olympics for the 1871 season, then made his way to Boston in 1872, remaining there for the next seven seasons. Leonard would finish his major league career in 1880 for the Cincinnati Reds, recording a lifetime batting average of .299 with 716 hits and 481 runs scored. As a fitting testament to his prowess as a baseball player, the Irish Baseball League award for the most valuable player naturally bears Andy Leonard's name.

Standing to the immediate left of Leonard, hands clasped together around the knob of a thick bat, was an unidentified ballist. Kneeling next to him we find 23-year-old John E. "Jack" Manning. Born on December 20, 1853, in Braintree, Massachusetts, Manning broke into the National Association in 1873 at the age of 19. During the 1876 season, Manning played 70 games as a right fielder, while batting .264 with two home runs. He would join the Cincinnati Reds in 1877 and post a 9–12 record as manager while playing shortstop for the last-place nine from the Queen City. Manning was the third player in major league history to hit three home runs in one game, accomplishing the feat on October 9, 1884, while playing for the Philadelphia Quakers against the Chicago White Stockings. Manning's professional career lasted until 1886, and he played for eight clubs.

Standing to the left of the crouched Manning stood the lithe figure of Timothy Hayes Murnane. Born of Irish descent on June 4, 1851, Murnane played 12 seasons in the major leagues but would best be remembered as the leading staff writer on the sport for the widely read and respected *Boston Globe*. His professional career began in 1872, when he played as the Middletown Mansfields' regular first baseman alongside Jim "Orator" O'Rourke. The 1872 campaign was his best, as he placed fifth in the National Association's (NA) batting race with a .360 average. He led the NA in 1875 with 30 stolen bases. He would finish his short career with a batting average of .261 and 336 runs scored. In 1884, he was the manager and first baseman for the Boston club of the Union Association, where he finished with a managerial record of 58–51 while hitting .235. Other honors would be given to Tim Murnane for his work as a sportswriter and editor, most significantly in the 1946 "Honor Rolls" of the National Baseball Hall of Fame, where he was one of 12 writers honored.

The last ballist wearing a white uniform with a noticeable "B" on the chest, and standing farthest to the left, was 21-year-old rookie "Honest" John Morrill. Born on February 19, 1855, to Irish immigrants in Boston, Massachusetts, "Honest" John made his professional baseball debut with the Boston Red Caps in 1876 as a first baseman. His career spanned 15 seasons, all but two seasons for the Red Caps, Beaneaters or Reds in his hometown of Boston. He is the only man to play for both Harry Wright and Mike "King" Kelly while wearing a Boston uniform. The zenith of his career came in 1883 with the Boston Beaneaters, when he batted .319 with six home runs while covering first base. Astonishingly, he also pitched two games that year with a 1–0 record and a 2.77 E.R.A.[8] Honest John also had a 33–11 record as manager of the Beaneaters after the mid-season departure of Jack Burdock, and would be the first manager to win a pennant after assuming duties mid-season.

The second photograph that was captured by W. H. Williscraft of the championship on the plaza match features in-game action. This is remarkable since the photography equipment of the day was not designed or intended to take action shots of any kind. We see a fairly good-sized crowd gathered on the plaza in front of the C. T. Rogers & Co. Prescott General Store and the shop of T. W. Otis on a pleasant afternoon in May of 1876. The four ballists from the Boston Red Caps stand out in their white uniforms in the right-center of the photograph. Three of the players in white seem to be in motion near the third base line, with the fourth Red Cap standing in the middle of the photograph.[9] Standing behind him is the left fielder,[10] clad a white shirt and dark blue or black trousers, standing just to the right of the flag pole on the left side of the photo taken during the home half of an inning.

Much about the match itself is left to imagination and the speculative nature that follows. We do not know exactly how many cranks from Prescott were in attendance, or how many were ladies. We don't know the nature of the game, how many errors were committed by one side or the other. We don't know how charged the atmosphere was, how much excitement there was surrounding and leading up to the much-anticipated contest. We have a few newspaper articles, two photographs and imagination to fill in the blanks left to us by history.

The article in the *Arizona Weekly Miner* that reported the results of this match mentioned no names of ballists from Boston. This omission, whether intentional or not, leaves the question of whether or not the Boston Red Caps were actually present for this match hanging over our collective heads. Even with an attempt made at identifying them in the first photograph taken after the match on the plaza in Prescott, questions remain about each player's on-field contributions that day. It is worth noting the discrepancy in the roster size for the 1876 Boston Red Caps, who were previously known as the Red Stockings. According to *The Great Encyclopedia of 19th-Century Major League Baseball*, the Red Caps numbered 17, including four substitutes and three additional hurlers. *The Baseball Encyclopedia, 9th Edition,* says the roster size was 11, including the regular nine and two substitutes, as was commonplace during that era. David Nemec's *The Great Encyclopedia of 19th Century Baseball* goes a bit further in providing the names of the additional ballists on the Red Caps in 1876: Tim McGinley, Sam Wright, Bill Parks, manager Harry Wright, and additional hurlers Joe Borden, Dick McBride and Tricky Nichols. With this in mind, it is entirely possible that the Red Caps, or Red Stockings as they were reported in the *Arizona Weekly Miner* article on May 19, 1876, could have been in Prescott and did participate in this match, as it appears that there may have been enough ballists for the club to send a group westward, while still competing in games during the early months of the inaugural season of the National League.

Several facts dispel the myth of the famous Red Caps of Boston being present for this match. Boston was scheduled to face the New York Mutuals on May 20 for one game, then travel to Cincinnati for a three-game series. The only route westward in 1876 that would have come anywhere near the Arizona Territory was the route that linked the Union Pacific and Central Pacific Rail lines and passed through the Great Plains and into the Utah Territory. The trip would have taken eight days to complete. The famed "Lightning Express" trip made by a group of stage actors headed to San Francisco and the Pacific Coast aboard a specially built locomotive and Pullman car wouldn't leave Jersey City, New Jersey, until

2. The Red Stockings Are Here! (Or Were They?) 49

June 1, 1876. That feat of travel would take 83 hours and 39 minutes, more than three days to complete despite a washed-out track in Utah. This special route would run non-stop to complete a very arduous, dangerous journey, as locomotives of the day were not specifically designed to run as hard as the Lightning Express would need to in order to cover such a vast distance in a short amount of time. Another factor that would prevent the Red Stockings from attending the match would be transportation to and through the arid land of the Arizona Territory. The Southern Pacific Rail Road lines wouldn't cross the Lower Colorado River and reach Yuma until the summer of 1877. Further north, the joint effort of the Santa Fe and Southern Pacific Rail Road companies wouldn't complete their joint line in Flagstaff until the summer of 1882, with the same line reaching the trading post of Williams on September 1. These events, significant in their own right for the future development of the state economically and socially, indicate that travel to the territory in 1876 from the East Coast would have been a lengthy and dangerous affair. Logically, no owner of a professional baseball nine would risk such a hot commodity on such a folly that wouldn't have made any money along the way.

According to the *New York Clipper*, the same Red Stockings identified in the Prescott photograph were playing their normal positions in a loss against the Mutuals in Boston at the South End Grounds on the afternoon of May 20. The infield and catcher that were allegedly in Arizona on May 21 were the subject of an approving post-match article in the *Clipper* which noted, "Leonard's play at second was excellent, as was that of Murnane at first and Shafer at third, while Morrill acquitted himself in handsome style behind the bat."[11] The lads would be in Cincinnati a few days later and would be back to their winning ways, besting the Red Stockings of the Queen City in all three games, including two shutouts tossed by Joe Borden.

It seems that the Red Stockings were not in Arizona, nor anywhere close. If the famed club wasn't in Arizona, then who were the nine young men who chose to don the uniform of the National League champions?

The article and box score offered by the *Arizona Journal Miner* offered different names from the Boston nine as being the on-field players for the Champion Base Ball Club. According to the *Great Register of Yavapai County for 1876*, all of them were residents of Prescott, holding various jobs. The confusing part in sorting out who these men were is that the *Great Register* made many spelling discrepancies in names of townsfolk, including the names of the nine gentlemen who comprised the Champion Base Ball Club. For instance, a third baseman by the last name of Schroeder is listed as possibly being a mining engineer, a baker, or even a part-time photographer working for W. H. Williscraft. Mr. Schroeder might have played in the game and took the photographs when the match was concluded. Other men making up the club were James Hickson Miles, a carpenter who played left field for the Champion B.B.C.; Leonard D. Sivyer, occupation unknown, who played shortstop and acted, along with second baseman Hat Pettibone and first baseman N. G. Wheeler, in the touring theatre group the "Prescott Minstrels," also called the "Prescott Amatuers" in the *Arizona Weekly Miner* and *Arizona Journal Miner*. Other members of the Champions were employed as painters or tinners, such as Nathaniel Parda Pierce, right field, and Charles Heenenan, the club's catcher and field captain.

The Prescott Minstrels were an active and popular local theatre group who made a tour of the Arizona Territory, leaving on January 28, 1877. The tour route saw them traveling to Wickenburg, south to Phoenix, Florence and Tucson before making an easterly swing through Globe and Gila County, then north through the military camps of Apache County and the Little Colorado areas before returning home many weeks later. The *Arizona Weekly Miner* endorsed the talent of the group, stating "If the people will give them 'half a show,' they will give the people a good show."[12] Three members of the Champions Base Ball club were with this traveling minstrel group, which raises the possibility that these three gentlemen-actors decided to impersonate the famous baseball nine from Boston during the championship match against the soldiers. Perhaps it was ego, or a neatly disguised attempt to rattle their opponents at match time by employing an intimidation tactic. Such an act was a well-planned and executed ruse, as even the writer for the *Miner* picked up on the difference, noting in an article published on May 19 that the Champions would receive assistance from the "Red Stockings" of Boston, with special emphasis on the uncharacteristically printed quotation marks. The main details left unknown would be how they obtained uniforms and which player came up with the idea.

No matter who played on both clubs, this match on the plaza between the soldiers of Fort Whipple and the Champions Base Ball Club of Prescott would mark a turning point in Arizona sports history. As the records and documents suggest, most if not all baseball matches played before 1876 were on military posts between random groups of soldiers or even specific units of regular U.S. Army troops. This match would mark the beginning of competition between towns and the soldiers stationed at the camps and forts nearby, as well as other baseball clubs in towns across the territory. It appears that no other club answered the challenge for the Territorial Championship that was subsequently issued by the newly crowned Champion B.B.C. These two clubs would not face each other on the diamond for quite a few years, with the Prescott B.B.C. awaiting formal reorganization until 1880. The soldiers on post at Fort Whipple wouldn't see action again as an organized nine until a few years afterwards.

The Championship of the Territory would not be openly contested again until 1887, in the first baseball tournament at the Territorial Fair that was held at the original ball grounds site near Phoenix along the banks of the flood-prone Salt River.[13]

In conclusion, the first Territorial Championship match contested by the Whipples and the Champions from Prescott would mark a unique chapter in Arizona history. Baseball would start to spread across the state as a result of this match being reported in the pages of the territory's largest newspaper in 1876, the *Arizona Weekly Miner.* The Boston Red Caps would, in their almost anonymous way, place an indelible mark upon Arizona and help encourage the spread of the game through the excitement generated by their alleged visit to Prescott. From here, the game would transition from being contested solely by the military, to being part of holidays and a matter of civic pride for many communities within Arizona. Sadly, no further information about both clubs and their formation can be found at this time. Despite the relatively short history of both early baseball clubs in the Prescott area, there is ample evidence that baseball had taken hold within the growing Arizona community. There is evidence and speculation that professional baseball was being followed with great interest in newspapers from cities across the United States such as New York, Cincinnati, St. Louis, Boston and San Francisco. Townsfolk in Prescott would be inspired, and would aspire to emulate their baseball idols on the diamond themselves. The future would be a bright and competitive one for both the military post and town, as indicated in the next chapter, and forged a storied history that helped establish baseball as Arizona's pastime.

Chapter 3

Town Rivalries Take Shape

The people who lived in the various towns, settlements and burgs in the Arizona Territory took a natural pride in their home towns. In the 19th century, the town's baseball nine was a source of outward pride that could be bragged about in the pages of the territorial newspapers along with letters sent to friends, family and acquaintances both inside and outside of Arizona. Newspapers were distributed in other Arizona towns, and those papers would find any reason to boast that their home city was the best, brightest and most desirable place to live in the land. Having a good baseball club enhanced a community's sense of pride. This relationship also fostered competition and nurtured rivalries to develop across Arizona. This competitive spirit would begin early and last throughout much of the territorial era of Arizona.

After the heralded Boston Red Stockings assisted the Champions of Prescott in securing the first Territorial Championship in the spring of 1876, baseball rapidly took hold across the Arizona Territory largely through military clubs playing their civilian counterparts. In the next few years, the game quickly spread to growing towns such as Tombstone, Tucson, Phoenix and Yuma. By 1880, the young territory had only 40,441 residents. This was less than half of New Mexico and far less than California. Most of them resided in these growing centers of mining and trade and within close proximity to military posts for protection from an ongoing threat of violence from Native American tribes that were campaigned against by soldiers of the U.S. Army under the command of General George Crook during the ongoing Indian Wars period.

The prominent newspapers of the day—the *Arizona Weekly Miner, Arizona Daily Citizen, Weekly Star, Tombstone Epitaph, Salt River Herald, Arizona Democrat, Arizona Sentinel, Phoenix Herald, Pinal Drill, Arizona Silver Belt, Mohave County Miner* and *Arizona Champion*—all at some point publicized and promoted the formation of baseball clubs to represent the towns that were the main focus of their journalistic efforts. These papers routinely ran short editorial pieces or even one-line entries admonishing their subscribers to promote their town as the best in the territory and to refrain from speaking ill about their beloved settlement. With this kind of sponsored message distributed to the citizens of the Arizona Territory, when the new game of baseball was introduced, most townsfolk saw the game as a vehicle to boost their town. This support included promoting banquets and masquerade balls given by home-town baseball clubs, such as the masquerade ball given sometime during the week of November 15, 1877, by the Phoenix Base Ball Club at Patton's Opera House in Phoenix.[1]

Yuma

The place heralded as the "birthplace" of baseball amongst the early towns of the Arizona Territory would be Yuma. The first known town to have baseball games between two clubs, on February 21, 1874, the town saw its first match between two nines composed of local inhabitants. The match was contested in front of the Exchange mercantile store on Main Street between two nines of "Prominent Young Men" of town, drawing the interest of many and creating quite a stir. The *Arizona Sentinel* reported that it was surprised to see "such an outcropping of so much energy" and was "pleased at the opportunity of adding so much interest to our local columns." The reporter also noted the dexterity of the ballists involved as well as the courage of the catcher and first sack to field the ball despite injuries sustained by both men that afternoon. The catcher for the first nine lost fingernails on three of his fingers, but despite the painful injury, he stubbornly stayed on the field of play, exhibiting great skill in catching the hurler's pitches. The article was favorable but raised some questions about why a ballist would be called "butterfingers" if he dropped a fly ball or about the need to slide head-first into first sack. Also interesting was the writer's report that the bases were nothing more than a "pile of rocks" and that sliding required "much nerve and nicety of execution."[2] The article vividly described the match's umpire being allowed to sit in an arm chair behind the catcher, with an umbrella for shade and perhaps a beverage of his choice for refreshment. Despite such details of the match, no box score or final tally was recorded. It appears that the writer was more interested in the happenings of the game and simply forgot to record the score.

In the same issue of the *Arizona Sentinel*, another short column noted that there was a strong intention of the citizens of Yuma to form a town baseball club as a result of catching the "spirit of Base Ball." The young men offered the position of umpire to the writer or editor of the *Sentinel*, but seeing the potential for injury in a previous match influenced the newspaperman to pass on the job. The coverage in Yuma didn't diminish in the coming weeks. Matches on February 28, 1874, and later on March 22, featured local players on two un-named nines that would compete in the grounds in front of the Yuma Exchange, located centrally on Main Street, with perhaps a wager or two between clubs. Notably, the games drew crowds, including many ladies, to watch the new game in town. As in previous articles, the writer failed to give a detailed account of the score or action inning by inning, but did report that the "native boys" were victorious by a wide margin. A challenge for another game was issued for the following afternoon by the winning club, and readily accepted.

The good humor and gentlemanly manner of the contestants had caught on, helping to fuel the popularity of baseball in Yuma. For example, on March 7, 1874, after a quick lead by the "native nine," the regular nine quickly acknowledged defeat and called the game finished by the end of the third inning. In a gracious demonstration of sportsmanship by the losing club, the Captain of the same "native nine" took the liberty of buying rounds of beer for all ballists that played that day at a saloon on Main Street.

The *Sentinel* realized that baseball was very popular in town and wanted to promote the game as a way to gain territorial recognition and pride. In a few short years, the paper would have ample opportunity to do so by reporting matches between the C.A. Earnest Base Ball Club of Fort Yuma and the home-town Yuma City Club or "Red Shirts," as discussed in Chapter 1. However, baseball would disappear from Yuma for nearly ten years, finally re-introduced on March 20, 1886, with the editor of the *Arizona Sentinel* noting that "baseball fever has made a start in Yuma and soon will have full swing of the burg" and would replace the Yuma Indian game of "shinny." The Native American bat-and-ball game was played on a large field with contestants using a longer stick with one crooked end, much like a modern hockey stick. The ball, similar to a baseball in size and construction, was kicked or tossed into the center of the field. The players played "on the sticks," meaning the only means of moving the ball towards the goal was to use the stick to bat or push it up field. It was a rough game where intentional tripping was commonplace, with no rest periods over a match that usually lasted several hours. Victory was awarded to the first side to score a goal by launching the ball through a pair of sticks lodged in the ground. This version of field hockey was immensely popular amongst the Yuma and Mohave Indians as well as several other tribes across the United States. It is very possible that during the long absence of baseball in the Yuma area, this game was played until the resurgence of the National Pastime in 1886, when two picked nines of cowboys would take the diamond.

Baseball wouldn't be played regularly in Yuma for an entire year, as no games were reported in the *Sentinel* during 1887. Games commenced again with these two nines facing each other in the spring of 1888. The long-awaited rematch was a complete blow-out as the Caballeros, led by Joe Redondo, were determined to win the rematch. They did so by an impressive final tally of 45 to 15 in an error-filled contest in the fields of local rancher Don J. M. Molina. The play of the two nines was no doubt sloppy, prompting the *Sentinel* to urge the nines to practice some before further entertainment of the locals. The paper even brazenly suggested that both nines' form made the game more of a "spectacle" than serious sport.

In a letter published on the front page of the *Sentinel* on December 1, 1888, an inhabitant of Mohawk Valley aptly named "Gentle Annie" made the first mention of an obscure baseball club named the Mohawk Plungers. Gentle Annie related the recent drought of baseball games played by the Mohawk nine, speculating that their regular opponents, possibly a Yuma team or a nine from neighboring ranches aptly named the "Amblers," had quit the field for "nursing the wounded and applying cold-water bandages to the enlarged heads of its 'doubty' champions."[3] There was a Christmas game scheduled between the Plungers, who had continued practicing, and the Yuma Base Ball Club. The game never occurred, with Gentle Annie sounding off about the Amblers possibly abandoning their club permanently and the application of the Plungers to a league in a follow-up letter to the *Sentinel* published on January 5, 1889. A few weeks later, in a separate letter written by an anonymous author called "Hayseed," the *Sentinel* noted that a return match for $100 per side was arranged between the Mohawk Plungers and the Amblers from Texas Hill. The Plungers were so confident in their baseball skills that a representative boasted that they would like to travel to the distant burg of Phoenix to try the Phoenix Base Ball club. In response to this heady exhibition of 19th century bravado, the *Sentinel* added to a budding rivalry between the Texas Hill Amblers and the Mohawk nine, declaring, "The Mohawk Plungers (base ball club) challenge any club in the Territory, but would prefer to meet the Texas Hill Amblers,"[4] possibly implying that the Mohawk nine weren't as good as they thought. After an exchange of barbs and taunts the two clubs were set to meet on the field for a match, though it seems to not have taken place.

Baseball activity in Yuma continued to wax and wane over the coming years, with clubs disbanding, then reforming again in 1892. For the next decade, the story would remain the same. Games would be a part of the Fourth of July festivities as well as Thanksgiving and Christmas, between local nines and on occasion against soldiers from Fort Yuma on the California side of the Lower Colorado River.

Tucson

With the increasing baseball activity in Prescott of the Champions Base Ball Club, and the Whipple Base Ball Club, as well as in the streets of Yuma, the next frontier town to embrace the national game was, to no one's surprise, Tucson. The "Old Pueblo" settlement dated back to March of 1856, and in the following years Tucson was a stage station of the Butterfield Overland Mail Route connecting Los Angeles, Yuma and further east to the settlement of Franklin, Texas, now known as El Paso, with early mail service and a rudimentary stage route delivering freight and travelers.

The earliest mention of baseball appeared in a column on December 21, 1872, in the *Arizona Citizen* as a public announcement that "Lovers of the game of baseball, are invited to meet this evening in the dining hall of J. Newgrass to organize a club for active service." The *Citizen* writer was confident in noting that attendance at the meeting would be enough to fill the club's roster, with equipment readily available for a pick-up match to be played after the meeting that evening. No record exists of that first ball game in Tucson, who the players were, or if interest in the game took hold. It seems that interest in baseball went dormant for several years. The first team formed in Tucson was the Lone Star Base Ball club sometime in the fall of 1877. Their first opponents were the Worth Base Ball Club of Fort Lowell. The *Arizona Weekly Star* announced that both clubs would meet in front of the school grounds in Tucson, the game to commence at 1:30 p.m. sharp on Sunday, December 2, 1877.[5] Unfortunately, the result of this match is unknown and lost to history. Baseball would remain part of the landscape in the Old Pueblo, even drawing attention from noted frontiersman, saloon keeper, and diarist George O. Hand. In his *Saloon Diary of Old Tucson*, his entry for Sunday December 15, 1878, noted that he was up early and it was cold, but "There was a baseball game and a horse race today."[6] Following the early entry in Hand's private journal, there was a match between the "Greaser" and Gringo" nines. The match took place on the Military Plaza in town on Christmas Day and was reported in the following edition of the local paper as the first known Christmas baseball match in Tucson. The *Arizona Weekly Star* noted that the game saw little skill displayed by both clubs, and that the Gringo nine were victorious. The column did not mention whether any of the participants in the match were soldiers from Fort Lowell. No score was given.[7] If baseball caught the attention of someone as seasoned as George Hand, then there must have been quite a stir created by those who watched these games as the popularity of baseball spread through the Old Pueblo.

The following summer, the *Daily Arizona Citizen* reported that a baseball match was contested on July 4, 1879, as a part of the holiday festivities in Tucson. The match featured two nines selected from volunteers.[8] Subsequent issues of the *Daily Citizen* failed to report the action of the match or a final score. The sporadic games would continue until the following October, when two new clubs emerged on the scene, ready to compete with each other and clubs in neighboring towns. Continuing with the idea of participating in national holidays, the two new clubs faced each other on Thanksgiving Day, 1879. The *Arizona Daily Citizen*, continuing to support baseball, published a story that the two clubs were to be called the "Citizen" and "Star" nines.[9] The paper noted that "considerable interest is manifested" and that both clubs were practicing for the upcoming match. The paper also divulged the lost names of ballists being considered to represent the Citizen nine: Requa, Farell, Snyder, Roche, Goodfriend, Hereford, Clum, Reed, the Moroney brothers and a gentleman named Frank.

Two weeks later, the names of the players officially chosen to play for the Citizen nine on Thanksgiving Day were published by the *Daily Citizen*. The two clubs had arranged for a series of games to be played for the "Star Cup," no doubt a handsomely carved or engraved trophy to be displayed by the winning club in the window or storefront of a favored patron. The first match, scheduled for November 27, 1879, would commence at 10 a.m. on the Military Plaza in downtown Tucson. The men competing for the Citizen nine, selected from the earlier named group, were as follows: Requa, first base; Hereford, shortstop; Moses Lully, catcher; Roach, hurler; Goodfriend, second base; Mark Lully, third base; Wood, left field;

C. Moroney, center field; T. Casselli, right field, and a ballist with the last name of Nichols acting as the club's only substitute.[10]

The two clubs finally clashed on the field on November 27, 1879. From the basic box score printed by the *Daily Citizen*, it appears that a combination of poor fielding and prolific striking created this high-scoring affair—31–30 in favor of the Citizen nine. The paper remarked that "the game was not marked by any brilliant fielding."[11] Through nine innings, it came down to the wire, adding to public interest and excitement. The score was close, ending in a one-run victory for the Citizen nine, with mention for Renshaw, Gillette, and Pomroy of the Star nine as the most notable that day. For the Citizen club, Roach and Requa were good in striking and gained praise for solid fielding as well. For the victors, the play of Farrell deserved the praise given. Through nine innings, Farrell scored/drove in seven runs, while not recording a single out. The coveted Star Cup was taken to Schusler's Store on Church Street to be put on display on behalf of a proud Citizen nine. The obligatory return match was tentatively scheduled for December 7, 1879.

December 7 came and went, with no word on a return match from the defeated Star nine.[12] Eager to test their mettle against other clubs outside of the Old Pueblo, the Citizens nine challenged the Phoenix Base Ball Club to a match on New Year's Day, 1880, under the new name of the Tucson Base Ball Club. At stake were a Peck & Snyder Regulation Dead Ball and a purse of $100 that was furnished by the proud citizens of Tucson. As confident boosters of the Tucson club, the *Arizona Daily Citizen* was more than happy to print the open challenge, no doubt hoping for territory-wide circulation. From the simple box score for the first game to decide the Star Cup, and the signatures printed in the following edition of the *Daily Star* that issued the challenge to the Phoenix B.B.C., it appears that both the Citizen nine and the Star nine combined forces in December of 1879 to create the upstart Tucson Base Ball Club. Three of the nine players for the new club were from the defeated Star nine, with one of the two substitutes also being from that club. Perhaps this was discussed at a general meeting, open to all persons interested in the New Year's game between Tucson and Phoenix, at Levin's Park Hall at eight o'clock on December 18, 1879.

One week later, a response from the Phoenix Base Ball club was sent back to the Tucson club via telegraph, saying they would meet the Tucsonans for a game, but with elevated stakes. It was proposed that a purse of $250 per side be put up, while the winning club would bear the expenses of the trip for their foes. It is unknown if the new terms for the match between the Tucson and Phoenix nines were agreed upon, but the *Daily Citizen* reminded its readers that the long-awaited return match to decide the final possession of the Star Cup would take place on January 1, 1880, at 2 o'clock in the afternoon on the Union Grounds, on the Old Military Plaza. While details of the match were awaited by readers of the local newspapers, it appears that the Clerks of the Military Department Headquarters had formed a baseball club and were getting in practice "on the sly."[13] With disappointment, the *Daily Citizen* mentioned that the New Year's game between the Tucson and Phoenix clubs was not played as advertised, instead the Phoenix Base Ball Club would be in a contest with the soldiers of Fort McDowell for a match on January 3, 1880, in Phoenix.

The following summer, a large fire destroyed a significant section of town, including the newspaper office of the *Tucson Citizen*. The loss, as reported on June 17, 1881, in the *Phoenix Herald*, totaled $4,000. In today's dollars, the loss would total $93,731.03. Surprisingly, the business equipment, paper and building used by the *Citizen* was not covered by any insurance. Fire was a constant danger in the towns and military posts of territorial Arizona. Fires could spread quickly, and the towns lacked any kind of fire-fighting equipment other than utilizing a bucket line to pass water to douse the flames. Fires usually consumed a significant section of town, resulting in a big economic loss and interruption of normal daily life. This fire interrupted business interests and social happenings, including baseball games, until the town could be rebuilt. Baseball in the Old Pueblo ceased, and would be reorganized again under the direction of former Tombstone resident Bob Lewis in 1882. In May, the Tucson B.B.C. selected grounds to use for an upcoming series with Tombstone. They chose a "handsome, level plat of ground on the road to Silver Lake, about a half mile from town"[14] for the upcoming series with Tombstone and for future games for the reorganized nine. The Tucson series would be an interesting series for the new nine. The *Arizona Weekly Star* of May 11, 1882, noted that a brilliant struggle was to be had and comfortable seats with awnings would be made available to shade the many ladies expected to be in attendance. The next day, the names and positions of the ballists from both nines were printed along with a few pre-match notes to push the level of excitement for the first game of the series. As would be expected, the *Arizona Daily Star* mentioned that "The betting is about even, there being no backwardness in accepting wages offered."[15] Clearly, the games would be just the tonic that Tucson needed in recovering from the catastrophic fire that ravaged the town just a few months earlier.

The *Daily Star* also noted that there would be "Herdic" coaches running from the intersection of Congress and Meyer Streets, in downtown Tucson, at 25 cents for a one-way trip for those who lacked personal transportation. "Herdic" coaches were horse-drawn buses or cabs that could seat up to eight persons comfortably, and were the forerunner of the modern-day cab. Locally, this service was offered by the Tucson Land and Herdic Coach Company. Founded on November 16, 1881, the new transportation company filled a need to get customers to and from the new train depot built the previous year. Over the remainder of the 1880s, service became so sporadic that by 1891, plans were made to implement a railcar line throughout metropolitan Tucson. The Herdics were a vast improvement over previous modes of transportation as they could deposit their customers curbside, instead of leaving them in the middle of a muddy street as was common with earlier horse-car service. The excitement felt locally was so strong that everyone living in the Old Pueblo would make a strong effort to attend the game, ensuring that enterprising young businessmen would try to capitalize on the crowds any way they could. Lastly, it was mentioned that both clubs would leave the Palace Hotel together, riding in several coaches with a lively "Tally-Ho!" To push the growing baseball frenzy to new heights, there would be no admission charge to the match.

Finally, the much-anticipated match between the Tombstone and Tucson Base Ball Clubs took place on Friday, May 12. Coverage of the match appeared in the *Arizona Daily Star*, which had been covering all aspects of baseball leading up to the match. There was an enormous crowd in attendance, with many standing along the base lines in foul ground and "many enjoying the scene from carriages and coaches." The weather was perfect. The crowd was on edge. The ballists were nervous. A charged wagering atmosphere meant quite a bit of money exchanging hands, with a fever-pitch in odds coming in the later frames of the contest. The Tucson lads took the field first, clad in white jerseys and knickers with blue hose and trim. The Tombstone nine were dressed in similarly styled jerseys and knickers, but wore red belts and hose instead. In the top of the first, the Tombstone nine scored two runs and Tucson answered with a run of its own in the bottom half. Both clubs featured hard-throwing pitchers, each trying to outdo his opponent from the box. Hitting that afternoon was lively, and the scoring went back and forth with several lead changes that drove the tension of the cranks in the stands to new highs every inning. Oddsmakers in attendance scrambled to accept money after each inning as the odds on who would win were changing quickly. Late in the match, the hometown nine pulled ahead for what looked to be the last

3. Town Rivalries Take Shape   61

time, setting off a wild celebration with cranks from Tucson throwing the bats used by their nine into the air. Their joy would be short-lived as the clubs were soon tied at 13 runs with darkness setting in. There were protests from both sides that the match should be declared a tie. However, the substitute umpire, R. E. Kearon, decided that the game should continue. The Tombstones rallied in the top of the tenth and scored seven unanswered runs for the victory. The charged atmosphere caused several ugly fights in the crowd. In response, and maybe to keep the peace, the umpire decided to call it a draw since the game went into extra innings. When the Tombstone Club departed the next morning for a return trip home, no word had been relayed about the award of the sums of money wagered during the match.

The next day, the decision of the umpire that finished the match was printed in the *Arizona Daily Star*. Mr. R. E. Kearon quoted Rule 44 of Spalding's Base Ball Guide for 1882 as it related to a draw game. This allowed the game to be declared a draw on account of darkness and all wagers cancelled. A few days later, a challenge for a customary return match, to be played in Tombstone, was reported in the *Daily Star*. The editor scoffed at the challenge, saying "There will be an acceptance, of course."[16] On May 19, a short reply letter written by the Tucson Base Ball Club to the Tombstone Base Ball Club was printed in the newspaper. The president of the Tucson Base Ball Club, Mr. Percy Thompson, apologized for an unsatisfactory result of the first match between the two clubs and pledged his club would do everything possible to make things right the next time. Mr. Thompson skirted the challenge, saying it was doubtful that a skilled nine could be raised for the return match. A similar blurb in the *Daily Star* concerning the baseball series noted that it would cost the Tucson nine an estimated $300 to make the trip south to Tombstone. The *Arizona Weekly Star* called for the citizens of Tucson to support the club in hopes that enough money would be raised to send the group to defend the town's honor and reclaim some of the lost wagers from the first game.

While the Tucson club was busy practicing for the return match in Tombstone and raising the needed funds to get there, a large, devastating fire broke out in Tombstone on the afternoon of May 25, 1882. Starting on the rear lot of the Tivoli Gardens on Allen Street, the fire spread quickly, consuming most of the block between Toughnut and Allen Streets between Fourth and Fifth Street. The fire jumped across town, eventually reducing three prominent hotels and the offices of the *Tombstone Nugget* newspaper to ash. The office of the largest paper in town, the *Epitaph*, was also damaged. Damages at the time were estimated to be at least $500,000. The devastation brought business to a halt and paused any activity of the Tombstone Base Ball Club. The entire town was nearly consumed over the course of one afternoon and evening. The series for the second Territorial Championship of Arizona would be postponed.

Rebuilding the town would take time, but in June the tough citizens of Tombstone took a respite from their labors for a town picnic on the banks of the San Pedro River. The Tombstone Base Ball Club staged for a practice game, drubbing their opponents 23–3 in what the *Weekly Epitaph* described as "almost too one-sided to be called a match."[17] Even in a town as tough as Tombstone, the "Town too Tough to Die," baseball could heal wounds and restore a sense of normalcy after such a devastating loss to business and life. Eventually the town was rebuilt, life resumed at a somewhat normal pace, and baseball returned the following November in a continuation of the series of games to decide the championship of the territory. After receiving numerous challenges in the fall months of 1882 from an eager and persistent Tombstone nine, it took the club captain and secretary of the Tucson B.B.C. almost a month to accept. The teams finally met for the final match on December 2 at Doling's Park in Tombstone. Despite much practice and a change in venue to much more suitable grounds, the boys from the Old Pueblo couldn't quite get the win over Tombstone, with a final tally of 17 to 12. Very strangely, baseball would fade into memory for the next several years. It wasn't until 1888 that Tucson had a baseball club to compete against other cities in the territory.

If a single family could be elevated to the status of "Baseball Royalty" in the Arizona Territory for simultaneously loving, promoting and playing the national game, it would be the Drachmans of Tucson. It isn't known who organized the meeting on April 14, 1888, at City Hall or if any of the Drachman brothers were present to reorganize baseball in town. No local games were reported for the rest of the year, except for the *Citizen* relating that on May 21, the Tombstone Base Ball Club defeated a strong Albuquerque nine, 4–3. The following summer of 1889, the *Arizona Daily Citizen* described the Junior Pioneer baseball club as having "a standing chip on their shoulder and are spoiling for a game."[18] They were brash enough to issue an open challenge to any active club in the territory. The challenge was finally answered on Sunday, June 30, by another new club, the Tucson Tigers. The first match would end in favor of the Tigers, 22–21, with the victors winning a $5 purse. As a baseball custom of the era, a return match with elevated stakes was arranged for the following Sunday. To illustrate the overly excited nature of the rowdy crowds in attendance, violence in the seating areas was common. Sometime during the Junior Pioneers versus Tigers match, a "Chinese crank was hit in the head with a quirt."[19] The assailant was quickly jailed to await a hearing in front of Judge Meyer on Monday morning. Two weeks later, baseball action would explode as the *Daily Citizen* reported three games played on the plaza. The main attraction was a re-match between the Tigers and Junior Pioneers, who exacted a measure of revenge, though owing to the intense heat of mid–July in the Arizona desert, few spectators were in attendance. By August, a new club entered the Arizona baseball scene. The Zeckendorf Nine, as they were called, was formed by pioneer retailer Louis Zeckendorf, who opened a retail location in Tucson in 1866. The Zeckendorf Nine would win their first match against an unknown opponent on August 11, 1889, by a whopping tally of 19 to 8.

By late August, the baseball scene in Tucson was getting as hot as the weather. The Junior Pioneers and Tigers went win-for-win against each other, and neither club could win two games in a row. The *Arizona Daily Citizen* noted the local sporting scene's growing interest in baseball, commenting that "the small boy that cannot come out to the Plaza with a red cap and belt, is looked upon as decidedly behind the times."[20] Finally, the newspapers acknowledged that baseball's popularity in Tucson and southern Arizona was important as Arizonans desired to keep in step with all current and popular interests. By the end of the month, Tucson had five baseball clubs: the Young Pioneers, Tucson Tigers, Jerry McGintler Nine, Fort Lowell Base Ball Club and the aforementioned Zeckendorf Nine. Even the South Pacific Railroad had a ball club that played games against the Jerry McGintler Nine, sometimes called the J.P.L. Club by the *Citizen*, in the fall of 1889. Tucsonans didn't have to travel far to witness the games, as all of the contests for the season took place on the Military Plaza in the middle of town, located between Fifth Avenue and Scott Avenue and 11th and 14th Streets near the railroad depot in the center of town. A perfect spot for so much baseball action! This was the first evidence of any town in Arizona having enough interest and population to support so many baseball clubs at any one time, making the first local league possible. Baseball in Tucson had hit its zenith.

The Tucson Base Ball Club was loosely re-organized in May of 1890. The Drachman brothers and Zabriskie brothers comprised the core group of a "picked nine" that would represent Tucson in ball games for a new league announced in the *Arizona Daily Citizen* on May 24, 1890. The clubs from Phoenix, Tombstone and Fort Lowell were in the new organization, with Tucson's new home grounds located at Levin's Park, east of

Game at Elysian Grove, Tucson, c. 1900. (Arizona Historical Society, Tucson)

town. The park would later be re-named Carrillo's Gardens, then Elysian Grove. The ball club's official headquarters remained so until 1915, when the park was officially closed down. The Tucson baseball club had rented the grounds to become recognized as a serious competitor, and a formal meeting to elect officers was held on May 13. Through early May, the nine played practice games and an early series with Tombstone, losing badly. George Kelly, writing for the *Arizona Citizen*, noted that there were some "solid business men being in it,"[21] along with a confident declaration that the club would be champions. He even managed to sneak in a barb, warning Phoenix to take note of the new Tucson Base Ball Club. Their first win was against a scrub nine in a practice match on May 18, 10–2. In June, the club had completely new uniforms tailored by a local seamstress, Miss McKenney. The lads would take the field clad in uniforms of "steel grey with bottle green trimmings."[22]

Amongst the 25 initial members of the Tucson B.B.C. was a young railroad worker named Emanuel "Manny" Drachman. Manny came from a large family, ten children in all, born to Phillip and Rosa Drachman. By the age of 13, he was good enough to start playing on the local town team, which usually was an aggregation of the best players in town. Described as "five foot nine and 202 pounds,"[23] he loved to fight and was a well-known "baseball nut" to his family. It had been rumored that Manny was the strongest man in town. Working in the blacksmith's shop for the Southern Pacific Railroad had developed his physique as an asset he would use on the diamond to slug the ball along with opposing players who wanted to exchange fisticuffs during or after the game. He would be joined on the club by his brothers Mose and Harry. Mose Drachman initially worked at odd jobs which included being a traveling salesman for the Arbuckle Coffee Company for Southern Arizona. Harry was a clerk in town for Steinfeld's Store, where he learned the mercantile business. While not an active player on the club, a fourth Drachman brother was involved in promoting and developing baseball in Tucson. Sam Drachman, who operated a Men's Club consisting of a pool hall and cigar store on Congress Street at Stone Avenue, would be instrumental in promoting and supporting the early Tucson Base Ball Club. No doubt the store would have been a prime location to hang posters advertising baseball games. On June 27, 1890, the *Daily Citizen* reported that a series of games between the home town club and the Tombstone B.B.C. would take place over the Fourth of July holiday. The results of the three-game series, pitting the hometown team against their rivals from Tombstone, was mixed. Tucson lost two of the three games, both by a wide margin. Despite suffering a 16–3 loss in the first match, hurler Manny Drachman struck out 14 batters. No doubt Manny used his curveball to devastating effect, having learned the pitch from a professional hurler who took a liking to him when the young man was only 15 years old. It was rumored that Manny was the first pitcher in the territory to throw a curveball successfully.

The earliest surviving photograph of the Tucson Base Ball club was taken on August 11, 1890, by famous Arizona Territory immigrant photographer Henry Buehman. Not only was he a noted cameraman, he was also employed as a dentist, moving to Tucson in 1874. His work as a photographer varied in subject matter from Native Americans, nature stills, buildings and architecture, to the more mundane studio or "cabinet" photos of early Tucsonans. Occasionally, he took a photo or two of baseball games and the young men who played them. This photo was taken on the grounds of Fort Lowell, looking at one of the Officers Quarters along a line of cottonwood trees that are still standing. The match featured the home nine versus the soldiers from Fort Lowell, on the grounds at the military post. The victory went to Tucson, 13 to 10. There were 26 combined errors and 28 stolen bases. Manny Drachman caught the pitching of Dave Hughes, both standing in the photo taken to commemorate the event. The *Arizona Daily Citizen* noted that 15 wagon loads of cranks

Tucson Base Ball Club at Fort Lowell, August 10, 1890: Standing, left to right: E. Hutton; Emanuel Drachman; Abe Goldbaum, Secretary; B. J. Zabriskie; Frank Smith; Dave Hughes. Seated/lying, left to right: Mertz; Harry A. Drachman; J. Blinkhorn, manager; Mose Drachman; Walter Zabriskie. (© Jeremy Rowe Vintage Photography, vintagephoto.com)

made the journey to Fort Lowell to cheer on their nine, with group and individual photos being taken.[24] There would be a return game played on the Military Plaza in downtown Tucson, as the grounds at Levin's Park had been flooded and were in no condition to host a game.

Boosted by victories against the soldiers, an open challenge was sent to Tombstone. A committee, led by Manny Drachman and club manager J. Blinkhorn, met the delegation from Tombstone, who arrived on a freight train due to a passenger car derailment in Mescal, for the next series of matches. The first game was contested on the afternoon of September 5, with the first Grand Ball of the season to follow that evening to cap off the first day of the fiesta. The first match was an enormous success for Manny Drachman and his fellow ballists. The *Daily Citizen* praised the hometown club as looking "neat as pins" wearing their new gray and green uniforms for the contest. Tucson hit to all parts of the field, with 14 runs scored in the seventh inning alone. Tombstone made a valiant effort but fell short as the final tally was 33 to 7. The weeks of hard practice had finally paid off, with Manny Drachman using his curveball to astonishing effect, with the paper commenting that "Drachman's curves curved as never before."[25] The return match the next day was cut short after two innings due to an intense dust storm that quickly swept through town. The only detail reported was a final score of 5 to 3 in favor of Tucson. The final game of the series was played on Sunday, September 7. Manny pitched the game, and as in the previous matches, confounded the strikers from Tombstone with an effective curveball. The *Daily Citizen*, giving the third match of the series more detailed coverage, credited Drachman's hitting and pitching on the same biblical scale as the prophet Moses. When the umpire declared the game over by shouting "All out!," the score stood 20 to 9. Tucson had swept all three games against a strong opponent. The Tombstone lads packed their bags and departed on a late train that was delayed by rain and washouts along the line. The excitement caused by the series drew out the other clubs in the area to play before large crowds. The Tigers and Junior Pioneers battled on September 14 to a final score of 11–9 in favor of the Junior Pioneers.

In the following weeks, the Tucson nine played practice games with the soldiers at Fort Lowell in preparation for the tournament at the territorial fair in Phoenix in October of 1890. The three-game series between the Phoenix B.B.C. and Tucson B.B.C. was advertised in the local newspapers of both towns as being for the Territorial Championship. Tucson would win two of three games to claim the crown. Dubbed the "Regular Club" by the paper, they would see plenty of action the following season, including facing a new nine aptly named the Pastime B.B.C.

The 1892 campaign saw the Tucson B.B.C. continue their winning ways as the dominant club of southern Arizona. By 1893, word had spread to all parts of the territory that the lads in grey and green were a very good baseball club and would play anyone, anywhere. The 1893 season proved just as successful as the previous two had been. The club faced challenges from local nines such as the newly formed Pastime B.B.C., along with games that renewed inter-territory rivalries with Tombstone, Phoenix and El Paso. In a split-squad practice match on May 22, 1893, at the new ball grounds, the first known "hidden ball trick" in Arizona baseball history occurred. Harry Drachman, playing third base, coaxed his younger teammate Walter Zabriskie off the bag by imitating a throw towards the hurler or first base, well out of view of the base runner. Despite the fake throw, Drachman had the ball neatly tucked under his arm. When the young Zabriskie stepped off the bag, Drachman quickly retrieved the ball from its hiding spot and applied the tag for the out. The many spectators seated under the shade of the trees that lined Carrillo's Garden must have been equally surprised at what had happened, thus enjoying seeing such a fine play. The *Daily Citizen* added praise, commenting, "In addition, the ground itself is excellent."[26] In June, a serious proposal was received for a series of games with a newly revitalized Phoenix Base Ball Club. To get the point across, the *Phoenix Gazette* boasted of the strength of the newly reformed club, adding they would "walk off with the cake."[27]

The home nine spent the week before the first match of the series engaged in hard practice. Finally the two clubs met on the diamond on July 3, 4 and 5, under sweltering conditions as the thermometer hit an average of 108 degrees. The wool uniforms both clubs wore during the era must have felt restrictive and heavy under such heat. Tucson emerged victorious in the first game, 27–18. Phoenix tied the series by winning the second game on the Fourth of July, only to fall the next afternoon by a lopsided tally of 19–8. The Tucson B.B.C. and the newspaper declared themselves "Champions of the Territory" once more. An offer from El Paso was kicked around, with the idea of meeting for a couple of games in nearby Benson, Arizona. The details could never be agreed upon, resulting in no games with El Paso in July. Instead of staying home and waiting for the next challenge, the newly crowned territorial champions decided to head north to Tempe and an LDS settlement known as Stringtown. Initially an offer was made of $100 guaranteed against a forfeit, with the match to be played for $500 per side as secured by the Tempe Bank. The *Daily Citizen*, now engaged in consistent coverage of the increasingly popular territorial champions, noted that Tucson was the challenged club and would have choice of the grounds for the match.

The Tempe club either backed out or arranged to have the Stringtown nine take their place for the series commencing on August 1, 1893. Both the *Daily Citizen* and *Arizona Republican* boasted about their home team in fine 19th-century fashion. The *Tombstone Prospector* chimed in, saying "If Tucson base ballists are nursing the idea that their team is the champion of the territory, Tombstone will take the conceit out of them if they make too much noise."[28] With all the hubris of the territorial newspapers being thrown back and forth, the terms of the match were finally agreed upon. The stakes would be $250 a side, a $500 total purse for the match. As both clubs prepared for the game, the Tucson B.B.C. accepted a challenge from a new local club called "Stein's Nine" for a keg of San Francisco lager beer. The practice game was played on July 23, with the Tucson club victorious, 11–6. The same day, the local nine secured a keg of beer to wash away the grit and grime of a well-played practice match. The *Daily Citizen* published a letter to the Tempe club, demanding $50 in forfeit money. The *Daily Citizen* and *Arizona Republican* seemed confused about the name of the opponent. On July 24 the *Daily Citizen* said the next opponent was from Tempe, while the game reports on July 31 through August 2 referred to the "south side" boys as being from Stringtown. It is quite possible the best players were selected to form a combined nine, as was common practice of the day.

The series was played in Phoenix at East Lake Park, with results wired back to Tucson via telegraph. Clad in worn-out grey uniforms with fading green trim, the visiting nine secured an easy win against their counterparts, who were clad in white flannel uniforms with red stockings, by a score of 18 to 1. The *Daily Citizen* noted that the "Stringtown men were brawny big men,"[29] and that their hurler sent in fastballs like they were being shot from a cannon. Manny Drachman took the box for Tucson and, as evident by the final score, used his trusty curveball to good effect. Stringtown's only run came in the eighth inning on a wild throw that sailed over Gaff, covering second base, and going through the legs of the center fielder, allowing the unnamed batter from Phoenix to race home. The post-match notes in the *Citizen* mentioned that the pitcher for the Stringtown nine had a hard time keeping his feet on the ground while delivering pitches. Sometime during the game, Mose Drachman walked the ball out to his brother, pitcher Manny Drachman, only to hide the ball under his arm without anyone knowing about it. The *Citizen* noted that he "put his man out" but wasn't rewarded for the trick play as the umpire never saw the tag. Later in the game, second baseman Gaff did the same trick but was successful in recording the out. After the match, both Manny Drachman and, umpire Denton drank some lemonade provided to the visiting club and, soon after ingesting the drink, became ill. A doctor was summoned and, while a heated argument arose over the cause, both men were set right and calm was restored.

The second game of the series went ten innings with Tucson emerging victorious, 11–10. Manny Drachman did not pitch that day, as he may have been still recovering from drinking the tainted lemonade that may have been planted to remove him from action during the next two contests. The third and deciding game saw a low attendance, with Tucson securing the win, 15–9. Frank Smith pitched for Tucson in replacement of Drachman and by all accounts was good in the box, as he recorded three strikeouts in the bottom of the ninth inning to secure the win. For the second time, a trick play by second baseman Gaff was used to pick off a runner at first base. The Tucson Base Ball Club was a solid nine, not afraid to use trickery and deceit to their advantage to win a ball game. Fellow Tucson resident, owner/publisher of the *Arizona Daily Star* and newly appointed Territorial Governor L. C. Hughes was even on hand to offer his congratulations to the victors.

The season for the Tucson Base Ball Club wound down, as most of the players on the roster returned to their jobs, already having asked for quite a few days off to pursue baseball glory. The series against El Paso had proposed dates of August 27–29. While the regular club took time off from the baseball circuit, the junior clubs resumed regular Sunday games against each other. Eventually the Tucson Base Ball Club would disband, introducing other clubs such as the Tucson Grays, the Tucson Royals and the Elysian Cubs. As the population of Tucson grew in the latter half of the 1890s, the need for traveling to games rapidly diminished. Local competition was steadily rising, with numerous games to be had. The future of the game in Tucson would also see the University of Arizona entering local competition under an official baseball program in 1904. The games at Carrillo's Garden, later re-named Elysian Grove in 1903 by new owner Manny Drachman, continued until 1915. The park held sporting events of all kinds, from boxing and wrestling to outdoor music and the first motion picture shown in Arizona. The ball field was located on the west side of the park, and eventually the Grays and Royals would begin a bitter inter-city rivalry.

Phoenix

The earliest baseball happenings in the youthful and growing burg of Phoenix were briefly mentioned as "present amusements"[30] that were taken in by citizens in the cool hours of the May evenings in town, according to the upstart newspaper, the *Salt River Herald*. Later that June, the *Salt River Herald* noted that one Mr. Shaw, while indulging in a game of baseball, had broken some of his fingers while trying to catch the ball with just the tips of his fingers. The writer quipped that the injury would bench "uncle F."[31] for at least two months. Poor uncle Shaw. Two weeks later, the editor of the *Herald* boldly suggested that the best nine in town be selected and that a challenge to the club from Fort McDowell be issued for the upcoming Independence holiday on July 4, 1878. Unfortunately, the match never took place, and over the next several months, as summer waned into fall and winter, the local boys of Phoenix continued to engage only each other in friendly contests of baseball.

3. Town Rivalries Take Shape 71

In a popular journalistic practice of the day, newspapers printed letters received from all parts of the land. A letter written by a local who chose to sign the correspondence as "ADIOS" was printed in the *Salt River Herald* on July 6, 1878. The letter mentioned games of baseball along with other young men engaging in a relatively new sport called "quoits." Quoits was an interesting game that utilized flat river stones. The goal was to toss a ring or flat stone as close as possible to a stake. Today, we'd recognize its descendant—horseshoes. Apparently the baseball craze in Phoenix was in full swing, giving cause enough for the editor of the *Herald* to note that "Phoenix is blessed in one thing—a species of insanity termed as baseballism is almost unknown in this vicinity."[32] The editor was unable to say how long this affliction would affect the young men of Phoenix.

An official notice was printed in the *Arizona Daily Citizen* on November 18, 1879, noting that all the necessary tools of a fully organized club had been formed and that the new club therefore issued an open challenge to any club in the territory. In December, the Phoenix B.B.C. received a challenge to play on the grounds of the Tucson B.B.C., for terms listed earlier. The days passed, and in a follow-up column on December 26 published by *The Phoenix Herald*, it was noted dryly that the Tucson club had backed away from the original challenge, and after offering an undisclosed excuse had then refused to play. The column also mentioned that the club from Fort McDowell would be in town in a few days' time to play a match against the new club from Phoenix.

It is unclear as to the real reason why the Tucson club shied away from their original challenge to the Phoenix nine for a game on their home grounds. There seemed to be enough interest, and a wager of $100, no small sum at the time, to back up the seriousness of the lads from the Old Pueblo. Regrettably, we may never know the real reason behind the cancellation of this match. These nines would eventually clash on the diamond, creating one of the territory's most unique and intense rivalries that continues to this very day.

At the turn of the new decade, the Phoenix Base Ball Club emerged as a more organized club than any in the territory. It had regular monthly meetings and held elections for offices in the club's administration such as President, Vice-President and Secretary. As noted in Chapter 1, the Phoenix Base Ball Club met for the first time in match play the Norvall, commonly misspelled as "Norvell" by the *Phoenix Herald*, on February 27, 1880. Along with the Chaffee Club of Fort McDowell, the three clubs would engage each other on the grounds of the military post as well as the home ball field of Phoenix. The *Herald* also noted that for the Washington's

Birthday celebration, the only observance was a baseball match.[33] Held in Phoenix, it resulted in an extra-inning victory for the "boys in blue," 28–26 in favor of the Norvall Club of Fort McDowell. The townsfolk of Phoenix thought their club would be victorious, as heavy betting took place on the match. There is no indication about exactly how much money changed hands as a result of the final tally.

The earliest known club meeting was held on March 3, 1880, at the County Recorder Offices. An official notice was printed by the *Phoenix Herald* in which members of the club were notified that their presence at the meetings to discuss formal business of the organization was requested. The printed notice was signed by acting club President S. E. Patton and Secretary B. B. Kirkland.

As the weeks passed, few games took place. With the formation of a new club in the Phoenix area, the *Herald* noted on March 12, 1880, that the Young America Base Ballers had been requested to meet on the evening of March 10. It is unclear whether this was an adult club on par with the athletic ability and skill level of the Phoenix Base Ball Club, or possibly the first youth baseball club in the Arizona Territory. Nine days later it was reported that both the Phoenix B.B.C. and the Young America Club had engaged in games against both the McDowell Nine and Mesa City Club, with a defeat suffered by Phoenix and a first victory earned by the Young Americas. The newspaper eagerly reported a match between the two clubs in a week's time, suggesting that the Young Americas were an adult club, perhaps comprised of younger men in town. On March 19, 1880, the Young America Base Ball Club was reported as having traveled to Mesa City to compete with the local nine. A brief box score appeared in the *Phoenix Herald*. The Young America Club took an early lead and never looked back, securing a 45–32 victory in a heavy-hitting affair. In the same edition of the *Herald*, the Young Americas printed a formal "Thank You" to their gracious hosts and friends in Mesa City. It seemed that a good-natured rivalry had begun between the two clubs. Sadly, no other known games took place in Mesa City for at least another ten years.

In the spring of 1880, with the Phoenix Base Ball Club dominating the local competition offered by the Chaffee and McDowell nines, the club would be challenged by a selected group of ballists from the territorial capitol of Arizona, Prescott. April arrived, and with it a feeling that the home club was superior to the nine from the northern parts of the territory. The *Phoenix Weekly Herald* boasted, "It is too bad to go to so much pains only to suffer defeat." While awaiting a formal challenge from the Prescott nine, and with a notable air of arrogance about the club portrayed in the *Herald*, the men from Prescott would take the field against a confident Phoenix Base Ball Club and an equally poised following of cranks that rooted for them. In response, the *Weekly Arizona Miner* printed a sharp retort on April 21, calling the author of the *Herald* article a "parrot" and questioning the journalistic integrity of the paper. The *Miner* even went so far as to caution the Phoenix Base Ball Club against allowing such rude comments to be published on behalf of an otherwise respectable baseball club. It appears that the alleged challenge printed by the Phoenix newspaper was just that—hot air. A game was not arranged or played in 1880. If by some chance a game between the two clubs was played, there is no record of it.

It is interesting to note that the editor of the *Weekly Herald* had received a copy of the California Base Ball League's Constitution and Rules for 1880, as indicated in the weekly edition of May 7, 1880. Published by Liddle & Keating in San Francisco, this booklet covered the by-laws and playing rules of the semi-professional baseball circuit in California. Maybe the editor and citizens of Phoenix were following baseball developments nationally—more so than was reported in the pages of local papers. It was instances like this, brevities mentioned in the papers of the day, that encourages the idea that the larger towns in territorial Arizona were not completely cut off from the outside world. It also indicates that newspapers from Phoenix, Tucson and Prescott were being received by readers, and newspaper editors, in other states such as California, New Mexico, Utah and perhaps Nevada.

While the interested townsfolk and editor of the *Herald* scoured the Constitution and Rules for the California Base Ball League (C.B.B.L.), the baseball matches would come to a close for the season, to resume play later that fall. As a part of the Christmas festivities for 1880, the Phoenix B.B.C. took on the Norvall Club of Fort McDowell, their main competition at the time. With Mr. Charles McNeil acting as umpire and William Andrews partnered with Henry Wharton in charge of tally-keeping duties, the Christmas match between the two familiar foes was contested in front of a large crowd, with a sizable portion being ladies.[34] According to the newspaper recap, the Phoenix nine was in complete control through the first four frames, leading 9–0. The soldiers from Fort McDowell managed to push a run across in their half of the fifth inning, but their late-inning efforts would not be enough. The final tally was 13 to 9 in favor of Phoenix. The paper noted that many fine plays were executed and that the large crowd was appreciative of the effort and skill displayed by both clubs.

The boys from Phoenix would take the rest of January off to enjoy the holidays with their families, but would return to action on January 20, when they traveled to a match against the Chaffee Club of Fort McDowell. Upon a late return before the *Herald* went to press, it was reported that the Phoenix nine played a very good match. In a sparking hurling performance, Hellmich, who had also played first base for the Phoenix club, managed to hold the Chaffee club to a mere 12 runs. By today's standards that is a high number, but in 1881 the ballists played barehanded. Dropped catches, missed ground balls, and line drives that were avoided were a normal sight for any spectator. Even though the home club at McDowell suffered defeat that day, they still showed their guests a measure of hospitality and kindness that bore mention in the follow-up article in the *Phoenix Herald*.

With the reputation of the Phoenix club growing along with the town's heralded brass band, the club reaped the benefits of an adoring territorial press. The *Herald,* ever boastful of the Phoenix nine, noted that the club in Tucson was monitoring their games in the paper, and wondered why the two clubs hadn't yet met on the field of play. The *Arizona Gazette* boldly proclaimed on February 1, "The Phoenix Nine can 'everlastingly whitewash' both of them" after noting a disappointing score in the Fort Lowell–Tucson B.B.C. match two days earlier. Several newspapers in the territory began exchanging barbs in an attempt to one-up each other in promoting their local clubs. The Phoenix newspaper printed several good exchanges in advance of the game against the Picket Post club. The Phoenix B.B.C. made its way south to play the Picket Post Nine, also known as the Pinal Base Ball Club, on February 26, 1881, contested on the grounds of the Phoenix Club. The Pinal nine handed Phoenix a "rather rough defeat,"[35] as seen in the final tally of 30 to 12. The home club offered to play a return match at elevated stakes but was declined. Their visitors, perhaps sensing that they might lose the next match and a considerable amount of money, quietly left town.

It wasn't until March of 1881 that the much-anticipated first match between the Phoenix and Tucson clubs would finally—after many challenges and taunts thrown at each nine by the other—took place. The Phoenix nine held a meeting on the evening of March 10 to discuss taking on the unknown ballists from the Old Pueblo. Word of the match quickly spread through both communities, including a letter from Tucson that was published in the *Phoenix Herald* on March 15. The author, who signed the letter "L.F.," commented that "the Phoenix Base Ball Club will be put on mettle by the Tucson boys as near as I can find out, though I have not seen them play."

3. Town Rivalries Take Shape

Amid frequent rain-storms in the area that week, the Phoenix nine set out for the match in Tucson the same day that the "Letter from Tucson" appeared in the *Herald*. Even the much-lauded brass band in Phoenix was threatened by the frequent storms, as the citizens of Phoenix frequently attended outdoor concerts by the band, which competed for the attention of Phoenicians alongside baseball. The weather threatened to make the ball games the following evening a damp affair. The Phoenix club, in great anticipation of the match, had even abandoned plans to stop in the towns of Pinal and Silver King on a brief barnstorming tour on their way to Tucson. A few days later, through special dispatch to the *Herald*, the result of the first match was announced. Though they made a courageous and gallant effort, the Phoenix B.B.C. would go down in defeat to the Tucson nine, 14–9. The match was heavily anticipated in Tucson and drew a large crowd. The lads from Phoenix gained favorable opinion through their skillful play, despite the unfavorable outcome that afternoon. In relaying the final score to the hometown cranks on March 18, the *Arizona Gazette* lamented that "the flags around town are at half-mast." The return match was contested the next afternoon. The Phoenix nine quickly rebounded from the opening loss, securing a 15–10 victory to even the series at one game each. To close the festivities offered by the host club and city, both clubs and their supporters met at the Elite Hotel, where a sumptuous champagne dinner was held, complete with a lengthy speech by the U.S. District Attorney, who bestowed some kind of "gift" on the visiting Phoenix nine. The club departed on the 19th-century version of the modern-day "red eye"—a 3 a.m. train departing for the Maricopa station.

A month later it was proposed that a game be played in Tucson for a finely engraved silver ball and ornamental silver bat. The game was never played, and another challenge from a new baseball club in Maricopa that was printed in the newspaper that month was also deemed a joke. The Phoenix club would never be the same, suffering a string of stinging defeats that eventually caused them to disband. Even the *Phoenix Herald* commented on April 15, 1882, saying "All our Territorial Exchanges make mention of baseball matches about to take place. Where, oh, where is the Phoenix B.B.C.? Did their last defeat wipe them out entirely?"

Apparently the defeats suffered by the Phoenix club were enough to make early Phoenicians forget about baseball for quite a long time. The *Phoenix Herald*, in relating the score of a match between the Prescott and Fort Verde clubs on May 20, 1881, originally asked the question "what has become of the Phoenix club? Has it wilted?" Months later, the *Arizona Gazette* begged the club to "wake up and teach those fellows a lesson in the national game"[36] after printing the results of the Tombstone versus Tucson matches in the spring of 1882. The club disbanded, completely disappearing from the pages of the local newspapers. During the almost five-year absence of baseball, the town saw some tough times. Chicken pox and smallpox outbreaks and several devastating fires hit the town hard. Even the *Arizona Gazette* was prompted to note that times were difficult. All was not lost, and to alleviate the despair felt by their fellow Phoenicians, the townsfolk decided to form a Library Association and the Maricopa County Fair Association in the fall of 1884. The sporting events covered were foot and horse races. One local, Mr. Lucius C. Copeland, became the first Arizonan to try to master the first steam-powered bicycle on the frozen dirt streets of downtown Phoenix. Later that fall, at the first Territorial Fair, he would demonstrate the same steam-powered Star bicycle he was testing months earlier, to an astonished crowd.

In February 1887, the *Arizona Gazette* said there would be some practice matches held on the home grounds, presumably on the same area used for the newly established Territorial Fair. The newly reorganized club challenged a team from Fort McDowell to two games on February 13–14. Phoenix won both contests by a wide margin. As noted in the *Daily Alta California* on February 16, 1887, the score of the first match was 9–2, and the second was 21–8. As the practices continued, the members of the baseball club went about town, collecting money to host the Fort Lowell B.B.C. in a series of games in April. Sensing the excitement building, the *Arizona Gazette* noted that the Phoenix club had acquired two "curved pitchers and two reliable catchers"[37] in order to make the games more difficult for the visiting soldiers from Fort Lowell. The match was advertised as being for the Territorial Championship of 1887 in a series of three games. It is worth noting that no other newspaper in the state printed any kind of protest against the series or the winner, so the results would stand. The Phoenix Base Ball club won both games, 9–7 and 14–7. Tragedy struck the Phoenix Base Ball club on the evening following the second match. Sergeant Muntz, who played third base for the Phoenix club, was thrown from his horse while trying to cross the Maricopa Canal on his way back to Fort McDowell, where he was stationed with the 4th Cavalry. According to the *Sacramento Daily Union* of April 14, 1887, he was "stunned, and taken to town, but never regained consciousness, and died this evening." Despite the tragedy, the *Arizona Gazette* pushed to have baseball games added to the event calendar for the Territorial Fair held in October, calling the idea a "winning card."[38]

The Phoenix Club wouldn't have any new local competition on the

3. Town Rivalries Take Shape

The Bee Hive Nine, and early Phoenix club sponsored by store owner E. H. Winters, July 4, 1890. Photograph by early frontier photographer John P. Rhodes. (© Jeremy Rowe Vintage Photography, vintagephoto.com)

diamond until 1890, when an upstart club, the Beehive Nine, would challenge them to a match on July 4. The new club was sponsored by local merchant E. H. Winters, who opened the Bee Hive store in May of 1890. Naturally, he wanted to take advantage of the fervor of local baseball cranks, hoping to draw business into his shop. The *Arizona Republican*, an upstart newspaper that year, noted that "A new baseball nine is being organized for the express purpose of defeating the Phoenix boys. It will require some very good material to do that."[39] The Beehive nine challenged the Phoenix club for a match with the purse of $50 offered by the managers of the Fourth of July planning committee. To test the waters, both clubs played a practice match at Patton's Park. Only four innings were completed, leaving the score tied at eight runs per side. It seemed that Phoenix might have met their match for the holiday contest.

The Fourth of July holiday in Phoenix was an especially extravagant affair. Businesses were decorated with all manners of flag-inspired bunting, union flags flew wherever a mast could be secured, and the people were especially joyous on the nation's 114th birthday. One participant, as noted by the *Republican*, used his or her bicycle to weave red, white and blue-colored streamers through the wheel spokes, giving off a wave of color as the wheels turned. Mr. Seelig, owner of a local cigar shop, even got into the act by draping the flag around the Indian Princess statue on display at his storefront, adding that she was "the Goddess of Liberty."[40] The game would be called at 4 p.m. with the hope that the two clubs would be able to return to town to take part in the parade, followed by a spectacular fireworks display on the grounds southeast of City Hall. With the line-ups announced by the *Arizona Republican* on July 3, both clubs were set for battle on the diamond at Patton's Park. In front of a large crowd, the Phoenix Base Ball Club humbled their would-be challengers, 16–2. To commemorate the event, the Beehive Nine stopped by a local photography studio used by John P. Rhodes to take a club photograph before heading out to Patton's Park for the afternoon match. It is the earliest known photograph of a Phoenix baseball club found to date. An estimated 1,500 visitors, along with hometown Phoenicians, crammed the streets for the holiday.

The Phoenix Base Ball Club took a hiatus for the remainder of the summer, to re-convene for practices on a vacant lot east of the Lemon Hotel, and held a meeting to discuss the upcoming tournament at the Territorial Fair of 1890 at Goldman's corner. The Phoenix club took several ballists from the Beehive nine into their ranks, most importantly pitcher Lee Gray of Tempe. The nine began practices for a tough series against the Tucson Base Ball Club, led by ace hurler and master of the curveball—Manny Drachman.

Over the next decade, the Phoenix Base Ball Club would compete under different names and would see less competition from clubs across the territory. The newspapers sometimes referred to the nine as the "Alfalfas," after the crop most prominently grown by farmers in the Salt River Valley. Eventually the Phoenix Base Ball Club permanently disappeared from any kind of competition, but it had paved the way for other clubs in the Phoenix area. The Phoenix B.B.C. were true pioneers of the game, helping other towns like Tempe and Mesa establish their own interest in baseball as early as 1890.

By the fall of 1895, the club was under the direction of local businessman and baseball enthusiast Dave Goldberg. That season saw the first baseball association formed with the idea of incorporating strictly local competition and drumming up sponsorship funds to put on territory-wide tournaments like the one held on November 24–26 that hosted clubs from Albuquerque, El Paso, Fort Grant, Williams, Winslow and Prescott. The Phoenix nine spent several weeks playing practice matches against a

3. Town Rivalries Take Shape 79

Game in progress at East Lake Park, Phoenix, ca. 1895. Note the wide-open space available for play and the lack of a modern pitcher's mound. Also note the position of the umpire, standing directly behind the pitcher. (Arizona Historical Society, Tempe)

club from Tempe, referred to by the *Arizona Republican* as the "south side club." Most notable in that tournament were the games between Phoenix and Prescott, as captured in a live-action image showing both clubs on the diamond at Patton's park, clad in dark uniforms. The roster for the match was printed in the November 24 issue of the *Arizona Republican*, which made a point of noting that four of the nine were soldiers from Fort Whipple. The hometown lads would have the benefit of wearing new uniforms for the match.

The local merchant association and prominent citizens took "subscriptions," or donations, to fund a prize purse and expense fund for such a large gathering of baseball clubs at East Lake Park. The first action of the tournament saw Phoenix coast to two easy wins over Prescott, 9–0 and 22–2. The newspaper noted that Prescott's pitcher didn't do that badly, but had no run support. Popularity for the game remained high, enough to encourage Dave Goldberg, the club's manager, to arrange games with Fort Grant, Fort Whipple and the Phoenix Indian School. Before leaving town, both the Prescott and Phoenix baseball clubs celebrated the games played with a banquet at Fireman's Hall in Phoenix. The *Arizona Republican* recounted that a good time was had by all in attendance, enjoying copious amounts of food and local beer.

Over the coming years, the Phoenix Base Ball Club would disband, reorganize, then disband again, as was usual with baseball organizations in the Arizona Territory. Their names would change, at least on the pages of local newspapers, and their influence would stay within the local area. By 1899, the club was known as the "Rough Riders." The club faced new competition from the local farming settlement known as Glendale, with the first match between the two taking place on December 1, 1899. The Rough Riders would emerge victorious by a tally of 16 to 11 in what the *Arizona Republican* described as "an equally matched game of baseball"[41] held at the grounds in Glendale. The prize was a professional model ball and bat of unknown make or model. Afterwards, in continuation of 19th-century tradition, the victors were taken to a local hotel and treated to dinner by their hosts. The return match, contested a month later on New Year's Day of 1900, saw the Glendale nine take the field in new grey uniforms.

After being served a full-course turkey dinner by the local ladies group, who had taken an interest in baseball and in promoting the local nine, a sluggish Phoenix club took to the field and were defeated, 9–7. In reporting the outcome of the match, the *Arizona Republican* cast a shadow of doubt over the ladies group, claiming their hostesses "are responsible for some of the slow playing done by the Phoenix boys."[42] Whatever the excuses might have been for losing that day, the victory encouraged the Glendale club into considering itself a full-fledged baseball club, complete with traveling privileges. Due to the very inconsistent coverage in the pages of the *Arizona Republican,* it isn't known what the future held for the new club from Glendale.

The next decade would see baseball in Phoenix grow, with the club changing names multiple times. There would be many other clubs starting in Phoenix—youth nines, Mexican teams, and company-sponsored baseball clubs came and went—all the while making East Lake Park home to all the action.

Tombstone

The newspaper readers in Tombstone, no strangers to baseball themselves, had been following the taunts that were exchanged by the Phoenix and Tucson nines in the spring of 1881. The printed jabs continued well into February that year, when the *Arizona Weekly Gazette* related a story printed in the *Tombstone Epitaph* sometime around February 21. The *Epitaph* added a jab of its own, stating "it is suggested that in case the invitation is accepted, the Phoenix boys be invited to come over to the metropolis, and see what they can effect when pitted against Tombstoners. What say you, Knights of the bat?" A few weeks prior, a single line that read "Tombstone now has a base ball club" had marked a quiet beginning of the Tombstone B.B.C.[43]

The rough nature of the 19th century version of baseball certainly fit in with the raucous environment in Tombstone in the early 1880s. Most of the players on the early town ball team were hard-rock miners who lived in small, damp and drafty quarters. Their days were filled with backbreaking labor, extracting rock to be sent to the nearby mills for processing into copper, silver and occasionally gold ore. Their work was very dangerous and often fatal. Baseball was a wonderful way to relieve the tensions of working a mining claim in the wild boom town of Tombstone, Arizona.

Despite the surrounding saloons, brothels and gambling houses, Tombstone attracted the attention of a young preacher from Salem, Massachusetts, named Endicott "Cotty" Peabody. Educated in England, Peabody came west after accepting an invitation to take charge of a Presbyterian ministry in Tombstone. He arrived on January 29, 1882, after a seven-day train ride from Boston. He noted that the previous church had burned down and the lack of an effort in rebuilding, which forced services to be held at the Miners Exchange Building in town. The miners took a quick liking to Peabody, who was just as tough as they were and in excellent physical condition. In a letter to his cousin, Fran, Peabody mentioned being included in the local discussion on baseball, saying "I asked 2 or 3 miners to come by my rooms to talk over baseball with a view of setting up a club."[44] He joined the founder of the Tombstone Base Ball Association, George Rice, and other gentlemen in a match on February 23, 1882. Later that week, riding to the park on a borrowed horse, he took part in a baseball match with a group of miners from the Merrimac mine referred to as "Merrymacers."[45] The journal entry suggests that baseball was played at the various mining camps that dotted the desert countryside around Tombstone.

In preparation of the championship match against the Tucson B.B.C., the baseball club participated in a picked scrimmage match on March 2, 1882. Peabody was asked to captain his side, only to lose the match by a few runs to a nine led by Tombstone B.B.C. manager George S. Rice, a prominent figure in town who managed the Knoxville mine. Two days later, Peabody was back on the diamond in an effort to get to know the men he was ministering to. He described the game on March 4 in his journal as a "capital game. Ball cut to pieces so had to shut up." This passage illustrates how rough and rocky the ground was that was commonly used for baseball games around the Territory. Journal entries over the coming weeks by Endicott Peabody confirmed that he was a talented athlete and was developing into a powerful hitter. In an entry posted on March 10, he noted that he saw the local bishop, then played in a game of baseball, bragging he was "in rather good form, hitting 3 times & one to the fence & made a rather swaggering catch." The detail of hitting "one to the fence" indicates that the ball grounds at Doling's Park were enclosed at one time. The grounds also featured a race track for horses and a full saloon, readily available to quench the thirst of hard-playing ballists and their cranks after nine innings on a dry, rocky and dusty field. However, such a slight clue from Peabody's journal leaves much for interpretation and debate. He often wrote letters home to his cousin, Fran Peabody, describing his activities within the development of the church and his aspiration to form his own baseball club. An entry on Wednesday, March 22, 1882, saw him playing first base in an afternoon match, dispelling the widely held myth that baseball games were strictly an event for holidays or a Sunday afternoon.

By the end of March 1882, the Reverend Peabody had gained the respect of his fellow Tombstoners. Having played ball regularly over the previous month, he pressed forward with the desire to organize a club, relating in a letter to his cousin Fran dated March 30, "The townspeople take quite an interest. Somebody told me that a man looking on at the game exclaimed 'Why is that the minister there? Well, I'll be damned if I don't think more of him than I did before.'" The game had taken root in Tombstone to the point where townsfolk used it as a measuring stick of sorts in sizing up newcomers. Peabody continued to travel to all parts of the area, visiting mills and mines in an effort to grow his flock. He even took part in a game at the renowned Boston Mill, where the game was played in over 90-degree heat between the Tombstone B.B.C. and the San Pedro boys. The match even made the pages of the *Daily Epitaph* on April 29, 1882. He also participated in helping to level the baseball grounds. It was alleged that he was asked to umpire games in Tombstone, due to his upright character and impressive physical reputation as a first-rate boxer. However, none of the newspapers during the first half of 1882 mentioned him having officiated a match.

Endicott Peabody left Tombstone forever in early June, much to the disappointment of local folk who had come to like and accept him. After a questionable affair with his cousin, Fanny, the two were eventually married in 1884. Peabody became an educator, eventually founding the famous Groton School for Boys after returning home to Groton, Massachusetts.

After winning a widely advertised and reported series of games for the Territorial Championship of 1882 from their rivals from Tucson, the Tombstone team took a hiatus until the following summer, when the Red Stockings of Tombstone would face the Grand Centrals on July 4. The

3. Town Rivalries Take Shape 83

Tombstone Weekly Republican reported on July 7 that "Quite a number of ladies graced the occasion by their presence" at the match held at Doling's race track outside of town. Incidentally, the ball field that was used for many years is located on Allen Street at the "Y" junction heading out to the Schieffelin Monument. Today, a faint outline of the baseball diamond and race track oval can be seen on the Google Maps satellite view of the area. The game on the patriotic holiday was a glorious affair that drew a large crowd to the park. The Tombstone B.B.C. dressed in their usual white uniforms with red stockings, while the San Pedro boys took the field in what was described as a "sans souci, go as you please garb, that, while it did not present so gay an appearance, had sufficient pocket room to hold the $200 in stakes."[46] Dressed to the nines in period baseball attire or not, the San Pedro boys won an error-filled contest that morning, 20 to 17. Suffering defeat silenced the regulars of the Tombstone B.B.C. for the remainder of July. In their stead, the Grand Central nine took on a picked nine on July 21 with the usual large crowd in attendance to see another error-filled contest which Tombstone won, 30 to 23. Baseball was a clear favorite attraction in Tombstone. The Tombstone nine reshuffled the line up to take on the newly formed club from Fort Huachuca on August 4, 1883. The first match for the soldiers of the post ended in defeat by a wide margin. The remainder of 1883 would see the Tombstone B.B.C. and the Grand Central nine go back and forth in a series of regular games. Three members of the old Tombstone club would often change sides. One of the original members of the Tombstone club, third baseman Bob Lewis, would be instrumental in reviving baseball in Tombstone in 1885 after the craze in the area took an unexpected break.

From there, baseball was sporadically played, as noted by miner and frontier diarist George Whitwell Parsons. March 26, 1885, was a cold afternoon, however according to Parsons the baseball game "attracted the whole town pretty nearly. Huachuca soldier boys played the Tombstone boys and beat them. Score: 18 to 25. Many ladies out." While not overly organized into a proper baseball club, the game was alive and well in Tombstone. The appearance of ladies at the ball games furthered the interest of the young men who played on the various clubs across the territory, in addition to having them refrain from the fighting, swearing, rowdyism and drunken behavior that was prevalent among professional ballists of the age. The games between the soldiers of Fort Huachuca and the Tombstone nine continued for many years. Successes marked a point of pride for the frontier mining town.

Tombstone dominated the early games between the two, until a unit change took place at the post. A new unit of soldiers had been ordered west to replace the post's regular company. Once the new unit was on post, a challenge was quickly issued to Tombstone. In a dubious series between the two, as related by Arizona pioneer Katherine Bagg Hastings, Fort Huachuca exacted some revenge. In her words, there "was a great gathering of fans to see Huachuca humiliated."[47] After the match, Tombstone strengthened its roster and scrounged up more money to wager against the soldiers. The return match was set for the following Sunday. Ms. Hastings noted that again the Tombstone nine went down to defeat, losing several thousand dollars in the process. Controversy was ignited after one of the soldiers, in a drunken admission, let the secret out that the battery for the Huachuca club were two semi-professional ball players who had recently enlisted with the U.S. Army. Enraged, the citizens of Tombstone quickly raised $500 and wired the manager of an un-named semi-professional club from Los Angeles with the instructions to send the best hurler and catcher the money could buy. The following Sunday, two young men showed up in town. The soldiers put up large sums of money, and even upped the odds on the match to 2-to-1. The game started with the normal Tombstone lineup quickly giving up two runs. The Tombstone manager changed batteries, sending in the ringers, who struck out the side, helping Tombstone to make a miraculous comeback and win, 5 to 3.

The rivalry between the Fort Huachuca soldiers and future incarnations of the Tombstone B.B.C. would last for decades. All of the games were lively affairs, attracting all of the color of town and post, as spectators usually dressed in their best attire.

Nogales

The border town of Nogales would come to the baseball scene in Arizona late. Well, later than its nearby sister cities of Tombstone and Tucson. Baseball in Nogales got a jump start as the new club faced off against Fort Huachuca for a couple of games on October 16, 1886. The contest was a more friendly introduction into the competitive arena of territorial baseball, as the wager on the match was only $1 per side.[48] Nogales lost, 9 to 6, at home but quickly arranged for a return match at elevated stakes for the following Sunday. Meanwhile, the Tombstone nine practiced hard while following the match reports in the *Daily Tombstone*, which printed the full box score and detailed game account on October 18. Interested individuals could catch a special train departing from the Fairbank station in Tombstone the morning of the game. The railroad charged a special fare for the round trip. If one couldn't afford the train fare, a gentleman called "Sandy Bob" ran a stage to and from Nogales. The return game featured wagers at $200 per side and train loads of cranks traveling from as far away as Benson. The practice that the Nogales nine put in during the week would not be enough as they fell for the second time, 20 to 14. The game report must have been a colorful one, as the results were printed on October 25 in the *Sacramento Daily Union*. The third game of the series was set for Thanksgiving day, allowing both clubs time to sharpen their skills. The *Daily Tombstone Epitaph* voiced support for the idea in a short blurb about the series printed on October 27.

Nogales newspapers changed hands no less than six times from 1886 to 1893. All of the newspaper microfilm for this era has been lost, so a large gap of this town's history remains. Nogales would play a few games with Fort Huachuca, Tombstone and later Bisbee in the coming decade. The focus in town would be the development of a local circuit, furthered along in 1907 by a soldier from Fort Huachuca who moved there after being discharged from the U.S. Army.

Prescott

Townsfolk sporadically played games against the soldiers from Fort Whipple as early as 1872. The baseball action in Prescott was hit and miss before and after the renowned first "Territorial Championship" match of 1876. After the intense excitement of the contest on the plaza in downtown Prescott between the Champion B.B.C. and the soldiers from Fort Whipple, baseball vanished there until 1880. Perhaps the long absence stirred fond memories in the townsfolk living in the territorial capital to revive a once-favored pastime, or maybe it was the sudden coverage in papers such as the *Phoenix Herald* and *Arizona Citizen* that encouraged a return to active baseball. The long-running *Weekly Arizona Miner*, on April 16, 1880, printed a notice for a meeting of the Prescott Base Ball Club at the library, inviting all interested to be in attendance. While organizational meetings took place, some of the local boys couldn't wait to play. Dubbed "the Prescott Boys"[49] by the *Arizona Democrat*, a smaller publication, they took to the diamond against the soldiers of Fort Whipple, winning 23 to 17. The annual May Day celebration saw festivities including baseball, in addition to a performance by the brass band from the post. Having fully organized a club, the Prescott nine went about obtaining uniforms, and a contest was proposed. Medals would be awarded to the "three best average players"[50] who showed the most skill during a series of practice games between interested young men who joined the club. The idea clearly was to find the best talent for the first nine, or the starting lineup of the club. Such an idea even caught the attention of the *Phoenix Weekly Herald*, which reprinted the article a week later. While waiting for the new uniforms, Prescott played another match against Fort Whipple, but no score was given in any of the newspapers. In addition, it isn't known who won the medals from the board of directors for displaying the best baseball skills.

The home field for this club was in a clearing in West Prescott. The site was ideal but prone to wind and dust storms that often postponed and canceled games. Even the spring gales that whipped through the area weren't enough to stop the first-known Arizona baseball tournament reported on April 30, 1880, featuring both clubs. One tournament game reported by the *Weekly Arizona Miner* said, the boys from town "got away with" the win, 39 to 28. Baseball fever had clearly struck the area.

The first wind-related interruption for a match in the area was on May 15, against an unknown opponent. While the match was delayed one week, the editor of the *Arizona Miner* chimed in about the uniform selection for the new club, saying "we would recommend any color for the suits but pumpkin." While local matches with the post and practice matches continued through the rest of 1880, the *Arizona Weekly Miner* published a short article noting the "New Base Ball Rules" for 1881 on December 17, 1880. Among them was the pitcher's box being moved back five feet, from 45 to 50 feet from home plate. The number of balls called before a walk would be seven, strikes to remain at three. No substitute runners were allowed. New scoring rules would change how box scores should be taken down, while a runner could be tagged out after a foul ball if the ball, made by Spalding and officially adopted, was handled by the pitcher first.

The winter snows finally melted enough for the first games of the 1881 campaign to take place, once again pitting Prescott versus Fort Whipple. At 1:30 p.m. on Sunday, April 30, the two familiar foes took to the field to renew the popular rivalry that would last for another decade and a half. The Whipple nine exacted some revenge, winning 19–17. The two clubs played on a weekly basis for the rest of the spring, especially on days when the soldiers had been paid and were in town "scattering greenbacks."[51]

A new club emerged on the scene in April of 1881, labeled the "Verde Nine" by the *Arizona Daily Miner* and other territorial exchanges, though it isn't known if this club represented the military post of Fort Verde or one of the mining camps. The *Daily Miner* had received numerous challenges on behalf of the Prescott club, so many that the paper felt compelled to urge the club "should put itself to practice," adding "Let them organize at once and go into training."[52]

The Prescott B.B.C. held another series of practice games on their home field in West Prescott. The games were a method to "shake down" the young men to be chosen for the regular nine in an upcoming match with the club from the Verde valley. There was plenty of baseball going on in and around town, so much that even the *Phoenix Herald* commented on April 29 that there was "plenty of baseball at Prescott," in an effort to motivate the Phoenix Base Ball Club to play and practice more often. The anticipated game finally occurred on May 16, almost a month after a challenge was issued by the Verde nine. The boys from Prescott were soundly defeated, 66–29, in possibly the most lopsided match in territorial era baseball in Arizona. The match was noted by the *Phoenix Herald,* which dryly commented, "Even our boys would be ashamed of such a score."[53] The *Arizona Daily Miner* printed a short note before press time about the match on game day, noting that the home nine were being waxed and that the catcher for the Verde club had a badly split finger. The game report published the following day broke down all the action, including the 21 runs scored by the visiting Verde nine in the top of the second inning.

The home team was discouraged after such a drubbing, no doubt, and made attempts to strengthen the club in the coming months, only to suffer defeats against the Verde nine in July. While the regular nine struggled to win, two new clubs, the "Milligans" and the "Rifles," formed loosely organized clubs to compete in a game on the established ball grounds in Prescott. The *Weekly Arizona Miner* was optimistic, adding "some very fine playing may be expected."[54] No game was reported in the following issues.

The Prescott, Whipple and Verde nines competed against each other well into the 1890s. In 1885, an unknown hurler for the Fort Whipple Base Ball Club allegedly started using the curveball in games against Prescott. One such recorded instance came in a match on August 24, 1885. The *Weekly Arizona Miner* commented, "The town boys were not accustomed to the curve racket." Somehow, the pitcher for the soldiers either figured out how to throw a curveball effectively or was taught by another player who knew how to use the deceptive pitch. The Whipple nine used this to defeat the boys from town, 31 to 23. The games continued for years, and the first known wager of $100 between the two sides was on May 6, 1886. No score was given in the papers, so either the home team was defeated or the game never happened due to a lack of money for the wager.

In the 1890s, while most of the baseball clubs and associations across America were building formal, enclosed ball parks (some with gas/phosphorus lighting for night games!), most of the Arizona Territory didn't have an enclosed baseball ground of any kind. Either Tombstone, Tucson or Prescott was the first town in the territory to implement the notion of enclosing the ball diamond. However, in the journals of Presbyterian minister Endicott Peabody published in an excellent work titled *A Church for Helldorado* by S. J. Reidhead, mentioned that in a game on March 10, 1882, he had hit "one to the fence." Newspaper accounts in Tombstone were sketchy about specific games, as many contests were happening between scratch nines around town. Either way, these early communities saw the importance of having a dedicated baseball ground, complete with fencing and perhaps a small grandstand for the local cranks. The same diamond would see plenty of action over the coming seasons by clubs from the post and as far away as Williams, Flagstaff, Albuquerque and El Paso. The development of the railroad line through Flagstaff in 1882 made travel for baseball games much faster. The railroad made it easier for baseball nines from far-away towns to come for a tournament or holiday match.

Most of the ballgames for the next decade reported in the local press were the contests in special events such as the Territorial Fair and the Fourth of July. Prescott hosted a few lavish holiday celebrations, complete with all of the holiday activities any western town could think of. The Fourth of July celebration in 1895 lasted an astonishing six days. No expense was spared that year, as the organizing committee in Prescott offered cash prizes ranging from $25 to $250 for foot, horse, and bicycle races, along with shooting events and a "hose team" race, which pitted fire companies from neighboring towns against each other. The bash featured a baseball tournament in which the famed Albuquerque Browns faced the two local clubs. The first match was scheduled for July 4 between the Fort Whipple and Albuquerque clubs, with the winners to take on Prescott the following day. The visiting Browns proved their mettle, winning 8 to 4. The Prescott club never even stepped onto the diamond, forfeiting the match on a successful protest lobbied by Albuquerque for adding a few players from Fort Whipple to their roster. The visitors walked away with $250 in prize money and some kind of a diamond belt. On July 10, the *Weekly Journal Miner* complimented the Browns, saying "It is a fine nine." Outside of this singular fiesta for the nation's birthday, few of these games seemed to match the excitement, hoopla and controversy of the Arizona Territorial Fair.

The Territorial Fair

As briefly mentioned earlier, the citizens of Phoenix decided to organize the first Territorial Fair in the fall of 1884. It was held in late October or early November and was an exposition of agriculture and mining exhibits from across the Arizona Territory. The fair was held at the Territorial Fairgrounds adjacent to the Salt River, on Central Avenue just two miles south of Phoenix. Baseball made its initial appearance as a side attraction in 1887. The first matches at the fair would be a series of three between the Phoenix Base Ball Club and the Fort Whipple Nine. The *Arizona Gazette* reported on October 18, 1887, that the visiting club was comprised of ballists from both Fort Whipple and Albuquerque. With a purse of $250 at stake, each club would put their best athletes on the diamond in hopes of winning glory and a nice sum of cash. The *Gazette*, in anticipation of the matches between the two clubs, added that "Our base ball boys will make the fur fly when the proper time arrives."[55] The next day's edition promised that the Phoenix lads were equal to the task even though the soldiers from Fort Whipple were in fine trim. The game drew a large amount of interest amongst the townsfolk of Phoenix, including many betting pools being formed before the first match, with the soldiers from Fort Whipple favored to win.

The three matches were contested for the championship of the territory for 1887. The first match, on Monday, October 17, 1887, made the first page of the *Gazette* in response to the large amount of interest shown during the previous week. The newspaper noted that the Phoenix B.B.C.'s starting hurler, Powers, had been injured and could not play, being replaced by a young gentleman from California named Hopeman, employed by Goldman & Company of Phoenix as a clerk in the general store. The match started with the Phoenix B.B.C. scoring eight runs in the first three frames to Fort Whipple's four. In the fifth inning, the soldiers scored a single tally. The hurler for the visiting nine, Kortman, was able to hold the powerful Phoenix B.B.C. to a mere four runs in the remaining six frames. The final tally was 12–5 in favor of the hometown club. The score was also reported in the *Arizona Weekly Miner* on October 18, 1887, to keep the readers in Prescott apprised of the championship match that featured their local nine from the military post. The article in the *Gazette* relayed that the finest fielding play of the match was turned in by the shortstop for the Phoenix B.B.C., Thoman, who speared a hot line drive by the utility ballist for the Whipples named Love that was headed to short left field. Thoman quickly made an accurate throw to first to double-up center fielder Osterman. It took two hours and 20 minutes to play a full nine innings. The second match would commence the following morning.

On October 19, the *Phoenix Gazette* printed an article titled "Don't Squeal Boys," wherein a scandal surfaced regarding the first match of the Territorial Championship. The directors of the Territorial Fair Association, who had organized the entire event including the baseball matches, decided to disqualify Hopeman, the replacement hurler for the Phoenix B.B.C., because he was not an official resident of Phoenix or the Arizona Territories. There was also a rumor circulating amongst the citizens of Phoenix and Prescott that Hopeman had once pitched professionally for the California Base Ball League, a new league that started in 1886. Hopeman (Hapeman, in some sources) would make his first appearance in a series of games for the Tombstone Base Ball Club in 1887, after a large sum of money was put up by the boosters of the nine to secure his services from a professional club out of Los Angeles in hopes of getting even with their regular opponents from Fort Huachuca. Albert G. Hapeman, misspelled as "Hopeman" by the *Arizona Gazette,* pitched in the California Base Ball League, a forerunner of the PCL, from 1886 to 1890. He began with the Sacramento Altas and later took the box for the Stockton club in 1889. A good pitcher who kept Stockton close in tight games, he was known for being lazy. Hapeman's antics earned him two $25 fines in 1889, for being late and talking back. The editorial charged the Whipple-Albuquerque nine with "not being able to cope" with the Phoenix nine and advised that if this was the case, then they should quit the field and admit defeat without protesting about one of their competitors. The article defended Hopeman's intentions of residing in town and his right to compete for the local nine. The editor added, "if we were the soldier boys we would stand up and take our medicine without squealing."

The next day, the *Gazette* called for fair play amongst the two nines and refrained from blaming the umpires of the first match. Word of the controversial ballist reached Prescott, and in the *Weekly Arizona Miner* printed a letter from "Justitia," airing his (or her) feelings about the controversy surrounding the first match of the championship. The letter said the Phoenix B.B.C.'s action of importing a professional hurler was "about on par with the fellow who steers his friends against a crooked game."[56] The editor deemed the letter exactly what the Phoenix B.B.C. deserved for the foul act. "Justitia" called into question the motives of the citizens of Phoenix, questioning their honor and accusing them of "highway robbery." The letter gives a clue about the tactics of the day in 1887. It was common for clubs to hire "ringers," or highly skilled and experienced players, to give a decided edge in a match or tournament with prize money at stake. In this case, it seems that the Phoenix B.B.C. might have done the same, despite no concrete evidence of such a conspiracy perpetrated by the host club.

The letter written by "Justitia" also gave the Whipple nine another name for their club, calling the ballists from Fort Whipple the "Whipple Reds." The letter also revealed that the prize money of $250—no small purse during that time—was provided by the Agricultural Club of Phoenix. The letter added that the manager of the Phoenix B.B.C. was guilty of bribery, as would be the hurler for unfairly pitching for the Phoenix nine. This wouldn't be the first controversy in baseball games in territorial competition. In a match between the Prescott B.B.C. and Fort Whipple B.B.C. on October 8, 1895, a member of the Prescott nine used a foreign substance to help him in catching fly balls. S. P. Bartley, a local businessman, reportedly used Golden Gate Baking Powder on his hands to help snare any ball, as the *Arizona Journal Miner* described it, "that was over knocked from the plate."

With the dark cloud of controversy seemingly over with, and the first match of the championship called off, the second match of the series was played on October 20. The following day's *Gazette* buried the account in a column that listed other sporting events and labeled the match as an exhibition game. The intense dispute over the Hopeman issue had caused the directors of the Territorial Fair Association to cancel the championship of the territory for 1887 and sanction the second match as an exhibition. The prize fund of $250 would be returned to the Agricultural Club of Phoenix. The match was won by the Whipple Reds, 17–8, with the paper noting that the young men who competed in the match showed much energy and spirit. The article promised to include more details about the match in the next issue. The last game of the fair never happened, however, as the hard feelings caused by the Phoenix nine hadn't cooled off enough.

The 1888 Territorial Fair would not include baseball in any events. The bad blood from one year prior was long remembered by the clubs from Tucson, Tombstone, Prescott and Fort Whipple.

The Fair in 1889 was initially planned to include a three-club tournament between the Phoenix Base Ball Club, the Tombstone Base Ball Club and the Aztecs of Yuma County. The opening-day match of the 1889

Territorial Fair featured the Phoenix B.B.C. and the Aztecs of Yuma, as announced in the program printed on October 17 in the *Arizona Daily Gazette*. The paper noted that the match would begin at 10 a.m. and anticipated a good game. No report was given of this match, which raises the question of whether the game was played. On the next day, the *Gazette* announced that the second match would pit the Tombstone and Phoenix nines against each other, while noting that the clubs were experienced and well matched. The match resulted in a victory for the Phoenix club, 10–5. The *Gazette* reporter noted that the baseball match was surprising to those who attended due to the assumption that the Tombstone nine would win easily, but by some miracle the Tombstone nine "let go entirely, and allowed the Phoenix boys to win with ease."[57]

The third match of the Fair, the second between the Phoenix and Tombstone Base Ball Clubs, ended in a victory for Tombstone, 19–12. The *Gazette* failed to include any box score or description of the match itself, citing lack of space in that edition. Ironically, that same issue, the score of the first game of the 1889 World Series between the New York Giants and the Brooklyn Trolley Dodgers (renamed the Bridegrooms due to so many of their young players being newly married that season), with Brooklyn winning, 12 to 10. The *Gazette* printed the scores of the 1889 World Series, following the national interest in the Series, which the New York Giants won in nine exciting games. Back home in the Arizona Territories, the Phoenix nine had hired help from San Francisco, paying a $50 premium to a battery from California. This would cause kicking in the papers for several years to come, proving problematic for fair organizers seeking to attract baseball clubs to Phoenix. Even in the late 1880s and 1890s, no one wanted to play with a known group of alleged cheaters.

The following year marked a new decade, and the baseball matches for the Territorial Fair would continue. In 1890, the championship of the territory was contested between the Phoenix and Tucson Base Ball Clubs. On October 13, 1890, the *Arizona Daily Citizen* proudly announced that the Tucson club would travel northward to "cross bats with the team of that place, in a series of three games, to be played at the fair for the championship of the territory," under management of R. Rainsbury, who would lead the ballists and oversee any cranks that wanted to join the excursion. The round-trip fare on the Maricopa Rail Road cost $9.80. Any interested cranks of the Old Pueblo were directed to sign up for the trip by adding their name to the list at Black's Jewelry store, located at 113 Congress Street.

In anticipation of the upcoming contests, the Phoenix Base Ball Club held practice games as early as October 6. The first match was played at Agricultural Park, called Patton's Park in the Phoenix papers of the day, on October 16, on a pleasant, 76-degree day. Both the *Arizona Daily Citizen* and the *Arizona Republican* reported the action, including lineups and the final tally. The Tucson club arrived on the evening of October 16 and were met by the officers of the Phoenix B.B.C., Mr. Goldberg and Mr. Kibbey, who graciously led them to the Central Hotel. The first match would commence at 10 o'clock the following morning on a well-groomed field, umpired by H. H. McNeil and George Spangenburg.

This would be the first time Phoenix and Tucson faced each other in many years. Plenty of taunting had been built up prior to the games through the newspapers, and both the *Arizona Republican* and *Arizona Daily Citizen* proudly exchanged barbs, each paper boasting of the prowess of its respective club. The *Daily Citizen*, in keeping up with the shenanigans of the Phoenix club in territorial games of seasons past, cautioned the would-be opponents that "if they do go, an understanding should be made that the club [not be] part San Francisco and part Phoenix, as was done to the Tombstone nine at the Fair a year ago."[58]

For 1890, a three-match series between the Tucson Base Ball Club and the Phoenix Base Ball Club for the Territorial Championship would be held at Patton's Park on a Friday, Saturday and Sunday. The *Gazette* listed the positions of players from both clubs as follows: "W. Zabriskie, Catcher; E. Drachman, Hurler; M. Drachman, First Base; B. Zabriskie, Second Base; R. Rainsbury, Third Base; W. S. Kengla, Short Stop; Frank Smith, Left Field; Harry Drachman, Center Field and E. Hutton in Right Field for the Tucson Base Ball Club. For the hometown Phoenix nine—D. Goldberg, Catcher; A. P. Walbridge, Hurler; T. Downey, First Base; W. Widmer, Second Base; L. Grey, Third Base; A. Thoman, Short Stop; B. McNulty, Left Field; B. Stockton, Center Field; and F. Kibbey Right Field."

Getting to and from the games at Patton's Park in Phoenix meant riding the horse-drawn trolley cars operated by the Valley Street Railway Company. The route began on Central Avenue and Washington Street, working eastward to 16th Street, where the cars would unload passengers for the ball game and pick up anyone wishing to return to town. A one-way fare was five cents, with the car line making 11 round-trips per day.

The first match of the championship series commenced on the morning of October 17. Both sides were in good spirits on the makeshift diamond at Patton's Park. Tucson scored twice in the first frame, while Phoenix didn't score until the bottom of the second inning, when Tucson third baseman Rainsbury made two errors, which resulted in two runs.

Frank Kibbey reached third base on an error, with left fielder McNulty being put out at first base. First baseman for the Phoenix nine, Downey, would score an ace on an error of Zabriskie. The article isn't clear about which Zabriskie made the error, as there were two on the field that day. The scoring increased in the fifth inning with errors being made by the Tucson nine, with two charged to Zabriskie, allowing a run to score despite a second strikeout recorded on the Phoenix catcher, Goldberg. At the end of the fifth inning, the tally remained close, Phoenix leading 10–9. The Tucson nine scored one run in the sixth inning, four in the seventh and one in the eighth, while Phoenix recorded just two runs over the next three frames and trailed 15–12 heading into the ninth inning. Tucson went down in order in the top of the ninth. Phoenix started its half with McNulty smashing a double. Downey followed with a single and Goldberg hit a line drive to second base and was put out at first while sending McNulty to third. Widmer lifted a fly ball to the shortstop for Tucson, who caught it and relayed the ball to third base, catching McNulty off the bag for the double play and the final out of the match. The final score was 15–12 in favor of the Tucson B.B.C. The paper noted that Frank Smith, playing for the Tucson nine, was the youngest ballist on the field of play, and that amongst the spectators were several young ladies on horses, who watched the game and undoubtedly encouraged the young men from Tucson to give their finest effort.

The second match at Patton's Park on October 18 saw a spirited game between the two clubs. About 300 cranks were on hand to witness the game, which began under cloudy skies with cool temperatures. The game was a wild one, full of errors, timely hitting, stolen bases, strikeouts, bases on balls and a hit batsman. The reporter provided a detailed account for all nine innings, including a box score that appeared in the October 20 edition of the *Arizona Republican.* Tucson scored five runs in the first frame, starting with a base hit and stolen base by E. Drachman. Smith flied out to Thoman for the first out, and Drachman tagged up and advanced to third. The next batter, Zabriskie, reached first on a base on balls, which in 1890 meant four balls. This rule had changed in 1889, as in previous years it was as many as nine balls called for a walk. Zabriskie promptly stole second and later scored on a single to left field. Hutton was safe on an error charged to right fielder F. Kibbey. R. Pacho, a new left fielder who had replaced Frank Smith, stepped to the plate with the bases loaded but struck out. B. Zabriskie, playing center field that day, hit a scorching line drive to right field to score two runs. Tucson scored two more runs, ending the first frame with a commanding lead of 5–0.

The Phoenix nine opened their half of the inning with successive singles by catcher D. Goldberg and pitcher Lee Gray. Second baseman Widmer popped to second, and Phoenix failed to score. Tucson got only a single and stolen base by Drachman in the top half of the second frame before two strikeouts and a pop-out to first. The bottom half of the second inning ended just as quickly with no runs being scored.

The third inning went quietly for Tucson, with Hutton leading off but being put out on an assist by Walbridge, who was listed in the box score as both a pitcher and a center fielder. R. Pacho reached first on an error by catcher Goldberg, but was forced out at second. B. Zabriskie hit a towering fly ball for the third out. The *Gazette*, had thoughtfully named the Phoenix Nine were now nicknamed the "Alfalfa's" by the press, perhaps describing the Phoenix Nine's play or their individual professions. In the bottom of the third inning, Kibbey hit a sharp ground ball single to right field, only to be tagged out at second base. Goldberg bunted, but the pitcher, E. Drachman, cleanly fielded the ball and made a quick throw to first base for the second out. The article failed to describe the third out, moving on to the top of the fourth inning.

Drachman was struck by a pitch and awarded first base, another first in recorded baseball in the Arizona Territories. He advanced to third on a passed ball by Goldman, and scored a single to left field by third baseman R. Rainsbury. Tucson showed no signs of letting up on the Phoenix club scoring, on two errors, two stolen bases and several base hits off of Phoenix's hurler, Gray. Tucson now led 9–0 heading to the bottom of the fourth.

The Phoenix B.B.C., consistently described as the "Alfalfas" by the *Gazette*, finally ended the shutout on Widmer's single to center field, a stolen base, a passed ball and a wild throw by hurler E. Drachman, who fired the ball to third base in an attempt to pick off Widmer, who seemed to be napping. Finally Phoenix had a run on the board. Thoman walked, but the inning ended on a foul-out and a pickoff at first base. The tally now stood at 9–1. Tucson recorded three more runs in the top of the fifth inning on solid hitting and more stolen bases. Tucson added more runs as the game progressed, while Phoenix could never quite find their footing offensively or defensively. The final tally was 15–9 in favor of Tucson. The hurler for Phoenix, Lee Gray, recorded an impressive ten strikeouts on the day. The Phoenix catcher recorded eight passed balls, giving the Tucson nine ample opportunity to score.

The last game of the series was played on October 19 and reported in the *Gazette* on the following day. At 2:55 p.m. Tucson sent one of the

Drachman brothers to the plate to lead off the game. He doubled, and Smith struck out for the first out. Drachman advanced on a passed ball, only to be stranded there. In this game, the boys from Phoenix turned the tables on the visiting club from Tucson. Their leadoff hitter, D. Goldberg, reached first on an error by first baseman F. Drachman. The Phoenix hurler, Gray, followed by hammering the ball to deep center field for a triple, scoring Goldberg and giving Phoenix an early lead. The next batter lifted an easy fly ball to Zabriskie in center field, but he muffed the catch and allowed Gray to score. Cuber and McNulty drove in two more runs for Phoenix and at the end of the first inning, the score stood at 5–0. The second and third innings saw no scoring, but in the fourth inning, Tucson recorded three runs, only to see Phoenix tally twice in the bottom half of the inning. In the seventh inning, Phoenix scored three runs to take a commanding lead. Despite Tucson scoring four late runs, Phoenix won, 13–8. The series closed with Tucson claiming two victories and Phoenix salvaging their pride by winning the third contest. The Tucson B.B.C. would claim the Arizona Territorial Championship for 1890.

The Phoenix B.B.C. would print an open challenge for a baseball match on Thanksgiving Day, asking that any interested club in the territory write to club secretary Maurice Fleishman. There were no takers on this challenge, or at least none printed in the local newspapers for November of that year. The next tournament for the territorial cup would be contested on the grounds at Patton's Park, later known as East Lake Park, in 1895.

There was no baseball in the fall of 1891 due to a catastrophic flood that completely decimated the Territorial Fair grounds and large parts of Mesa, Tempe and Phoenix. The waters of the Salt River rose dramatically overnight and, on the morning of February 19, 1891, a loud roar of rushing waters awakened the residents of these riverside communities, announcing the worst flood that the territory and state has ever witnessed. Many days of rainfall, added to a large snowmelt, had caused the normally sanguine Salt River to rise an unprecedented 18 feet. The destruction leveled homes along the riverbank, wiped out the ball field at the fair grounds and completely demolished the Tempe bridge. Naturally, residents focused on reorganizing and rebuilding their lives, forgetting baseball.

The Arizona Territorial Fair would not resume until 1905. By then, reviving the fair became the mission of a citizens' group which formed the Arizona Territorial Fair Association in 1905. Financed by its members, the group, led by hotelier J. C. Adams, purchased the present location for $9,200. The Association immediately developed the property, adding two racetracks, a grandstand, and a wooden fence around the grounds. To aid the Association with their 80-acre development, the Territory of Arizona created a Fair Commission. With a legislative appropriation of $22,500, the Commission constructed two buildings on the property. After renting the property from the Fair Association for $10 a year, the Fair Commission purchased the property in 1909 for $30,000. With statehood granted in 1912, the State Fair Commission continued the work of the Territorial Fair Commission in presenting the annual fair, which continues on the same site to this day.

Conclusion

Baseball was played and widely promoted by all of the larger towns in the territory by 1890. It has been often said that any town in the old west needed three things to survive: (1) saloons; (2) an opera house; and (3) a good baseball club. A mix of patriotism and hometown pride fueled the promotion of baseball to represent any town in the land as being better than the rest. At first, townsfolk were reluctant to support the game, as tales from Eastern newspapers warned about how rowdy and drunken ball players tended to be. Once the game took hold in the territory, competition was fierce, as recounted in the games and surrounding events earlier in this chapter. In these early days, travel was a necessity to find competition. Celebrations for the Fourth of July and Decoration Day held special importance to these communities. Everyone observed them, mustering as much patriotic pride as they could. The earliest example of baseball matches on the Fourth of July was in 1879 between two "Independent Nines," as reported by the *Arizona Daily Citizen* in Tucson. These holidays would be a mainstay for the game, but not the only time games were played. Eventually the organizers of the Territorial Fair would make baseball a "side attraction." The games were competitive, if not overly controversial in nature. With large cash prizes at stake, the clubs did everything they could imagine to win the tournament and title of Territorial Champion.

In 1882, a census taken in Phoenix revealed that there were only 2,764 residents.[59] During that period, it was common practice for smaller communities, like Tempe and Mesa, to pick the best ball players from both towns to represent them on one combined club. As the years passed, the population for towns like Phoenix, Tucson, Tombstone and others grew in connection with the opening of the Southern Pacific and the Topeka-Kansas & Santa Fe Rail Roads. Traveling at first increased, then faded away. By 1900, baseball clubs weren't traveling nearly as much as they had five, ten or even 20 years prior. There was simply more competition to be had at or closer to any club's home grounds. The press started offering more detailed and dedicated coverage to baseball in general, noting the names of the various clubs, where the games were being contested, and the young men on the rosters for the afternoon. By Admittance Day in 1912, baseball was everywhere. Everyone played baseball, at schools, on official town clubs, and at the few military posts still active.

There were plenty of sandlot games where any group of people would pick sides, throw the base bags down, and play ball. The town rivalries that began on the make-shift baseball diamonds in the territorial era still continue today. The games were certainly rough in nature, with the unpredictability of cheating by opposing clubs, umpire bribes, the hiring of "ringers," and even instances where cranks discharged firearms into the air to distract the opposing fielders, made baseball a truly wild affair in a rough land. Phoenix and Tucson still square off in amateur, scholastic and collegiate baseball games. Bisbee and Tombstone celebrate one of the oldest rivalries in the nation, one that began on a rough patch of ground with a bat and ball over 100 years ago. For Arizona, the national game of baseball is truly at home.

CHAPTER 4

Women and Minorities on the Diamond

Baseball and America are quite a bit alike. Mark Twain, celebrated author of the Victorian era, was once asked to give an honorary speech at Delmonico's Restaurant, then a gem of bustling New York City. The speech was for the celebrated return of Albert Spalding's ambitious and history-making World Tour of 1888–1889. Twain described baseball as "the very symbol, the outward and visible expression of the drive, and push, and rush and struggle of the raging, tearing, booming nineteenth century!" Twain was right, and the early games of the territorial period in Arizona did share the same qualities he observed about the era. They were rough, raging and sometimes violent contests played out with bat and ball. However, baseball also had an ugly color-line barring the admission of Hispanic and African American athletes into its ranks of professional players.

Once considered a "gentleman's agreement" of sorts, the policy adopted by the early amateur clubs in New York, Pennsylvania, New Jersey, and the New England states simply barred inclusion of African American ballists. On October 16, 1867, the Pennsylvania State Convention of Baseball held its annual meeting in Harrisburg, and members openly denied admission to the black Pythian Base Ball Club. The National Association of Amateur Base Ball Players (NAABP), then the largest governing body of organized baseball and forerunner of the National Association (NA) and eventual National League (NL), followed suit by adopting a bylaw for club admission that banned "any club including one or more colored persons."

While this held true during the transition of baseball into more open professionalism, there were a few key years when formal agreements among clubs in the National Association and National League were dissolved, primarily in 1871, 1878 and 1884, that allowed some African American players to join the ranks of professional clubs that toured the country, playing in the largest of ball parks—cathedrals of sorts—in front of scores of rabid fans.

If there was a true pioneer of integration in baseball, it was John W. "Bud" Fowler. Born in Cooperstown, New York, on March 16, 1858, to John W. and Mary L. Jackson of Fort Plain, New York. His father was a barber, and the family moved around quite a bit, drifting from the upstate New York community of Cooperstown to parts of New England. Fowler learned to play ball on the school grounds of Cooperstown Seminary and, by age 20, he had matured to fill out a 5-foot–7-inch frame that carried a lithe and speedy 155 pounds. By then, he called himself Fowler, not using his birth name of Jackson. He threw the ball with terrifying accuracy and range on a strong right arm that, like his father's, gained strength from toiling as a barber to supplement his income as a ball player. He also wielded an effective bat, hitting right-handed. As he gained experience on local diamonds, his effort and dazzling display of speed and talent paid off when, as a part of a "picked nine" from Chelsea, Massachusetts, he was selected to pitch against none other than Tommy Bond and the reigning National League Champions, the Boston Red Caps, in an exhibition match on the afternoon of April 24, 1878.

Fowler was brilliant in the match, frustrating the more experienced professional nine from Boston, who begrudgingly played in foul weather without their usual uniforms. He tossed a three-hitter, allowing only one run in the 2–1 victory. He bounced around from town to town for several years in an effort to piece together a career in baseball. In 1884, the Toledo Blue Stockings of the American Association signed the first African American ball player to its roster, Moses "Fleetwood" Walker. He made his professional debut on May 1, 1884, as a catcher in a game against the Louisville Eclipse. He went hitless that afternoon, while recording four errors in a season-opening loss, 5–1. Despite a dismal performance that afternoon, he had officially broken baseball's color-line. He would play in 46 games in 1884 for the Blue Stockings, batting a respectable .263 as a solid place-hitter. The following season the Toledo club folded, and Walker went back to the minor leagues, finding short work with the Cleveland organization before signing with Waterbury, Connecticut, remaining there until the end of the 1886 season. From there, he went on to play for the Newark Little Giants in the International League, where he caught fellow African American hurler George Stovey. They would form the first known African American battery in baseball history.

4. Women and Minorities on the Diamond 101

Due to frequent injuries that were common to catchers in the 1880s, Walker missed a scheduled exhibition match on July 14, 1887, that would have placed him on the same field of play as the legendary Adrian "Cap" Anson of the Chicago White Stockings. His teammate and hurler, George Stovey was also given the game off under the guise that he was "sulking," in order to avoid any kind of conflict with Anson that might have prevented the lucrative exhibition match. Anson was well-known in baseball for being a bitter racist, and in his later years managing the White Stockings he wasn't afraid to show it. Mysteriously, the International League Board of Directors voted 6–4 to exclude African American baseball players from future contracts. It would seem that the color-line in baseball was becoming more entrenched, and Walker's days in baseball were numbered.

During the next off-season, the International League modified its ban on black players, causing Walker to sign with the Syracuse franchise for 1888. That September, Walker had his second incident with Cap Anson. When Chicago visited Syracuse for a post-season exhibition game, a very lucrative proposition at the time, Anson refused to start the game when he saw Walker's name on the scorecard as catcher. Syracuse relented and someone else did the catching in Walker's place. He remained in Syracuse until the team released him in July 1889. Shortly thereafter, the American Association and the National League both unofficially banned African American players, making the adoption of Jim Crow–type policies in baseball complete. Fleetwood Walker left baseball in 1891. He went on to be a hotel and movie theatre owner and later filed several patents regarding film projector technology.

Closer to home, Maricopa County recorded a scant 20,457 persons in Tempe, Mesa, Phoenix and outlying areas. According to Official U.S. Census Data, there were only 150 African American residents in Phoenix in 1900. Even with the towns of Tempe, Mesa, Lehi, Stringtown, and Glendale counted along with Phoenix there were fewer than 200 African American residents in Maricopa County. Like the color-line in professional baseball, the towns in early Maricopa County, along with the other population centers in the territory, were segregated. Considering that the population in territorial era Arizona was sparse, the number of baseball clubs in the beginning were few. Most of the time a "picked nine" was chosen from the best players that showed up to compete or took any interest at all in the game.

The earliest mention of a minority baseball club appeared in 1878 Tucson. What the *Arizona Weekly Star* called a contest between the

"Greasers and Gringos" was held on the Military Plaza in the heart of Tucson. An error-filled contest didn't impress the reporter, who quipped, "the game was principally remarkable for the lack of skills displayed."[1] Early accounts in Phoenix allude to baseball being played by boys of all ages. An unnamed fan who called himself "Adios" wrote to the *Salt River Herald* in the summer of 1878. While not specifically mentioning whether the lads "engaged in the usual varieties of play. Some with bat and ball."[2] were of any specific color, the letter by an otherwise observant resident of Phoenix offers a few clues, such as the number of young boys speaking Spanish to each other. The author of the letter, titled "What Shall We Do?" mentioned that these lads held the interests of "our country in embryo." With this in mind, maybe the Mexican boys felt left out of the ball games. Whatever the reason, minorities would also contribute to changing the game of baseball during this period in Arizona's history.

To illustrate the views of the communities where minorities were living, one needs to look no further than the pages of any local newspaper. Phoenix was known for many firsts, including the first ice cream parlor in the Territory in 1882. The *Phoenix Herald*, expressing its own views of the conflict still being waged across Arizona as the Indian Wars played out, printed a front-page headline in April of 1882, saying that the number of "Good Indians" was equal to the number of insurgent Native Americans killed by the U.S. Army. Playing on a baseball club during these early times was certainly a risky affair for minorities. Minorities in the early Arizona towns desired to assimilate into white culture. Mexicans, Indians and blacks all saw baseball as a means of acceptance as being "more white." These early settlers wanted to learn English (if not already spoken), vote, run for office and run businesses in white communities that were gaining in population, wealth and political influence so that they too could have the same prosperity as their Anglo brethren. Remembering the three keys to a successful town being alcohol, theatre and sports, playing on a winning ball club was a good way to gain acceptance, especially if you were talented with the glove and bat.

The early territorial newspapers were less than accepting of the notion. When the games featuring Mexican nines were reported, terms such as "greasers" and "tomale" were used to describe them in an unflattering tone. During the 1870s, sparse baseball action was reported, a game here and there summarized by the newsmen covering a town or county. The 1880s saw more newspaper coverage, including lineups and rudimentary box scores. No mention was made of minorities on the rosters until 1886, when a series of games was held between clubs labeled "Mexican" and "American" for the Slaughterhouse Championship of the Yuma Valley.

At the time, the Native American game of shinny was very popular amongst the citizens of Yuma, representing the major sport in town for almost a decade. In 1886, even the *Arizona Sentinel* offered a long-overdue farewell to the game in an effort to usher in a revived interest in baseball. Presumably, after re-organizing and practicing their fielding and batting skills, the "Caballeros Mejicanos" of Yuma officially issued an open challenge to any club in the area for the championship of the Colorado Desert. Another cowboy group named "The Dudes" readily accepted the challenge, with a purse of $90 at stake. The contest immediately drew wide interest as the park in back of the local slaughterhouse was used. The Slaughterhouse Athletic Association oversaw the event, assuming the task of preparing the grounds and constructing a grandstand for spectators. Trains ran to the event every 14 minutes and charged an all-inclusive fare of $2.25, which included a reserve area seat at the ball game. Refreshment stands were also in place, to quench the thirst of local cranks on their way to and from the match. Post-match festivities included a sack race for a silver mug trophy and a boxing match that evening. A full day of athletics indeed!

The Dudes won the match on April 3, 21 to 10. The *Arizona Sentinel* noted that "The game was hotly contested and displayed the fact that Yuma could raise a nine that would be open to all comers."[3] The victorious "Gringos" would win a rematch against their Caballero counterparts despite spotting them a 15-run advantage. The "bad feelings" between the two clubs that were perceived by the *Sentinel* wouldn't be resolved until April 28, 1888, when the paper called on both Mexican and American nines to start practicing again and eventually settle matters on the field in a proper "Tug of War." The game that transpired on the grounds of Don J. M. Molina's field was described by the *Sentinel* as "the most wonderful ever played." The Mexican nine outplayed their opponents in grand style, winning 45–15.

Tucson's baseball history is lengthy, consistent and rich. Despite the many clubs that competed there, any kind of baseball played by minorities wouldn't reach the pages of the *Citizen* or *Star* again until September 1889. A group of young men, presumably white, named themselves the Young Pioneers. The *Arizona Daily Star* advertised the upcoming match on November 29 between the Young Pioneers and their Hispanic counterparts, dubbed the "Tomales," for a purse of $10 per side. This was a re-match of a contest in late September, when the Young Pioneers were victorious by a wide margin. The December 2 edition of the paper reported a 36–6 victory for the Young Pioneers in the re-match. It isn't known what skill level, organization or amount of practice the young Mexican nine had. Judging from the score, they were out of practice or may have been specifically picked to ensure an easy victory for the Young Pioneers. The *Daily Star* offered few clues and no explanation.

Years later, in August of 1893, the *Arizona Daily Citizen* noted that the youth of Tucson had taken a more distinct interest in baseball than the adults in town and that $35 had changed hands between "the Tamales, or Mexicans, and the Juniors, Americans."[4] To continue the rivalry between the two ethnic groups, another game was scheduled for the following Sunday with a $20 prize for the winning club. No article reported that a return match was ever played, so we are collectively left to wonder who won or if it was even played.

Phoenix itself staged its first formal match between a minority nine and an Anglo club on May 31, 1890. The match was reported by the *Arizona Republican* as being "a very good game." At Phoenix Park, the Apaches competed against a skilled Phoenix B.B.C., losing 14 to 7. The *Republican* noted that a Phoenix player named Cubre had three base hits. The Apache nine quickly vanished from the pages of the *Republican*, and it is not known if the club ever played again. Later that fall, a game was played between the Lemon Hotel nine and "Mexicanos."[5] No game report, box score or final tally was reported. Outside of Phoenix proper, the small farming and ranching community of Glendale was finally getting into the baseball craze that had afflicted Phoenicians for decades. The first matches that the Glendale nine competed in were against a Mexican nine that was routinely playing a Phoenix club known in 1900 as the "Rough Riders."

Tombstone, now affectionately called the "town too tough to die," certainly has seen a fair share of baseball action in its long history. One of the town's main rivalries, as discussed in previous chapters, has been against the soldiers from Fort Huachuca. Plenty of controversy, game fixing and even blatant cheating by both sides has marked the games since the earliest days of the rivalry. In 1893, the competitors met for a match at Fort Huachuca. According to the *Tombstone Prospector*, the match fell through after one of the Tombstone nine didn't show up, preferring to spend time with his sweetheart instead. To fix matters, a replacement player was suggested, to the objection of the baseball team comprised of colored soldiers from the 24th Infantry. It appeared that no game would be played that afternoon. As a solution, drawing from the two baseball clubs on post at the time, a challenge was issued from the white soldiers of Troop E, 2nd Cavalry. The challenge was accepted and the 1 o'clock start time was upheld and the game commenced. Despite a distinct lack of practice on the part of the Cavalry men, the score was a close, with Tombstone winning, 12–8.

Although there would be several minority and integrated clubs by 1910, all had a connection to the Tempe Crimson Rims club. The Crimson Rims took their place in Arizona history as not so much the first integrated club, but as an integrated club that had continuity. They played for several years primarily against other clubs of the Salt River Valley, namely clubs from Mesa, Stringtown, Lehi, and Phoenix. Tempe was known as a "Sun-Down Town," meaning it was not safe for blacks, Mexicans or Indians to be out on the streets of Tempe after sundown. Late-night assaults and robberies against minorities were commonplace. Hotels and restaurants would take out advertising in the pages of the *Tempe Daily News, Mesa Daily News* or *Arizona Republican*, assuring the public that their establishment hired only white hotel staff and waiters. Professional opportunities during this chapter of Arizona history were less than enterprising for minorities.

This didn't stop baseball from developing amongst colored nines. The towns along the Salt River were prospering in the "Gay Nineties," fielding several new clubs to challenge the well-established Phoenix B.B.C. On February 7, 1890, the *Tempe Daily News*, then a small paper covering Tempe and Mesa, noted, "We understand that the Tempe baseball nine has challenged the Stringtown nine to play a match." Without enough players to field two complete clubs, the game never took place. The boys from Tempe redoubled their recruiting efforts in order to field a solid nine to face future challenges for baseball supremacy against other scratch clubs in the area and, on occasion, visiting nines from Tucson. Later that month, Tempe assembled a full nine to face the Phoenix B.B.C. with the 1 p.m. start moved back an hour and a half to allow for a large crowd that the *Arizona Weekly Republican* estimated as "fully 1000 spectators."[6] Tempe won the toss, which may have been a coin toss, a bat toss or even using a flat rock. The umpire would spit on one side and call "wet or dry?" for the captain of one club to call, to decide which club would bat first.

Phoenix started the game at bat, presumably at Patton's Park in Phoenix. Tempe had yet to select and prepare a home ground for baseball, while Patton's Park had plenty of space for cranks to take in the action on the diamond. Through the third inning, the score stood 7 to 6 in favor of Tempe. The next five frames saw no scoring as both hurlers settled down, exhibiting skillful pitching. By this time the large crowd had surged to a record throng and, as noted by the *Weekly Republican*, "had continually grown in numbers, had by this time closed in on the outfield, and when a ball went outside of the diamond it was nearly impossible for the fielders to get it." The visitors took advantage of the situation, slugging a ball deep to right field, out of the reach of Griffin, driving in a crucial run. The ninth saw two more runs cross the plate for Tempe, while Phoenix was held hitless. The famed curveball pitcher from Tucson, Manny Drachman, served as one of two umpires for the match.

The defeat at the hands of a new club didn't dampen the enthusiasm for the Phoenix B.B.C. Instead, the occasion launched a friendly rivalry with Tempe, including practice matches to sharpen their skills at the plate and in the field. Over the next year, the nine from Tempe helped spark interest with a new club from Mesa and Stringtown, notable Mormon settlements in Arizona. Both towns were early agricultural communities, with Stringtown deriving its name from the linear layout of its streets instead of the normal offset gridline design of most Mormon towns in Utah. A mixed club comprised of players from both towns played the Phoenix nine for many years to come. The Tempe-Mesa club's first match was played on May 13, 1891, a game that went 11 innings, contested on the east side of Patton's Park. The visitors showcased strong pitching by a young man named Lee Gray and his stalwart catcher, O. Stapley. Lee Gray was known throughout the area as a wonderful pitcher, and at one time had been asked to pitch for the short-lived Beehive Nine from Phoenix. The match was reported in *Arizona Republican,* which quickly took note of Gray's fastball, saying "[Gray] tried his best to knock down the backstop." The paper was equally impressed with his catcher, noting that Stapley possessed "Cinderella hands"[7] while handling the pitches that came blazing across the plate. Astonishingly, he had only two passed balls during the game. The "Alfalfas" of Phoenix stayed close until several fielding errors late in the game proved costly. The visitors claimed victory after 11 hard-fought innings by a score of 14 to 13.

Baseball in Tempe soon lost its appeal, disappearing from the pages of local newspapers until the fall of 1895. The Tempe club was originally scheduled to face the Fort Thomas nine, but failed to field a full club to play the match. They would forfeit $50 to the champions as agreed upon, to help cover travel costs incurred by the touring nine from eastern Arizona. The club reorganized and began competition with Phoenix in late September. The first match was a purely social event, with no stakes wagered. A 25-cent entrance fee was charged to help both clubs recover money lost to the territorial champions. The practice match on Sunday,

September 29, drew a large crowd that witnessed the newly formed club from Tempe go down in defeat, 22–12, to the more polished home club. The "Southside" nine would reorganize again over the coming month, recruiting better ball players for competition.

The rematch came on November 19 in Phoenix. The home nine marked this match as their last in old, tattered uniforms, with new ones scheduled to arrive before the next game. Tempe showed a stronger team this time out, even drawing praise from the *Arizona Republican* reporter, who wrote, "In fact it was the best team that ever came from the Southside."[8] The large crowd saw a better game from the visitors, who lost, 12–1. Playing only a few games over the next few seasons, the Tempe club saw sparse action, with regular members of the club coming and going. The end of the 1890s, a decade described as the "Gay Nineties," brought the most intense and diverse baseball action in Arizona history.

Phoenix and Tempe mixed it up again on February 6, 1899, with the *Arizona Republican* saying the two "played good ball." The spring months would again see a few games between old foes. August proved pivotal as five new clubs appeared on the local diamond and in local newspapers. The new clubs were the Cyclones, True Blues, Cracker Jacks, Union Stars and Tempe Crimson Rims, all of whom became active in 1899. These clubs were either fully staffed as minority nines or integrated clubs. The True Blues and Union Stars were Mexican nines, while the Cyclones and Cracker Jacks were described as "colored" by the *Arizona Republican*. The Tempe Crimson Rims were the sole integrated club in Maricopa County, featuring players from all races of peoples living in the Salt River Valley at the turn of the 20th century.

The 1899 campaign started on a rather mundane note, with the Tempe nine and a club known in the papers simply as the "DeMunds," engaging in practices and scrimmage matches through the spring and early summer. While the more organized nines were sharpening their skills for the season to begin in August, a landmark event occurred one month prior. A "Base Ball Challenge" was published in the upstart *Republican Herald* on July 20. A Mr. Stearns, the owner and operator of a popular local barbershop in Phoenix named the Fashion Barber Shop, "hereby issues a challenge to any team of white barbers." The prize would be two kegs of locally brewed beer, to be enjoyed on the ball grounds and paid for by the losing club. There was one catch to this offer. The kegs would be kept just off third base. To get a beer, one had to hit a triple. Stearns believed that it would "spur the players to their noblest efforts in running and sliding and prevent throwing off." The article listed the roster for the challenging nine. The *Republican Herald*, a weekly publication, also reported the white barbers of Phoenix and Maricopa County had declined the challenge.

This didn't deter the black barbers, who had enough ballists to play an entire game themselves for the two kegs of beer, starting at 2:30 p.m. Representing the "south side" was a team called Shirley's Bully's, while the men representing the "north side" were "Bolton's Possumalas." The selection of an umpire was a daunting task, as no one was sure how to handle the possibility of players getting more inebriated as the contest wore on. The local police force was probably on hand to search the contestants for razors, clubs and other weapons, to diffuse a potentially dangerous situation as wagers on the match ran heavy.

Prior to this match, minority clubs usually faced white competition. This was a first on two counts. It featured two black clubs competing against each other, and it was the first openly recorded reference to teams contending for and drinking beer on the diamond during a game. The game must have been electric! The *Republican Herald* failed to report a final score or any details. Imagination can fill in the large gaps in what might have happened during nine innings of baseball in late July with two kegs of ice-cold beer on the line.

In August, the newly formed Ash Fork nine issued an open challenge to the Phoenix B.B.C. for a large sum of $200–500 per side, while a Mexican club challenged a "colored nine."[9] There's no record of the challenges being accepted. However, a few weeks later, two other minority baseball clubs would face each other on the diamond.

The Cyclones, described by the *Arizona Republican* as "carrying a chip around on its shoulder for some time,"[10] issued a challenge to another minority club in the area, the True Blues. In ornate fashion familiar to the era, the True Blues responded in kind and a match was arranged for the following Sunday at Phoenix Park, commonly known as East Lake Park, on 16th Street and Jefferson Street a short carriage or rail-way ride a few miles east of town. After all the posturing by both sides through the newspaper, the game revealed the superior nine. In a well-attended contest, the True Blues emerged victorious, 28 to 12. Each club put up $50 and agreed to a best-of-three series for the $100. The paper noted that "there was more to play for than there has been at any previous game this season."[11] The game drew interest from the *Phoenix Daily Herald*, a chief competitor of the *Arizona Republican*. The *Daily Herald* offered a more detailed view of the diamond action and praised the victorious True Blues, declaring "the infield work of the Mexicans was brilliant."[12] While the

4. Women and Minorities on the Diamond 109

The Tempe Crimson Rims of 1899: Standing far left is Eugene Thomas. Seated to his left is Edward P. Carr. Lying in front of Carr is Chris Cresencio Sigala. (Tempe Museum of History)

minority clubs were busy mixing it up on local diamonds, the DeMund nine had issued a challenge to a nine from Prescott and was awaiting word regarding the anticipated match.

The True Blues emerged victorious over the Cyclone nine in the second game of the series, walking away with the $100 prize a week later by a final tally of 22 to 9. The captain of the victorious and now overtly confident True Blues, Augustin C. Bernal, called upon the *Republican* in person to boast of the victory and to talk about challenging the tougher DeMund club. With all the baseball action going on between three clubs in Phoenix, of which two were minority nines, the stage was set for the emergence of a fourth club in the area—the Tempe Crimson Rims.

The Tempe Crimson Rims were a novelty. The club was made up of white, black and Hispanic players, a true spectacle of the time, considering that as progressive as Arizona was in regards to politics and economics, there was still a distinct atmosphere of segregation. The club had humble beginnings in 1899. On Tuesday, August 21, 1899, the club met at the Tempe Bicycle Store on Mill Avenue and 5th Street to elect officers and choose a team name after notices had been posted in several issues of the *Tempe Daily News* and its sister publication, *Tempe Weekly News*. The club essentially was a more organized form of a town team that had played games against the Phoenix B.B.C. and surrounding nines in years past. The *Tempe Daily News* noted that "the battery will be the same, with Sigala 1b, Farish 2b, Schureman r.f., the other positions will be filled with new players."[13] Uniforms were on the way, along with equipment needed to begin play. The would-be athletes ordered equipment through the well-established retailer Pinney & Robinson, who sold everything from baseball equipment to typewriters, photo stock and assorted sporting goods. Located on 40 North Center Street (now Central Avenue) in bustling downtown Phoenix, the general goods retailer sold Official League Balls made by A. J. Reach, boasting that this was the official ball used by "Leagues of the East and by all ball clubs in Arizona."[14] To reassure readers of the *Republican* who may have been skeptical of such advertising, the ad for Pinney & Robinson added the same ball was "used exclusively by the DeMund team of Phoenix, Congress ball club, Tucson ball club, and all other leading teams." In addition to baseballs, the shop offered bats and gloves from Draper & Maynard and up-to-date masks and chest protectors.

In a supportive article on September 20, the *Arizona Republican* commented that "Tempe has the right spirit," having electric lights, many new businesses and homes, and a new hotel, all while constructing a new water and sewer system. The *Republican* commended the formation of the Crimson Rims Base Ball Club, noting that the uniforms cost in excess of $100, a princely sum in those days, ordered from Spalding Brothers & Co. Apparently the local bicycle store had an independent agent for Spalding that was unadvertised. The Crimson Rims held a first practice match against a scratch Mexican group. The *Tempe Daily News*, in covering the excitement of the new club, noted that it was more practice than actual competition. August was a busy month for the baseball enthusiasts of Tempe and surrounding areas. Even Mesa tried to reorganize its town team with "some $40 in the treasury left over from last year"[15] in an effort to capitalize on the new-found baseball fervor in the Salt River valley. By September 1, the rooters for the Crimson Rims had procured enough funds and building materials to level a baseball ground and construct a grandstand. The *Tempe Daily News* enthusiastically supported the club and the construction of the new ball ground by announcing that "there is no better advertisement for any town than a good baseball club,"[16] echoing the standard sentiment that held true across 19th century America. The newspaper and businessmen in town were hopeful that a successful baseball nine would draw visitors to patronize local restaurants, hotels, shops and mercantiles.

While the Crimson Rims were awaiting the arrival of their new uniforms for an upcoming match against the True Blues of Phoenix, the *Arizona Republican* mentioned that "Tempe is becoming noted for its baseball players"[17] in a column reporting a practice match between the lads of the Tempe Public School and the "Arizona Apaches" of the Phoenix Indian School on September 24, won 27–21 by the young Tempeans. Details about the young men who played for the Indian School have been forever lost to history, as no names were given in the *Republican* report. This isn't surprising, as most of the nines that had Mexican and black ball players were ignored in the local press, which avoided igniting backlash from the Anglo majority who comprised most of the business interests and readership of local papers.

The task of identifying ball players in the photograph of the Tempe Crimson Rims has become difficult because of the lack of coverage for the minority players of the day. For example, the sole black player, standing on the far left, remains a debated issue. A recently published work by Jared Smith, curator for the Tempe Museum of History, titled *The African American Experience in Tempe*, makes an excellently detailed and courageous attempt at illuminating the possible identity and family history of our mysterious ball player. He notes that the 1900 census was the first to record African American residents in and around Tempe. Three men, all in their 30s, were counted, though it isn't clear how many were not included. Among the possible candidates from the Green, Thomas, Noble, Fortson and Boggs families, one name stands out: Theodore C. Thomas. An early pioneer in the Tempe area, he was one of the three men counted in the 1900 census. He was actively employed as a barber though unable to write. Documents show the family originally being from Dallas, and Theodore enlisted in the U.S. Army, Troop I of the 10th Cavalry. It was likely that his service with the Army would bring the family to Arizona. Theodore was a good athlete, the starting pitcher for the nine of colored barbers that challenged any club of white barbers, while he was employed by R. S. Stearns of Phoenix.

Theodore and his wife Maggie had a son, Eugene, who was living in El Paso, Texas, at the turn of the 20th century. It was rumored that Eugene traveled to and from Phoenix on a bicycle, following the railroad tracks of the Southern Pacific line. That was no easy task in those days as bicycles were incredibly heavy machines with solid rubber tires, weighing in excess of 75 pounds. Eugene had the habit of wandering a bit, never really settling down. With his dad being a notable local ball player, it is likely that young Eugene could be the young man in the photograph, taking after his dad's interest and talents on the ball field. We don't know what position he played for the Crimson Rims, or any of his statistics. No mention was made in the local papers, nor are there any other supporting documents to confirm these suspicions. Identity aside, our mystery ball player certainly did his part in helping the Crimson Rims become the elite ball club of the Salt River Valley.

There are two other known men in this photograph, one white, the other Hispanic. Sitting to the left of Mr. Thomas was Edward Patrick Carr. He had traveled from Providence, Rhode Island, seeking the arid climate of Arizona to spend his last days while suffering from Lukins Disease, grave news given to him by his family physician in Woonsocket, Rhode Island, at the age of 16. Fate smiled upon young Edward Carr, as the move to Arizona had an immediate benefit to his health and extended his life. His condition improved while he lived with his sister and brother-in-law, John J. Hodnett, the local postmaster in Tempe. His interests in baseball and business became the foundation for the club's name, as he eventually purchased and operated the Tempe Bicycle Store on the Northwest corner of 5th Avenue and Mill Avenue in Tempe. He was a registered dealer for the Syracuse Bicycle Company of Syracuse, New York. Among the bicycles accessories and other wares sold by the shop, the famous "Crimson Rim" model bicycle was popular amongst Tempeans, ample reason to name the club the Crimson Rims.

Eventually the shop would be a full repair and sales location for the Syracuse Bicycle maker as well as carrying assorted baseball goods and other sporting items. Carr played second base, and from early game reports he played fairly well after healing from accidentally sitting in some carbolic acid that had been spilled in a box. The *Tempe Daily News* mentioned the accident as a footnote to an article reporting another win by the hometown nine against the Mesa Diamond Club on September 18, 1899. Luckily for the injured ballist, he would miss only a few weeks before rejoining the club in a push to contend for the Salt River Valley championship.

The *Tempe Daily News* and the *Arizona Republican* reported that Carr made his debut for the Crimson Rims on August 27, 1900, in a game headlined by the *Republican* as "Loose Ball Playing." In an error-filled contest, the Tempe nine out-slugged the Phoenix True Blues, 45–20. The reporter noted that the result was never in doubt in front of an interested and raucous crowd. The article mentioned few details about the match besides the line-ups with Ed Carr playing center field. He helped out his club by tallying two runs. Though the crowd was interested in the entire match, due to the number of errors it wasn't the "kind of game in which rooters delight." The return match was set for the following Sunday at Tempe, with an equally if not more enthusiastic hometown crowd expected to attend.

As early as March of 1899, the cranks and rooters who packed the grandstand, located near the center of town on Mill Avenue and Third Street in Tempe near the Cactus Manufacturing Company, would earn the reputation for being large and very noisy. For instance, on the afternoon of March 6, 1899, a large crowd of Tempeans crammed their way onto the baseball grounds to witness a match between the visiting Yucatecs and the Tempe nine. The hometown club was months away from reorganizing as the Crimson Rims, but this minor detail didn't prevent those present that afternoon from cheering with such great intensity, it would bear mention in the *Arizona Republican*. The Tempe lads secured the victory, 12–6, cheered on "by a large and noisy crowd. Horns tooted, the band played, boys, large and small, men, old and young, and women, white and brown, cheered and yelled themselves hoarse before the game was half through."[18]

Clad in new uniforms of heather grey with crimson red trim, the hometown nine set out to conquer the local baseball scene in 1899–1900 after finishing practice games against local scratch clubs and the boys from the Phoenix Indian School. The *Tempe Daily News* boasted about the Rims, declaring "The suits and other equipment of the Crimson Rims baseball club arrived this morning. The boys now have the finest outfit in the territory and their playing is expected to be equally as good as their equipment."[19] The local reporter had good reason to be proud as the club had soundly defeated the Diamond Club of Mesa the previous day in the Gem City, moving their record to two wins with one loss. By the end of September, the club won two more games, defeating the Phoenix True Blues and a local nine comprised of Mexican players dubbed "John Priest's Club."

In the game reports of these early matches, there is no mention about who the African American player was, even though the local newspaper printed the club roster several times. Each roster from 1899 through 1901 featured a different lineup. Young men of this era had other interests outside of playing for the Crimson Rims. Some were involved with running a business, like Ed Carr with his bicycle shop, or were employed, such as town clerk Fletcher M. Schureman, who played right field and third base.

The young men who comprised the Crimson Rims were a diverse and talented group. If there was an "All Around Athlete" award for the

Arizona Territory at the turn of the 20th Century, the hands-down favorite would be Chris Cresencio Sigala. In the featured photograph of the club, Sigala is in the foreground, lying on the ground along the left side, at Ed Carr's feet. Sigala was very athletically gifted, playing both catcher and hurler for the club nine while filling in as needed in other positions around the infield. When he wasn't playing baseball, he would anchor the right end position for the Tempe Normal School football team. His love for athletics saw him coach football at the Tempe High School for the 1902 fall athletic season, while actively promoting football at the Phoenix Indian School. In the Tempe Brass Band, he played the cornet. Not limited to sports or music, Sigala was also a member of the Tempe Democratic Club, meeting almost weekly to discuss the political and civic business of the day. To say this young man was involved in his community was an understatement. His baseball skills were very well known among the clubs in the Salt River Valley. On September 21, 1900, the *Tempe Daily News* reported his involvement in a series of games on behalf of the DeMund Base Ball Nine, playing first base against a strong opponent from Los Angeles. The paper stated, "Chris is one of the best ball players in Arizona." A week later, he pitched for the DeMunds while several other Crimson Rims watched in the stands. Sigala's benefit to the DeMunds would be short-lived. He rejoined his original nine as a catcher for a match on October 8, when his work behind the plate aided a tough win by a close score of 8–7 in yet another intense game played in front of a large crowd.

The Crimson Rims finished the 1899 campaign with a record of nine wins and one loss. The Crimson Rims used the first reported knuckleball pitch in a game against the Rough Rider club from Glendale on December 10, 1899. The *Arizona Republican*, in reporting the lopsided victory the next afternoon, added that the wily pitch baffled the Glendale strikers, adding "Several times, when the ball went by the batter, it seemed to whirl in any old direction just to miss the bat." The gods of baseball would smile upon the club for the 1900 season as well, despite an early defeat to the DeMund club on January 11. The disappointing performance on the rainy, cold afternoon wasn't a complete loss for the Crimson Rims. Their hurler, Robert Brush, astonished the crowd by knocking a home run blast clean across the railroad tracks, earning him a new pair of baseball cleats offered by the club's manager if anyone could perform such a feat. No doubt the typically large crowd in attendance was delighted to see the display of batting prowess despite the 10–9 loss. While the weather warmed up enough for the local roads to be re-graded by horse, Tempe leapt forward to join the rest of a technologically advancing nation when a telephone line was opened with Prescott on April 7.

Later that summer, a crude street sprinkler system was installed in an attempt at controlling the dust in downtown Tempe. The city was making strides in new technologies and ideas, despite being firmly segregated. To illustrate the all but unspoken color line in Tempe and other cities in Arizona at the dawn of a new century, a Tempe businessman placed an ad for his establishment in the *Tempe Daily News* on May 18, 1900, in which restaurateur Henry Frisch declared that his place was the "only restaurant in town with white help." With such an openly published position on race, it's astonishing that the Crimson Rims, a club integrated with both Hispanics and African American players, became so popular. In 1899–1900, the baseball games featuring these diverse young men always proved to be a big draw. Despite the color line, the Crimson Rims used the diversity found within its ranks to win ball games. Yet the local papers were reluctant to report on an interracial club, so the only game coverage local rooters saw was the telegraph report of a game between the Winslow and Williams clubs as reprinted by the *Daily News*.

The fall months brought cooler weather and a reprieve from a scarlet fever outbreak in the area that cancelled all games that spring. The same telephone line that had been set up in April was instrumental in communicating the details and duration of numerous quarantines in the town and nearby areas. Finally, as the collective health and fortunes changed with the weather, a renewed interest in the national pastime arose in the Salt River Valley. There was the unsettled business of the championship crown to be decided. No doubt the local cranks were itching for some baseball action, as play resumed on the local diamond on August 19. The Mesa Diamond Club visited the 3rd Street grounds as guests of the Crimson Rims for a long-awaited baseball match. The game "attracted quite a crowd of spectators among whom many were from Mesa"[20] for the "first" game of the season. A short memory erased a January loss to a strong DeMund club. An enjoyable time was experienced by everyone in attendance, with a victory for the hometown Crimson Rims, 13 to 10. The new season had started on the right track, a winning one.

As the weeks rolled by, the Crimson Rims would add victory after victory to their record against the True Blues of Phoenix, Mesa Diamond Club and a few scratch clubs from the surrounding areas that took to the notion that they could best the lads from Tempe. Their bitter rivals, the DeMund Nine, handed the club the first loss on September 14, 10–2. A return match was scheduled but was never played due to the "absence of several of the local players."²¹ To gain their competitive edge and confidence back, the Crimson Rims defeated the Mesa nine in what was labeled a "very ragged game."²² The *Tempe Daily News* reporter reassured his readers that numerous games with unskilled play could be witnessed before Tempeans would lose interest in baseball.

With star catcher and hurler Chris Sigala back in the lineup for the Crimson Rims, the stage was set for a three-game series to decide the Salt River Valley championship for 1900. In the first match in Tempe, the home nine won a close contest despite several fielding errors. The crimson-clad lads sealed the championship a week later, crushing the DeMunds in Phoenix, 10–1. The *Daily News* chided the Crimson Rims, remarking that with more practice they could best any club in the territory. This was a frequent practice amongst sports writers of the day, who were reluctant to try playing the game but had no problem chastising a player or club about the lack of skill exhibited on the field of play, insisting that the club needed more work. Humorously enough, things haven't changed in over 100 years of sports reporting. This was the last game the Crimson Rims played in 1900. A scratch nine from town accepted a challenge for a match by a club from the nearby Maricopa Indian Reservation, playing in a "pretty fair game"²³ a few weeks later. In a change of mood foreshadowing things to come in sports, the attention of the local rooters shifted from the diamond to the gridiron.

The following January marked a new year, a new millennium and an early start to the local baseball scene. The nearby LDS settlement of Lehi decided over the winter break to organize a baseball club and join the growing, but unofficially named Salt River Valley League. January 4, 1901, was their official debut on the home grounds in Tempe, where despite a valiant effort in front of a good crowd, the new visiting nine suffered an 8–6 defeat. The *Tempe Daily News* described the Lehi nine as "a new organization, but it has material in it to make one of the strongest nines in the territory." The two clubs wouldn't face each other again in a customary return match until late February. No score or game report survives. March ushered in better weather to encourage games against the True Blues. An unknown delay pushed the next match back one week to March 22. The Crimson Rims won the remaining spring games against the True Blues. Unfortunately, the only surviving hard copy—in ledger-bound form—of the local newspaper skips issues from May 24 to November 8, 1901. There is no telling what games were played or the results as the defending Salt River Valley champions continued to defend their crown. We don't know exactly how the 1901 season ended or who won the championship. Chris Sigala, the Crimson Rims star, would remain active on the local sports scene by organizing a Mexican-American football club in late November.

The 1902 season saw very little action from the Crimsons Rims, as most of their stalwart starters took up other pursuits. Tempe formed another club, the O.K.'s. There is little information about the lineup, coaching or uniforms worn by the O.K.'s. The club was mentioned in June as having accepted a challenge from the Congress Mining Company to travel north for a game on July 4 to help the mining camp celebrate the national birthday. The trip was a success, as the O.K.'s returned home with a 10–8 victory. Nothing else is known about the O.K.'s as no further games were reported. This club might have been a substitute nine for the regular Crimson Rims club, a common practice of the era. From here, the games became fewer and fewer as the club gradually disbanded. By 1910, the club and the home grounds once played upon were just a memory to Tempeans. Today, they are gone but not forgotten. Other nines of mixed and minority background would spring up, such as the Elysian Groves in 1904, Tucson Grays in 1906, Phoenix Colored Cubs in 1909 and the Phoenix Braves of 1915–1916. Each of these clubs would gain a little more local coverage and fame for being fine baseball clubs who put up fierce competition.

Among early Arizonans, the least reported minority to attend and, on rare occasion, even play baseball were women. Arizona's first taste of women playing baseball was in 1886, when a group representing the famed Boston Bloomer Girls traveled through Arizona and attempted to arrange an exhibition match against a club from Tucson to be held in the nearby railroad junction town of Benson. The ranching town was a key junction that tied Tucson, El Paso and Bisbee together with rail lines going both east and west. This was important for transporting supplies, settlers and visitors to these frontier towns, and for shipping cattle and smelted ore to the factories of the east. Around Christmas time in 1886, the *Daily Tombstone* printed a short blurb that asked "Why does not [sic] our baseball players organize and challenge the female baseball club that will pass through Benson very shortly?"[24]

Women have had an influence on the game since its beginning. In the earliest days, it was considered improper for a woman to witness, let alone play baseball. In 1880, a women's club formed by Smith College in Northampton, Massachusetts, was disbanded after a group of mothers united to pressure school officials, citing the impropriety of women playing in a sport that was, at the time, considered to be rough—played by hooligans, rowdies, drunks and womanizers. Despite society frowning upon

Boston Bloomer Girls in Oregon, Wisconsin, May 1908. (Oregon Area Historical Society)

and viewing women playing baseball as a novelty, several women's teams organized themselves to compete against men. The earliest was the Dolly Vardens of Philadelphia. Organized sometime in 1867, this club was comprised entirely of African American women. Not much is known other than that the uniform they wore was nothing more than a red calico dress over high-button shoes. Such a flashy outfit certainly garnered attention as a form of entertainment, not a serious sports club in Reconstruction-era America. It is debated whether this group of women were the first openly paid professional baseball nine, a few years ahead of the legendary 1869 Cincinnati Red Stockings.

Over time, women were not only allowed but encouraged to attend baseball games. The initial idea was that if a group of pretty young women were in attendance, it might encourage the young men on the field to behave and play their best. It was also hoped that the men in the crowd would exhibit more gentlemanly decorum, thus cleaning up the rough image of baseball on all levels. In addition to women's teams now appearing at private women's colleges such as Vassar and Smith, touring teams featuring women began to appear by 1890. Several major cities had their own "Bloomer Girls" clubs, the most famous being the group from Boston. In the fall of 1897, this club, comprised mostly of women players, toured the California coast, and wired a challenge to the Phoenix Base Ball Club for a match on November 21, at Eastlake Park in Phoenix. Word of this had even been printed in the *Weekly Arizona Journal-Miner* in Prescott, which noted that the challenge issued "will no doubt be accepted."[25]

With plans in place, the Bloomer Girls arrived on the morning train on November 21. There was considerable interest in the match around town. Game time was arranged for 3 o'clock that afternoon at Eastlake Park. The *Arizona Republican* printed the lineup for both clubs in the morning edition. Starring as a hurler for the Boston Bloomer Girls was none other than the famed Maud Nelson. Nelson was born in 1881 somewhere in the Italian Alps, eventually immigrating to the United States. She would take the name Maud Nelson over her Italian birth name of Clementina Brida. Not much is known about her before 1897. It is unclear how she was discovered by the Bloomer Girls club promoter from Boston, or how she learned baseball. Nelson started her baseball career in 1897 as a pitcher and third baseman for the touring Boston Bloomer Girls. Employing a terrific arm capable of lightning speed and control, she usually pitched the first two or three innings, then switched positions to third base. This allowed her relief pitchers to do the rest of the work, thus saving a good portion of her arm strength for the next game. The 1897 tour crisscrossed the United States, culminating with the feat of playing 28 games in 26 days. For the game in Phoenix, her club mates were as follows: Georgia Devore, first base; Julia Marlowe, third base; (male) Williams, catcher; Annie Jennings, second base; Carrie Roux, left field; LuLu White, center field; Nellie Bly, shortstop. Gussie Habuck and Rose Black served as substitutes. It was customary to have an average of three male players on a Bloomer Girls club, but it appears that there was only one in tow for the match in Phoenix. He was given the arduous task of catching the overpowering pitches of Maud Nelson using equipment that most would consider "sparse," all while trying to keep his name anonymous enough to avoid the attention of the local newspapers.

The match was covered by reporters from both the *Phoenix Daily Herald* and the *Arizona Republican*. The *Herald*'s coverage was a short paragraph buried amongst the other news columns, while the *Republican* ran over two pages and offered more coverage about the game but no official box score. The *Herald* described Maud Nelson's performance as "the pitcher being an adept and never made an error through the game, though she ran to every part of the diamond to assist her less expert sisters."[26] The equally supportive *Republican* remarked that Nelson was "much better in the box than it is supposed a woman should be."[27] The game, despite

Bloomer Girls versus a club from Oregon, Wisconsin, 1908. (Oregon Area Historical Society)

being more of a novelty than nine serious innings of competitive ball, drew a large crowd of 1,046 cranks, reportedly the largest crowd to witness any game in the short history of the ball grounds at Eastlake Park. The *Republican* noted that no less than 150 others had scaled nearby telegraph poles, trees and the fencing lining the park to witness the game, bringing the total attendance for the afternoon roughly to 1,200. The gate receipts totaled $380, with $285 going to the Bloomer Girls. The *Republican* was very complimentary to a few of the girls, giving them praise for beauty, grace and athletic skills while handling themselves in the most proper manner during their stay in Phoenix. The lads from the Phoenix Base Ball Club treated the game as more of a joke, with numerous sacrifice hits, lazy base running and generally sloppy play. Despite this lack of effort, the Phoenix club held on to win, 13 to 7.

A few days later the Bloomer Girls appeared in Santa Ana, California, to take on the local nine. A gentleman from Mesa, Dan Baker, was in attendance and telegraphed the results of the game to the editor of the *Mesa Free Press*. Despite the 11–8 loss, the Bloomer Girls put up another good showing, with Maud Nelson winning notable acclaim for her prowess in the pitcher's box. The *Santa Ana Standard* applauded her, saying "The best player in the outfit was their pitcher—a little, squatty, muscular daisy

4. Women and Minorities on the Diamond 121

who could catch or throw the ball with marked ability."[28] The *Free Press* also noted that several of the local young ladies had organized their own Bloomer Girls athletic club, but there were no further reports about this new organized women's athletic association. Despite the excitement caused by this first in Arizona history, it seems the notion of women playing baseball fizzled after the Boston Bloomers left town.

During all of the excitement of the 1899 fall baseball campaign, an auspicious occasion came about as a result of some regular meetings by a group of prominent Arizona women. On October 25, the *Arizona Daily Gazette* announced the 11th annual meeting of the Arizona Women's Christian Temperance Union (WCTU) at the Phoenix Baptist Church. All were welcome to attend meetings, starting the next morning. The movement to rid Arizona of liquor began in 1881 when Mrs. Glendenning, the wife of a U.S. Army officer posted at Fort Whipple near Prescott, organized the first chapter of the WCTU, likely after being frustrated by repeated instances of drunken soldiers getting into trouble on post. The sobriety movement slowly took hold, with a second chapter forming in Tucson in 1885. The "White Ribboners," as they were called, crusaded in the Progressive Era to rid Arizona towns from the evils of liquor. These fiery-tongued women wore pins resembling a white bow, to display their courage and commitment to this noble cause and to let those around them know some of their beliefs. Baseball may not have been a favored pastime of the White Ribboners from the WCTU chapters of Arizona, as most ball players of the day preferred to hit the saloon for a drink after the game.

Whatever the agenda was on the opening morning of the conference, matters were attended to and adjourned for an afternoon of wholesome refreshment. From correspondence sent to the *Arizona Republican*, it appears some kind of baseball match occurred on the afternoon before the WTCU meetings officially began on October 26. Observing from the corner of Monroe and Third Avenues in downtown Phoenix, a young baseball enthusiast reported that a very large audience witnessed a group of young women defeat their youthful male counterparts, 23–15. The newspaper reported that "twas a hot game."[29] The correspondent mentioned that the game was "interesting" but didn't mention in what manner. No other details of the game survive. Easily imagined is the group of young ladies at the WTCU meetings wanting to let off some steam and beat the local boys at their own game, possibly responding to a bit more teasing than they would like. No matter the motives, this game report provided ample proof that women were interested in more than watching the national pastime—they wanted to play!

The concept of women playing baseball was regarded as a novelty to some and more of a joke to others. The local Elks Club of Bisbee decided to challenge another Elks Lodge from Douglas to a baseball match in 1906 as part of the annual "Field Day" festivities. Each club was to dress in apparel akin to the famous Mother Hubbard nursery tale from a century prior. The game was billed as "McGregoresque" by the *Bisbee Daily Review*, noting there would be two matches on the afternoon and alerting readers to "a contrast between the burlesque and the game as it should be played."[30] The day's festivities were begun by a parade starting from the Opera House, in a long procession that wound through town. A large crowd packed the trains heading to the baseball grounds at Don Luis Park, where it was standing room only to witness the Mother Hubbard game and the exhibition between the "real" ball players from Bisbee and Lowell. The games were marked by the reading of a letter from President Theodore Roosevelt, who wished the local Elks much success for the year's Field Day activities. The *Daily Review* noted that even the local police were in on the fun, arresting people to solicit funds on a variety of charges. Everything from not carrying a gun to being too quiet was grounds for

Elks Day "Mother Hubbard" game at Don Luis Park, c. 1906. (Bisbee Mining & Historical Museum)

being tossed into the clink until enough money was produced to secure one's freedom. The makeshift jail that afternoon was set up in a remote corner of the park, not too far from the main grandstand, which by this time was jammed with cranks awaiting the games. One fellow, W. H. Brophy, acting manager of the Copper Queen Store in Bisbee, was arrested no less than 11 times! He was fleeced $2.50 for every "offense," totaling a whopping $27.50 in good-natured fines collected for the Bisbee Elks. The newspaper also estimated that every Elk in attendance was arrested at least once, all in good humor of course. With the side entertainment out of the way, the Bisbee "women" took to the field, performing admirably. The *Daily Review* pointed out two players of the Bisbee battery as displaying skill in pitching and catching, but no official score was provided for this match. The afternoon concluded with the Bisbee club defeating the Lowell nine, 5 to 3, in a closely played contest.

A few years passed before another Bloomer Girls club paid a visit to the Arizona Territory. In a brief tour of southern Arizona in mid–September 1908, the Boston Bloomer Girls returned on the homeward leg of their national tour. The first stop was in Yuma, where the grounds at old Meadows Park had been prepared, complete with canvas fencing to protect the female athletes, along with accommodations to seat 2,000 eager spectators. Word of the tour reached as far east as Bisbee, the *Bisbee Daily Review* printing an article regarding the game arrangements in Yuma on September 13, 1908. The *Arizona Sentinel* advertised the game on September 9, enticing readers to show up for the game. The advertisements worked as a large crowd attended the game between the Yuma locals and the Boston Bloomer Girls at Meadows Park on September 12.

Despite the printed box score, the commentary offered by the *Sentinel* revealed few details about the game. The score was close, with Yuma emerging victorious, 4–3, in seven innings. The *Sentinel* was complimented two ballists for the Bloomer nine, mentioning Lilly Booth pitching wonderfully for the first two frames of the match and a first baseman called Carrie Nation who was able to "make some very pretty plays"[31] while fielding the ball, thus garnering much applause and admiration from the crowd. It isn't known if the player who used that pseudonym for this match, and possibly the entire tour, was a man or woman. It was customary to have men playing with the girls' club, under assumed names to avoid any embarrassment. It was also possible that the young lady at first base was a WCTU or Anti-Saloon League member who chose to play under the assumed name. Despite the loss in Yuma, the efforts by the Bloomer Girls netted $214 in gate receipts. From there, the group departed on the Number 8 train heading for Bisbee to play a game a few days later.

The *Bisbee Daily Review* announced the arrival of the girls in a headline reading "Boston Bloomers Headed For Bisbee" on September 16, 1908. The idea was for the Bloomer Girls to take on the local club from the Warren District, despite the skeptical support by the *Review*, citing a recent loss against Douglas that placed the ability of the hometown nine in doubt and declaring that "a game with girls is the only one they can hope to win." The newspaper casually mentioned the success of the Bloomer Girls in surprising crowds with their ability to catch, run and throw. The article proved to be enough motivation for the Warren club to grind out an 8 to 7 win in front of over 1,000 people. No box score was given. The group reboarded the train and headed for Douglas on the last leg of the trip in Arizona.

Women's sports continued to be a novelty for many years. The Tempe Normal School (later Arizona State University) began to encourage basketball for girls in the latter half of the 1890s, citing it as a more genteel sport. For the era, it was. Baseball in this time frame was a rough affair usually played by men who were just as rough around the edges. Minorities gained more cultural acceptance in Arizona during these early years due to a keen desire to play THE only game in town. Baseball was everywhere in the Arizona Territory by 1900. Most towns had at least one club to represent it against neighboring settlements, while larger cities had several teams competing in local and regional games. Women and minorities simply wanted a chance to fit in, a chance to play the national game on the same field as the boys they'd cheer on Sundays. These groups of Mexicans and African Americans, along with their softer female counterparts, were up to the task of taking up the glove and bat against any opponent, on any diamond in the sun-drenched land. The clubs that competed were diverse, talented and an integral part of Arizona's early sporting history.

Chapter 5

The Company Nine

In the earliest days of the towns of Tucson, Phoenix, Globe, Miami, Bisbee, Prescott, Flagstaff and Yuma, there was a keen interest in developing commercial business in retail goods, agriculture, mining and lumber to support the material needs of a growing population that was coming to the Arizona Territory. The game of baseball would play a role in helping various mining companies, lumber companies, railroads and even newspaper publishers gain public attention and prominence in their communities and throughout the territory, while gaining bragging rights amongst competing town and company nines. The goal was to promote the town and certain businesses as the best in the territory, worthy of investment capital from outside sources, while maintaining a positive image within the local community.

As discussed in Chapter 3, the earliest company-sponsored clubs came to fruition in Tucson for both the *Weekly Citizen* and *Daily Star*. Both newspapers competed for readership, boasting of their journalistic prowess in commentary on everything from local, county and territory-wide politics, economic development and, of course, baseball games played on the local ball fields. They recruited and sponsored baseball clubs, even going so far as to arrange a series of games for the coveted "Star Cup" of 1879. The *Arizona Daily Citizen* was a big supporter and promoter of local baseball covered the games, and went as far as naming the two clubs. They were to be called the "Citizen" and "Star" nines.[1]

After quite a bit of posturing and trash-talk in both newspapers leading up to the game, the two clubs finally clashed on the field on November 27, 1879. The *Citizen* nine came away victorious, with the cash prize in hand as well as the coveted "Star Cup" that had been on display for weeks in local store-fronts in downtown Tucson. Eventually these two clubs would unite to challenge the Phoenix Base Ball Club, representing the Old Pueblo. Despite much talk in the papers, the highly anticipated match between the two clubs never took place. A decade and a half later, on March 12, 1894, the staffs of the *Tucson Star* and *Florence Enterprise* newspapers gathered for a game in Tucson. The game was more jovial than for any serious money despite the *Star* labeling its nine the "moral element" and their opponents from the Enterprise nine the "vicious element" in the box score. The Star nine emerged victorious in a less than skillful match, 11 to 10. The challenge was repeated in a follow-up article in the *Tucson Citizen*, but unfortunately for us, there was no report of a second game taking place.

Newspapers planted the notion in mining companies in southern Arizona that promoting baseball was a good way to build cohesion amongst the working men and, more importantly, keep them out of trouble. Hard-rock copper, silver and gold miners worked hard, lived hard and loved to spend their hard-earned cash in town at saloons, gambling halls and brothels to relieve the enormous tension felt every day in the dark, damp and dangerous underground mines. The work was back-breaking, and many men who chose a miner's life met their demise underground. The early settlement of Pinal City, now a ghost town near the present location of the Boyce-Thompson Arboretum, was once a thriving mining town close to the booming camp of Silver King. Located at the foot of the Picket Post Mountain, the town of Picket Post was founded in 1878 and renamed Pinal City one year later. The Silver King mine, living up to its name, primarily produced silver ore and by 1891 had extracted close to 42 million dollars in valuable metal. The mine was one of the most prolific—and short-lived—in the territory. Both towns had baseball clubs and frequently challenged each other to matches to be held in alternating locations a tradition still followed. The Silver King Base Ball Club had an unknown date of organization, with nothing printed in the *Weekly Pinal Drill*. The Pinal City Base Ball Club, otherwise known as the Picket Post B.B.C., was formally organized on December 13, 1880.

The new club elected officers, choosing H. L. Meyers as Club President; L. M. Cox as Junior Secretary; M. L. Cross as Treasurer; and H. E. Carlick as on-field Captain for the nine. The new club soon received a challenge from the Silver King club to decide the championship of Pinal County on Christmas Day. After the morning match, a "grand dinner will be given by the Pinal Club, at the Grand Hotel, Pinal, at 1 o'clock, p.m. to which all the members of the Silver King club are invited as guests of the Pinal Club."[2] The newly created Pinal Base Ball Club started off in grand style with post-match banquets in a tradition of at least the past two decades. The championship match did commence on Christmas Day, and the results were reported on January 1, 1881, in the *Pinal Drill*. The Pinal City won, 22–15, in a game that lasted three hours and 15 minutes. Afterwards, the hometown club escorted their visitors to the dining room of the Grand Hotel, where a sumptuous dinner with much toasting and good-natured humor was indulged in, with local magistrate Judge Rayment presiding. After being well refreshed, the two clubs returned to the baseball grounds to start another friendly game, but no report exists for the second match. The Pinal club met a few weeks later to discuss regular business matters and published a short statement of thanks signed by club president H. L. Meyers and junior secretary L. M. Cox, directed towards the businesses and townsfolk in the area who had been supportive of their efforts. It is interesting to note that Cox also played in the match for the Pinal County championship, going 2-for–4 at the plate, scoring two runs. The rudimentary box score in the *Drill* did not indicate what position he played.

The Pinal Club followed up these efforts with a Ball to be given on Washington's Birthday, February 22, 1881, at the Grand Hotel in Pinal City.

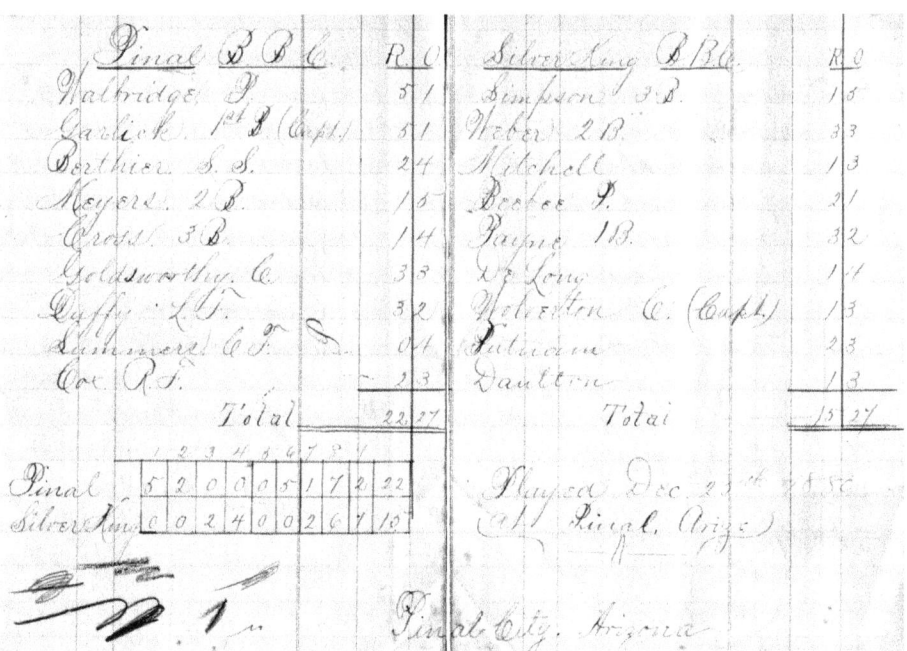

Handwritten box score for Pinal City versus Silver King, Christmas Day, 1880. (Arizona Historical Society, Tempe)

Tickets were sold through the members of the club and at Jay Brook's store in town, for two dollars apiece. The baseball match that took place on the 22nd was reported as a "test game" by the *Drill*, with the final score 14–12 in favor of the Picket Post nine, who played well despite high winds that kicked up enormous clouds of fine silt, confusing fielders, batters and the few brave cranks in attendance. After winning their second match in club history, both against the Silver King club, the ballists from Pinal City were treated to a lavish feast and ball that evening. Complete with post-meal cigars and brandy, the festivities were enjoyed by all, lasting until the early hours of the next morning.

Even in the early days of the Arizona Territory, news traveled quickly. Aided by the telegraph, the Phoenix Base Ball Club, upon learning of the Pinal B.B.C.'s formation and early success, soon challenged the upstarts from Pinal County. The *Phoenix Herald* announced on February 25 that on the following Saturday there would be a match between the two nines in Phoenix. On March 26, 1881, the Pinal B.B.C. emerging victorious, 30–12. A letter written by a correspondent named McClintock that was published in the *Pinal Drill* mentioned that the Pinal club was made up of ballists from both the Picket Post and Silver King nines. Not satisfied with the results, the Phoenix B.B.C. implored their guests to play another match the next afternoon, for $50 or $100 a side. The Picket Post club, thinking that they might have been lucky to win convincingly over the Phoenicians, thought better of the rematch and headed home with their well-deserved honors and enriched pockets.   The townsfolk of Pinal City and Silver King came together to form a large crowd to meet their conquering heroes at the Delta Stage station, where the club was greeted with music, a speech or two, and the nation's flag given to them by the *Pinal Drill* in appreciation of the victory over the Phoenix nine.

Three months passed before the Pinal B.B.C. saw action on the ball grounds again. Apparently too much time off slowed the club enough to suffer their first defeat at the hands of the Silver King nine on the Fourth of July 1881, 6 to 4. The *Drill* noted that the game "is said to have been the most closely contested game ever played in Arizona."[3] That claim would be repeated numerous times in newspapers for the duration of the territorial era. The *Phoenix Herald* printed the club's officers' names the following week, noting that the Pinal B.B.C. had taken on several new members to strengthen their ranks for the upcoming fall campaign. This would be the last published item about clubs from Pinal City/Picket Post and Silver King. It seems that baseball was a passing notion to these two mining towns, and the two clubs simply vanished into the mists of time.

Tombstone, the famous frontier town, had its fair share of rowdy miners who were interested in baseball as a way to relieve tension and make a few extra dollars wagering on the outcome. The local newspapers chronicled several matches between the miners of the Grand Central Mining Company, Congress Mining Company and Boston Mill versus the regular town club from Tombstone, unofficially called the Tombstone Reds. However, games featuring mine workers from the Tombstone area would be short-lived as the production of the mines would go into steady decline by 1885.

Even in the somewhat isolated mining town of Globe, further to the Eastern Superstition Mountains, baseball was a popular pastime as early as 1884. The local mining companies wouldn't encourage their employees to undertake the game for quite a few years, until the Old Dominion Mining Company played loose pickup games against the boys in town in 1892. Before then, Globe's main source of competition was the soldiers from Camp San Carlos, 22 miles east of town. That distance was considerable, and most road trips lasted several days through very rough terrain, unpredictable weather and lingering dangers of hostile Native Americans in the area. The rivalry was intense and would last for many years. The earliest known baseball games played in Globe by a company-sponsored nine was in late July 1892. The *Arizona Silver Belt* printed the notice on July 23, including the rosters for both clubs, in preparation for the early afternoon game the next day. The *Silver Belt* related that the miners for the Old Dominion Copper Company had taken the name of "The Walkers." The name may have reflected some aspect of their profession, or was given to them by the newspaper or collectively by the citizens of Globe.

The *Silver Belt* was a weekly publication. The game results were published one week later, unless a special edition was printed for distribution. The paper noted that the game was "something of a surprise" with little skill being displayed on the diamond. Despite providing no score, the *Silver Belt* reported there was plenty of offense and "run getting" during the game. Sid Coburn of the Old Dominion club had dazzled the newspaper men, having "caught in fine style, his work being surprisingly good considering that he had no practice."[4] The new player for the Walkers had caught the attention of the regular Globe nine, taking a spot as a substitute in a match with the soldiers from Camp San Carlos in the continuation of a long-running rivalry.

To say the men who worked the copper mines for the Old Dominion Copper Company were busy is an understatement. In May of 1892, the mine produced just over one million pounds of copper ore in 30 days of smelter operation. Shifts in the mines worked around the clock, excavating the precious earth to be refined, extracting valuable ore to be shipped to factories in the eastern United States. The output of the mines, and the related price of copper per pound, was the economic barometer for Globe and the entire mining district of Gila County, including towns like Pinal City and Silver King. The area would rise and fall from boom to bust year by year, often month by month. The mine would face tough times for the next few years, including a financial panic and a severe flood that wiped out a wood yard supplying the smelter furnaces. In January 1894, Globe benefitted from the construction of a railroad line from Fort Bowie to Globe as a northern spur from the main Southern Pacific line running from Tucson to El Paso. It would take five years to complete this extension. The mine would change owners and emerge into a new era of booming prosperity from 1901 to 1917. Baseball remained a diversion for the miners and would grow in popularity as time went on and the Globe operation increased in size.

The Old Dominion "Walkers" continued a new-found rivalry with the ballists from Globe in October of 1892. Sid Coburn returned to play for the Walkers as the starting catcher. The match was advertised in the *Silver Belt* to take place on the afternoon of October 2. Owing to the intense interest in the upcoming elections for political office in Gila County, the *Silver Belt* editor chose not to print any game report. Another baseball club formed by the mine would enter the local baseball scene later in November. The early matches of the Old Dominion Walkers and the new mining scrub nine went unreported, though the *Silver Belt* noted on November 12, 1892, that the games being played between the two clubs with "considerable rivalry." Local politics had, for the time being, completely shoved baseball off the pages of the local newspaper in Globe. The men from the mining company continued to play baseball over the ensuing decade, using the game to relieve tensions from working in the mines, a very uncertain profession for many reasons.

The development of the railroad in Globe was very important. The rail line ushered in a new era of production, allowing the company to efficiently ship out what was being produced in the mine. The new mode of transportation also allowed people to travel farther than they had thought possible, and in a shorter amount of time. By 1903, excursions to baseball games were a popular thing for local cranks in Globe, traveling as far as Cananea, Mexico, to see the hometown nine compete. Globe would hold a keen interest in baseball, fielding two town nines in addition to the clubs representing the mining companies. The Stars and Colts took their place on the local diamond in 1905, in a diverse baseball scene that grew into a local league between Globe and Miami. By February 1910, there would be baseball nines representing Globe, Miami, Copper Hill and Safford. The *Daily Arizona Silver Belt* previewed the baseball season, declaring "Great Crowds See Baseball Game at Miami" on February 15, 1910. The crowds packed all of the trains running to the game. Anyone who had an automobile or four-legged transportation was also in attendance. The highly anticipated match would pit the Park Brothers butchers, playing as the McClellan Steers, and the Miami Scrubs. From a game report in the *Daily Silver Belt*, it appears that the Steers were victorious after scoring 15 unanswered runs in the first inning. The Miami Scrubs never recovered despite a pitching change, sending starting hurler Thatcher to the "meat block." Despite the loss, townsfolk in Miami showed plenty of interest in organizing a club of their own, meeting a few days later at a local restaurant to elect officers and implement a plan to raise funds for proper uniforms.

The games for the league started in February and continued through the spring months while leaders from each club haggled over issues of scheduling and finances. One sticking point was the use of field space. The towns of Globe and Miami rubbed elbows with each other, with usable flat ground at a premium. The clubs from Miami and Copper Hill, the renamed nine from the Old Dominion Copper Company, wanted to use the grounds normally used by the Globe men as their home grounds, but objected to paying a share of the $200 cost required to maintain the field. Miami scrambled to find suitable grounds for home games in an attempt to defray club costs. There was plenty of action in Globe to watch, and the newly formed Globe Athletic Club (a.k.a. the "Athletics") tallied a win over Howard Jones' nine, 6–4, on April 5, 1910, in a game contested at School Hill. The Globe Athletics may or may not have taken their new nickname from an earlier bseball nine in the region, the Solomonville Athletics. While little is known about the club from Graham County, their exploits must have been remarkable enough to be remembered years later when locals adopted the name of "Athletics" to name the newly formed town team. The four clubs of this unofficial league would compete in many games throughout the spring months of 1910 although no formal organizing agreement was finalized. The local cranks from Globe and Miami didn't care, as long as the baseball was good, and attendance continued to be strong. The "Sunday Fever"[5] had hit Miami, with reported instances of barber shops being closed due to the ball games on Sunday. Most interesting was the call for jobs in the newspaper for players who would represent Globe. News of quite a few former semi-professional baseball

The Globe Athletics might have taken their name from an earlier team in the region, the Solomonville Athletics. The Solomonville Athletics of 1896/1897: Back, left to right: unknown; unknown; Andy Alexander; William B. "Wild Bill" Kelly. Seated: Frank Morey; Loprock; Charlie Thompson; unknown; unknown. (Arizona Historical Society, Tempe, William B. Kelly Collection)

players from the Arizona-Texas League would surface in the *Silver Belt*. Competition within the new league proved intense as each club scrambled to secure good ball players for the upcoming season. The rivalries between mining towns were as heated as ever, with one thing certain—baseball was alive and well in the Gila Mountains!

The Queen of the Copper Camps, affectionately known as Bisbee, lies deep in the heart of the Mule Mountains of copper-rich southern Arizona. Bisbee, at one time, was the largest city between St. Louis and San Francisco due to the large number of miners, merchants, outlaws, clerks, shady ladies, lawmen and their families who flocked to the new-found riches of the mining town between 1890 and 1920. As with Globe and Miami, copper was the main ore extracted in hard-rock mining operations conducted in underground, and later open-pit mining that would yield valuable ore to support America's continued growth in manufacturing. The miners in larger camps were known for drunkenness, gambling and consorting with sordid, "working class" women during off-duty hours to relieve tension from a hard day's labor underground. The mining companies in Bisbee needed an outlet for such pent-up, aggressive energy that would be more useful and far more reputable. As in Globe, the needed answer in Bisbee was baseball.

Early games in town surfaced in the spring and summer of 1892, when a newly organized Bisbee Base Ball Club challenged the Tombstone nine. The *Tombstone Epitaph*, the largest newspaper in the area during that time period, published the challenge on June 12, 1892. The Bisbee lads offered the choice of date and location for their first match. In the following week, nothing was mentioned about an actual date for the match between the two rivals. From the "Bisbee Notes" section of the paper, it appeared the boys from the copper camp were taking the matter seriously and were "busy getting ready to down Tombstone on the 4th. Every evening the sphere passes from hand to hand on our streets, and on last Sunday a game between two picked nines resulted in the close score of 10 to 9. Tombstone will have to get a hustle on herself this season to be 'in it' with the crack Bisbee club."[6] With clubs from Tombstone, Bisbee and Fort Huachuca preparing to battle it out on the nation's birthday, two games would be played on the Tombstone grounds dubbed "a treat" by the *Epitaph*.

Tombstone faced both clubs in the first doubleheader in Arizona history. The holiday in town would start the evening of July 3 and run all night in wild, noisy, patriotic glory before the games on the Fourth. The first match was a wild affair against a colored unit from the 24th Infantry from nearby Fort Huachuca. The match came down to the ninth inning, when Tombstone scored six runs. The soldiers could muster only two runs, failing in the come-from-behind effort by a final score of 23 to 20. With the players obviously tired, the next match was the much-talked-about game versus Bisbee. The game was started late, at four o'clock that afternoon, giving the hometown lads a few needed hours to rest. The Tombstone club took the lead from the beginning, holding on for a 20–14 victory despite a fist-fight near the ball grounds which resulted in an arrest. The grounds were packed with spectators, and several small boys perched on top of the wood and wire backstop, narrowly avoiding being hit on several occasions by foul balls. The festivities were wild, with several horse races held, resulting in a vast amount of money changing hands while everyone enjoyed the six kegs of Anheuser beer, courtesy of Tombstone Fire Engine Company No. 1. It was a great start to a long rivalry that continues to this day in high school athletic contests.

Over the ensuing decade, Bisbee and Tombstone met on the baseball diamond numerous times. Many games were played by youth teams dubbed the Pioneer Base Ball Club and the Bisbee Youngsters. Lovingly nicknamed the "Grave Yard Kids" by the *Epitaph* and its sister paper, the *Tombstone Prospector*, the teams played on holidays and every free day that was available. Bisbee fielded a good team that took on clubs outside of the normal rivalry, including Wilcox and Fort Huachuca. The earliest mining company club in the area represented the "Copper Nine" of Bisbee. On December 1, 1894, the *Epitaph* noted that a group of "baseball cranks" had made the trip to the copper camp for a match, returning victorious by a lopsided tally of 27 to 4. The mining camp wasn't ready for a club organized by miners for a few more years. By 1899 the copper mines in Bisbee were rolling along at a steady pace of production. There were several competing mining companies in Bisbee, with the Copper Queen Mining Company, the Copper King Mining Company, the Calumet & Arizona Mining Company and a couple of smaller outfits all vying for a share of the vast copper ore buried beneath the surface. At this time, mining companies could make money on ore that only contained 3–4 percent copper. Over the years Bisbee's population would swell, and by 1910 it was the largest city between St. Louis and San Francisco. With the influx of miners looking for work with families in tow, and the various barkeeps, rowdies, gamblers and prostitutes that followed, the mining companies sought outlets to keep the miners busy while maintaining a positive corporate image. Again, as in Globe, baseball was the answer.

Early fields for the mining camps were limited in size because most of these mining towns and camps were built into hillsides. Bisbee, Globe, Jerome, and Clarksdale would all have fields made available to the clubs that were scratched together as a direct result of mining company support. For Bisbee, the earliest known field was a flat of ground remembered fondly as Higgins Hill. There, the Copper Kings would play their home games. Alternate grounds would eventually be constructed near the stockyards further south of town and in the nearby border town of Don Luis. Bisbee wouldn't see a formal grounds designed for regular use until a suitable area was selected in the community of Warren in 1904.

The grounds on Higgins Hill didn't allow enough local cranks to attend, so another location was quickly chosen. The small border town of Don Luis, located seven miles south-by-southeast of Bisbee, was selected, offering plenty of flat, open space for a baseball field. It was relatively easy to get cranks to and from the games, as Don Luis was on a railroad spur line. The baseball season began with a few spring games in March and April, with the bulk of the season transpiring in the fall. The soldiers at Fort Huachuca tried to arrange a game on April 9, 1898, against the Copper

King Nine. An unknown delay would cause the soldiers from Fort Grant to play on that date on the new grounds at Don Luis.

The game drew two train-loads of people, and over 500 cranks saw Bisbee take on the soldiers in what the *Weekly Orb* described as not being "the best baseball game ever played," adding "but considering the conditions of the grounds and the high wind blowing all day, it was a good game."[7] Wagers were offered at 2–1 odds in favor of Fort Grant after they took the field, showing excellent throwing and fielding skills that caught the attention of the home crowd. Whoever bet on Fort Grant would be disappointed, as Bisbee built a lead in the sixth inning after trailing early and held on to a 21–15 win. The packed crowd included many ladies who graciously applauded every play on the diamond. Interest in baseball would be put on hold as collective interest shifted to the Spanish-American War. The *Weekly Orb* noted on May 8, 1898, that "baseball seems to have taken a back seat in our city and a militia drill will take its place." Baseball would have to wait until the following spring to reintroduce itself to the residents of the Queen of Copper Camps.

With time to organize and get back to the pleasures of the diamond, the Copper Kings got their first newspaper mention on February 12, 1899, when a short article appeared in the weekly edition of the *Weekly Orb*. The new baseball club practiced on new grounds located at Quality Hill on the following afternoon. Several weeks passed, prompting an article in the *Weekly Orb* reminding the ballists to appear on time with picks, shovels and garden rakes for leveling work to begin on the ball grounds. After the new grounds had been prepared for play, the Copper Kings arranged to meet the miners from the Copper Queen on the afternoon of March 6. No score was reported in the local papers, as it was most likely a practice game before starting in competitive play against other towns and mining camps.

The local rooters in Bisbee spent the summer months raising funds to help the club put the field at Don Luis in order, preparing for games against opponents from Morenci and local competition between a railroad nine and a club representing the Copper Queen general office. The *Arizona Daily Orb* mentioned that the new ball park was located near the stock yards, both in close proximity to the railroad line. With the season resuming in mid–August, the Bisbee nine welcomed a club from Morenci for a doubleheader. The August 18 issue of the *Arizona Daily Orb* noted that a new backstop had been constructed and put into place along with ropes to keep the standing-room-only crowds back from the baselines. The grounds were ready. The club from Morenci, numbering 14 players, replacements coaches and a mascot, was ready. The hometown nine were certainly ready, as were the local fans.

Trains to the morning and afternoon games ran from 8:30 a.m. to 1:30 p.m. schedule. Fare was 25 cents for a round-trip. A huge crowd of close to 1,500 cranks descended on the grounds at Don Luis to witness the morning game, the first between Morenci and Bisbee that season. The rabid Bisbeeans rooted their club onward to an 8–3 victory after leading 4–0 in the fifth inning. The second game crowd was larger as Bisbee's elite saw a wild affair with plenty of offense. The hometown nine fell short, 23–21. While the Morenci nine packed up to board the train home, talk of baseball was everywhere in town. The *Daily Orb* had also been following a series of games between Phoenix and Tucson. While the Tucson nine won two out of three games, there was much talk about a possible series between Bisbee and Tucson. While the details were being worked out, the general office nine from the Copper Queen Mining Company took on a challenge from the Arizona & South Eastern Rail Road (A. & S.E.R.R). The railroad ran several short spur lines in Texas, New Mexico and Arizona with several operational lines that ran across the Mexico border, staying in operation from 1888–1902. With the expansion of copper mining in Bisbee and Morenci, the railroad expanded to keep up with the needs of the mines while offering a more economical mode of transportation for tourists and a way to ship goods from eastern states more efficiently.

The local railroad workers challenged the office employees of the Copper Queen Mining Company for a game. The stakes were different. Instead of putting up a standard $50 per side, both contestants decided to play for elevated stakes—a princely $500 per side and a "first class supper at one of the popular restaurants," as penned by manager W. A. Harvey in the *Arizona Daily Orb* on August 23. The match took place in Don Luis on September 10. Clad in new uniforms, the Copper Queen office nine took the field to face their railroad competitors, utilizing the same battery as the Copper King nine. The *Daily Orb* printed odds and ends about the players who would take the field in a highly anticipated match. Among them was a rail road operator, Mr. Eby, who would play second base for the railroad nine despite suffering from an acute attack of typhoid fever. The jab printed by the *Daily Orb* painted him as a small man with feminine features, saying "Miss Eby is going to try to hit the ball—if she can do so." The undersized but stout second baseman got his revenge the following day, hitting a triple that would have been a home run had he not been ill, a courageous effort in the 6–4 loss.

Newspaper writers covering baseball in those days weren't always kind to players. In the accompanying column following the printed box score, the *Daily Orb* writer added that the third baseman for the Copper Queen Office nine's got hit by a pitch in every at-bat on the afternoon, saying "Strouf's being hit by the ball was a good thing for him, because he never could find it any other way. " A few lines later, he noted that Strouf had a sore left arm, thus making the long throw across the diamond difficult and accounting for his error. The return match was scheduled for October 23 at the grounds in nearby Naco.

The return match drew 980 excited fans from Bisbee, the surrounding area and as far as Benson, Arizona, for a hotly contested game on the Mexican border. Excellent play was displayed on both sides in the rematch, with the A. & S.E.R.R. winning, 7–6. As the large crowd was cramming the return trains, a shoot-out on the streets of Naco broke out between groups of Americans and Mexicans. It began as a fist fight on the Mexican side of the international border. The violence between the two factions escalated, with 40 shots exchanged, wounding three, including one miner from Bisbee who was trying to board the train to Bisbee. The locomotive finally pulled out from the station at Naco, returning home. The excitement wasn't done, as the violence continued after the passenger trains left for Bisbee. The correspondent for the *Daily Orb* observed, "the scene on the cars was one most pitiful; women and children fainting, screaming, calling for husbands, mothers and brothers, while a number went into hysterics."[8]

Interest in the national game amongst the locals in Bisbee continued for decades to come. Many company ball clubs would emerge, including machinists, clerks and brakemen forming their own nine to take on the other clubs. Baseball adapted well to the mining camps of Bisbee, despite the close calls while going to and from games. The game offered a better outlet for pent-up energies in these blue collar workers who spent day after dreary day underground. The development of baseball and the rivalries formed between mining camps and towns across Arizona was rapidly spurred on with the construction of the railroad lines that crossed the territory. Without them, towns like Bisbee, Globe, Morenci and even Winslow and Flagstaff wouldn't have taken shape. The building of the railroads heralded a new era of growth and expansion in Arizona, and along with it a new source of competition on the baseball grounds that by this time dotted the countryside.

Not all of the men who played baseball in mining towns across Arizona did so in anonymity. One young man would emerge from the mining camps of the southwest as a future star in the professional ranks, earning both fame and a dubious legacy. Described as a "professional malcontent," a six-foot, two-inch, 195-pound, rough and strapping young man named Arnold "Chick" Gandil found himself working part-time as a boilermaker in the mining town of Humboldt, Arizona, after leaving school at the age of 17. He got his start as the regular catcher of the mine-sponsored club, eventually winding up across the border in Cananea, Mexico, by 1907 as a result of financial problems that forced the mining company in Humboldt company to close. Working part-time for the Cananea Consolidated Mining Company, he continued as a boilermaker in the mines, while learning how to play first base between bare-knuckle prize fights.

Cananea was described as a "wide open" town in those days, and according to Gandil it "suited me just fine. I was a rough, wild kid."[9] The rough first baseman participated in bare-knuckle boxing matches for upwards of $150 per fight. His mean, callous disposition would follow him for the rest of his baseball career, even earning him a five-day suspension after he got into a fist fight with Tris Speaker on May 31, 1919. He had a few run-ins with umpire Ollie Chill, earning an ejection from a game for allegedly throwing a ball at the umpire while completing an "around the horn" relay after a strikeout. His conflict with Chill began when he was suspended for arguing balls and strikes on May 12, 1915.

Before his days as a professional ball player, the young Gandil played for the mining company nine against teams in Bisbee, Douglas, Tucson and El Paso. The informal league had organized and contracted teams with a $500 entrance fee, a paltry sum these days, but in 1906 a significant financial investment on behalf of the four (later five) clubs. Most of the clubs solicited investments from local businesses with promises of repayment through gate receipts from attracting cranks to watch a winning ball club. Each club also raised money to secure uniforms, sign players and negotiating open leases with the owners of ball parks to host their home games.

The 1907 season gave early indications of Gandil's skills as a premier first baseman. He gained notice from a minor league club in Shreveport, Louisiana. In his first professional season, he batted a respectable .267 with the club in the Texas League. His reputation as a trouble-maker and malcontent followed him to the California League, where in 1909 he risked being blacklisted from professional baseball by failing to report when ordered. Later that year he was arrested for stealing $225 from his new club in Fresno, California. Eventually, he was sold to the Chicago White Sox, beginning a tumultuous career in the big leagues. His nefarious

5. The Company Nine

Cananea B.B.C. of 1907. Standing third from left is Arnold "Chick" Gandil. Standing far left is Bert Whaling. (Arizona Historical Society, Tucson)

exploits with the infamous Black Sox are well-known, echoing his rough beginning in the mining towns of Arizona and Mexico.

    The importance of railroad development in Arizona cannot be overstated. The railways brought new settlers and supplies to foster growth from one corner of the territory to the other. Before the railroad entered the territory, 20-mule teams would haul freight and supplies over uncertain terrain, often getting stuck on mountainsides, mud and deep sand. River boats from the west coast were an important method of moving materials and supplies into Yuma, Ehrenburg, Camp Mohave and 17 other landings along the Colorado River. Steamboats named the *Gila, Colorado, Cocopah* and *Mohave* braved the dangerous currents of the Colorado to deliver passengers and cargo to western Arizona. Traveling to and through Arizona was just as uncertain, often braving dangerous territory. There simply had to be a better way to get men and material into and through Arizona.

    As early as May 1877, the sounds of clanging hammers rhythmically pounding spikes into the dry, rocky ground could be heard on the western outskirts of Yuma. For scores of Chinese railroad workers in the Yuma area, their work schedule in the summer months, starting early in the morning and concluding in the early afternoon, was deemed "sensible" by the local press[10] as it was "hot that summer as it was every summer."[11] After initial grading work was completed by crews of Chinese laborers, the daunting task of spanning the lower Colorado River began, but not without a bit of controversy and diabolical political maneuvering.

Competition was fierce between the Texas & Pacific and the Southern Pacific Railroad companies to complete a railroad line across southern Arizona in 1877. Completing a line that stretched from El Paso to California represented a windfall for transporting people and freight to America's golden coast, representing a financial boon to the victor who completed and controlled the line. Senior management from the T&P were seen around Yuma, working to stop the progress of the bridge being constructed by the Southern Pacific Railroad. The project manager for the SP, John Heaton, who oversaw construction, was killed in an accident while riding a hand car while inspecting the San Fernando Tunnel, located north of Los Angeles. Seth Green was quickly appointed to replace him so no time was lost in completing the work.

This change opened the door for leaders from the T&P to attempt to stall the SP's effort to finish the bridge over the Colorado River and enter Yuma. Over the next few months, several secret meetings and deals took place, some involving the U.S. Army's highest official in the area, General Irwin McDowell. Eventually, the SP was allowed to finish the bridge to avoid the "waste of their property" and to "open the way for passage of steamboats."[12] Orders were given to complete the bridge to allow boats to pass, but no rails were to be put down. Despite pleas from representatives of the Texas & Pacific Railroad, the bridge spanning the river was completed on September 29, 1877. The bridge lacked the rails to carry the first locomotive into Yuma, the Number 31, aptly named the "Arizona Express." Sensing that the men from the Southern Pacific Railroad were going to lay rails from the bridge into Yuma against orders from U.S. Army Headquarters in San Francisco, the T&P placed a lone sentry on the bridge. The work crews silently watched the sentry, waiting for him to fall asleep or be relieved of duty. Sensing that no ill plans were in the works, the guard was relieved at 11 p.m. Quickly the track crews sprang into action, laying track and rails from midnight until approximately 2 a.m. How the men were able to muffle the sound of hammers driving spikes into the ground is a mystery indeed!

5. The Company Nine

The work moved seamlessly until one man dropped a rail on the bridge, with the noise waking the few men stationed at Fort Yuma. The entire garrison descended on the workers completing the bridge, all with fixed bayonets. Work halted while Superintendent Green diplomatically handled the matter. Things were quiet until the soldiers saw that a carload of rails was rolling their way, providing little choice but to step aside to allow the car and the work to commence. Seeing that there wasn't anything to be done with such a small force, the soldiers went back to their barracks. The work happily and energetically resumed, with hammers singing out a singular tune that united rails and spikes. Finally, on the morning of September 30, 1877, locomotive Number 31 was able to steam its way into the area of Madison and First Street. Wild celebrations greeted the arrival of the railroad, a highly anticipated event for the townsfolk in Yuma. Another train decorated for the event also steamed into town, the Number 22, which eventually became the official locomotive named the "Arizona Express."

The *Arizona Sentinel* printed a special edition to commemorate the event. This opened the way for travel to the West Coast, as well as moving mail and commercial goods into and through the territory. A new era had been forged in Arizona!

From here the rails would slowly expand across the burning, dry desert to Tucson. From Yuma, the SP laid track through Gila City, Adonde, Mohawk Summit, Texas Hill, Gila Bend, Maricopa, Casa Grande, Picacho and finally Tucson. The first iron horse steamed into the Old Pueblo on March 20, 1880. Early Tucsonans were overjoyed to have the railroad in their town as several buildings downtown were decorated with bunting and plenty of celebratory banners crisscrossing the streets well above the dusty thoroughfares. Groups of dignitaries arrived that morning ahead of schedule and toured the town while the locals finished preparations for the festivities.

A few more years would pass before the railroad line was completed through Arizona. This important development opened Arizona to the outside world and ushered in a new era of travel to the territory. Passengers from both coasts would arrive, along with improved mail service. The availability of commercial goods coming to Arizona helped expand mining and lumber operations and the various mercantiles and businesses in town. The locomotive would feed the factories of the East with copper, silver and gold ore mined in Arizona. It was a big step forward, providing a population boom in Yuma, Tucson and Phoenix. As a result, the railroad workers assigned to maintain the rail yards and stations formed their own

Union Railroad Nine, c. 1894. (Tempe Museum of History)

baseball clubs to compete with local town clubs, work schedule permitting of course.

The earliest known baseball activity of a railroad nine occurred in Tucson on July 2, 1888, when a group of shopmen and other workers from the Southern Pacific Railroad faced a "picked nine" from Tucson at the Military Plaza in Tucson. Although no score was reported, the *Arizona Daily Citizen* described the affair as an exciting one, as the boys from town "naturally carried off the honors." This first match represented a humble beginning for baseball played by railroad employees in the Arizona Territory. More than a year passed until the next railroad nine stepped to the forefront of the baseball scene in Tucson. A new club was formed and on September 9, 1889, the first challenge was accepted between a club representing the Jerry McGintler Store, dubbed the "Jerry McGintlers" by the *Arizona Daily Citizen*, and the Southern Pacific nine. Action commenced on the large Military Plaza in downtown Tucson on Fifth avenue between 11th Street and 15th Street. It was a short distance from the new railroad depot built years prior by the Southern Pacific Railroad. An easy walk allowed the railroad men to enjoy an afternoon of sporting competition and camaraderie, with a few beers afterwards courtesy of one of the many saloons in the neighborhood.

Inexperience with the finer points of the game would handicap the SP nine on that afternoon as they were routed by the Jerry McGintlers,

38–11. This didn't dampen things, as the following week the *Daily Citizen* announced that "the Tucson League has organized with three clubs: The J.P.L., S.P.R.R. and L.Z. & Co."[13] The organizers, local merchants, promised a 30-game schedule for some kind of trophy that as of the announcement in the newspaper had not "been decided upon yet."[14] The same article mentioned that the J.P.L and L.Z. & Co. nines would open the season on the baseball grounds located on the upper portion of the Military Plaza, towards the corner of 11th Street and Fifth Avenue, in a series of games during the winter. If anyone in early Tucson didn't get enough sporting action on Sundays, there were regular bullfights, pitting man versus beast in a bloody contest of endurance and will, held every Saturday at the Amphitheatre on Stone Avenue.

The Southern Pacific railroad nine picked back up late in September in a return match against the J.P.L. club, also known as the "Jerry McGintlers," at the Military Plaza in an early afternoon match billed by the *Arizona Daily Citizen* on September 28, 1889, as "a game worth seeing." With the built-up anticipation for the return match featuring an improved railroad club, it is disappointing that no box score or game report was printed in the *Daily Citizen*. Meanwhile, the Tucson Base Ball Club had been reformed and took on the SP nine in a series of matches in October. In the first game, Tucson lost because of continual and strenuous kicking in the top half of the ninth inning and an outright refusal to continue the bottom half of the frame, even though they led 7–5.

Despite the outcome, the *Daily Citizen* noted that "The playing was good, and shows that Tucson ball players are rapidly improving and will soon be in condition to 'polish' with ease any nine in the Territory."[15] The return match one week later saw heavy hitting by Tucson bring an easy victory 20–5. The *Daily Citizen* noted that "Sunday's crowd was the largest ever seen on the plaza,"[16] though such claims in the newspapers of the day were frequent, if not overstated.

The railroad nine found time to practice and, on the following Sunday, battled the Tucson B.B.C. to a 16–16 tie. The game started late and was called at the end of seven innings due to darkness. In the final game of the series, the Tucson lads romped, 40–13. With word spreading through the Southwest that the trains between El Paso and Tucson were running regularly, it was reported that the El Paso baseball club was trying to arrange a tour through Arizona, in a front-page entry in the *Daily Citizen* on November 2, 1889. The paper also mentioned that the SP club had agreed to play the Junior Pioneer club the following afternoon in a friendly game, perhaps taking a break from the intense competition offered by the Tucson club.

Tucson B.B.C. with the Pearce Athletic Club, post-game photograph featuring Manny Drachman, seated left of catcher. (Arizona Historical Society, Tucson)

The railroads were helping to fuel the baseball action in Tucson. As mentioned in Chapter 3, one of the early avid and almost "baseball mad" supporters, organizers and ballists from Tucson was a young Southern Pacific Railroad blacksmith named Emanuel "Manny" Drachman. Although not clearly documented, it is very possible that Drachman had something to do with the resurgence of baseball amongst the railroad workers in 1889. Decades later his son Roy recalled, "Manny's ball playing days, of course, began when he was old enough to swing a bat. He had a natural talent for the game, and by the time he was thirteen he was playing on the 'town team' made up of the best players in Tucson."[17] The early game reports do not list a single lineup, so it's left to speculation on which clubs the young Drachman played.

The men who played for the railroad clubs were strong, tough and rugged young men prone to fighting at the slightest provocation on and off the ball field. Working on the railroad certainly toughened a man and often made him fearless. To illustrate this, we need look no further than a match between Cananea and Tucson in 1907 that saw post-game fisticuffs between Manny Drachman and a future professional catcher for the Boston Braves, Bert Whaling. The two frontier towns played a doubleheader on the Fourth of July holiday, with each club winning one game.

The third and final game of the series would be decided in Cananea. Despite the uncertainty of victory, the *Tucson Citizen* heaped praise on Manny Drachman, saying that he was "decidedly the best baseball general in the territory."[18] That was very high praise, as a catcher calls every aspect of the game, including what pitch is to be delivered, sets up the defense and makes pickoff attempts to catch a base runner sleeping.

Tucsonan Gus Bernal was also advertised as being in a prize fight with the "Mexican Mystery" for the championship of Mexico sometime the same afternoon. Nearly 300 eager cranks packed the train for the excursion south to watch the highly anticipated match between the two clubs. Dressed in dusters, white caps, and red handkerchiefs, the group intended to stand out from the natives at the ball park while rooting the Tucson baseball nine on to a much-anticipated victory. Nearly 3,000 people showed up for the game. Tucson was decidedly outplayed that afternoon, losing 22–7. The Tucson club did, however, receive a portion of the gate receipts to help cover travel expenses. The much-talked-about prize fight never occurred between the heavyweight Bernal and his mystery opponent. The confrontation between Manny Drachman and Bert Whalen had been brewing into a perfect storm of beer-fueled testosterone, finally reaching an ignition point in September of 1907.

While Tucson limped home to figure out how to defeat the strong team from Cananea, another series of games in Tucson was agreed upon for September, to be held at Elysian Grove. Both Arnold and Whaling (often misspelled as Whalen by the newspapers) were listed on the roster for the visiting club from the Mexican mining town. Manny Drachman took his usual position behind the plate for Tucson. The series was set up to celebrate Labor Day, complete with parades, speeches, decorations and refreshments. Tucson lost the first game after their left fielder, a gentleman named Dessie, dropped three fly balls, necessitating his replacement. A large group of people traveled from Cananea to watch the series, packing the grandstand to the point of overflowing onto the grounds in right field, where several plays were affected due to interference from spectators. The *Tucson Citizen* estimated the total attendance at more than 2,000 people. The final score saw Tucson lose, 9–2. The next game the following afternoon wouldn't be any better for the hometown nine from the Old Pueblo.

The *Tucson Citizen* reported that another enormous crowd "large enough to grace a National League game"[19] witnessed a confused Tucson club that barely scratched out two runs on the scoreboard over nine innings. The previous day's defeat demoralized the club, which seemed to switch players at each position every inning. As the game continued, each man would ask Drachman, the club's manager, where he should be playing. With tempers short, the stage was set for the confrontation between both catchers. Although not reported in the *Citizen*, a recollection recorded years later by Manny's son, Roy P. Drachman, has survived, telling the story. Apparently, during the fourth inning a strikeout ended the frame with Whaling standing on third base. While trotting back to the dugout, Drachman flipped the ball at Whalen, who didn't see the sphere coming. The ball struck him on the cheek, prompting Whalen to grab Drachman, spin him around and slap him across the face in retaliation. The entire crowd of thousands witnessed the blow, letting out a collective gasp. The smaller Drachman didn't back down for an instant. He stepped up to Whalen and said he'd "take care of the matter after the game."[20]

While the game report in the *Citizen* did not say who made the game's last out, the story as told by Manny's son paints a vivid tale. Manny came up to the plate in the last of the ninth inning with two outs and struck out, possibly on purpose. With the game over, Manny threw down his bat and reached out and forcefully removed Whalen's mask. The fight was on! The crowd roared as both men traded blows for several minutes. No one on either club dared interfere, and the crowd got louder and louder with each blow exchanged. Manny drove Whalen back against the backstop, continually landing heavy blows and eventually scoring the knockout. The hometown crowd was overjoyed, lifting Manny up and carrying him to a celebratory feast at the beer garden near the ball grounds despite losing the baseball game. The railroad lines in southern Arizona made series of games like this possible between towns like Tucson and Cananea.

In Yuma, the first major landing for the Southern Pacific in the Arizona Territory, the baseball action between the railroad nines and town clubs began around the same time action commenced on the diamonds of Tucson. The regular Yuma nine began practicing to play another railroad nine, the Mohawk Plungers, in games for a "heavy purse"[21] during the spring of 1889, a result of the Plungers overconfidently issuing an open challenge to "any club in the Territory."[22] While the clubs in and around Yuma were busy arranging games with each other, the *Arizona Sentinel* published two articles on the virtues and features of baseball and baseball bat-making in the May 4 and May 11 issues. There was quite a bit of "trash talk" coming from the Yuma B.B.C. but no real action on behalf of the club. A group of young men in town decided to put up the large sum of $100 for a game against the club.

The challenge was printed in the July 13, 1889, issue of the *Arizona*

5. The Company Nine

Sentinel, which asked, "What have our Yuma boys to say?" Across town, the *Sentinel* nine representing another group of baseball enthusiasts of Yuma extended a warm invitation to the employees of the SP for a match on the afternoon of December 15, 1889. No record exists of either match taking place. Missing coverage in the newspapers does not mean the games never happened. Newspapers were often fickle about what stories to print. It was common to have baseball coverage skip a few weeks until a favorable story that painted the hometown nine in a more favorable light could be reported to readers.

Over the next decade and a half, the railroad teams in Yuma would play games against the town clubs and from Fort Yuma on an irregular basis. Uniquely, the 1906 season saw the Fourth of July celebration use the grounds adjacent to the Southern Pacific line as a backdrop. A three-club "tournament" of sorts was held, with a club representing the railroad taking part in the holiday matches. In the accompanying panoramic photo of the game, taken on July 4, 1906, we can see that the game took place in the shadow of the Gila River levee, which in later years was drained and then occupied as a road bed for a spur line of the Southern Pacific Railroad. The *Arizona Sentinel* announced the preliminary schedule of events on June 23, noting that the game would take place on the morning of the national holiday. It was decided that there was enough time for only

Fourth of July game at Yuma, 1906. (Arizona State Library)

one match on the Fourth of July, so a playoff game of sorts occurred a week or two prior. Clubs representing the "Reclamation Boys" and the "Railroaders" (a.k.a. the Surveyors) played to see who would play the regular Yuma nine for a prize of $50 on the morning of the Fourth of July.

With the stage set for the prize match on the holiday, Yuma was ready for a grand celebration. The morning's festivities were in grand tradition reflecting a 19th-century taste for the outlandish, complete with patriotic bunting hanging from every home and storefront and the customary fireworks ignited everywhere. In a game that pitted the Colts versus a Surveyor nine from the SP, the interest was immense and drew "several thousand people."[23] The Colts emerged victorious, 8–5, claiming the prize money offered by the events committee.

Farther north, the towns of Flagstaff, Prescott and Winslow would have to wait until 1881 to welcome the iron horses from the Atlantic and Pacific Rail Road. After a brief halt to accommodate construction of a bridge across the expanse at Canyon Diablo, the railroad finally entered Flagstaff a year later. By the end of 1883 the rail lines stretched from one end of the northern part of Arizona to the other, much to the excitement of the local newspapers. The new road meant expedited service bringing goods and travelers in and out of the territory. It also meant a new chapter in baseball rivalries between Flagstaff, Williams, Kingman (a.k.a. Peach Springs), Prescott and Winslow. Flagstaff waited until May 16, 1885, for any mention of baseball to grace the pages of its own *Arizona Weekly Champion*. The newspaper quickly took hold of the growth that the "Skylight City" was experiencing and noted that the town should "step to the front" and organize a baseball club. In an article titled "Flagstaff Wants," the newspaper insisted that a brass band and a baseball club should be considered and quickly organized, saying "With our large number of young men and sporting men, these two things could easily be organized." Encouragement indeed!

Winslow, the first railroad stop in the northern part of the territory, had already organized a baseball club, boasting of their on-field prowess two weeks later claiming they have "a baseball club that can out bat, out catch, out run, out field and beat any club within 200 miles of them, for any amount of shekels that can be put up—by outside parties of course."[24] The first match for the new Winslow nine was reported in the same article, a game with a picked nine from Bangor, Maine. Winslow won, 32–8, leading the *Weekly Champion* to boast that the hometown boys had "cooled the spruce gum" out of their visiting opponents. The article mentioned that the pitcher for the winning nine was a railroad conductor named

Sechrist, the earliest known railroad man to play in a game of baseball in Arizona's formative territorial era. While reporting the action in Winslow, the *Weekly Champion* continued its call for a nine to represent Flagstaff. Citing many young men in town as suitable material for a nine, the paper went on to brag that surely "they would strike terror to the hearts of any of the clubs along the road."[25] The following summer, Winslow would issue an invitation to Flagstaff for a match during the Fourth of July celebration of 1885.

Flagstaff took the challenge seriously and began to organize and practice for the anticipated game on the nation's hallowed birthday. A letter penned by "Anon." and printed in the *Arizona Weekly Champion* on June 20, 1885, related that "The baseball craze is at its height now, and broken fingers, black eyes, and broken teeth are plentiful." It seems that practice was rough going for Flagstaff's catcher and first baseman, who after a liberal dose of "arnica and good nursing ... will be able to appear by that time." It seems that even the tough railroad men found that baseball was indeed a very rough game on their hands. The railroad would get in on the interest for the game, offering a round-trip fare of $4.60 between Flagstaff and Winslow for the holiday festivities. Like all Fourth of July celebrations, the events in Winslow for 1885 were grand. Ice cream, fireworks, and decorations marked the national holiday. Sadly, there was no baseball game included in the festivities, or at least none reported in the *Weekly Champion*. The newspaper pleaded with the residents of Flagstaff to organize a game for the following year's celebration, noting that the "youths of Prescott have the baseball fever." Baseball in Flagstaff and Winslow disappeared for the time being, until interest in the game was revived in the summer of 1887 when two clubs from Flagstaff were organized. Both Mill Town and New Town organized nines to play in practice matches on the flat just south of the railroad depot in Flagstaff.

Finally, on July 30, 1887, a game between the Flagstaff and Winslow nines took place after much back-and-forth taunting in the pages of the *Weekly Champion.* The Flagstaff nine walked away victors that afternoon, 16–14. The Winslow grounds were "a little to the east of the town are excellent and the game was closely contested."[26] Betting was lively, and the score was tied going into the seventh inning. Flagstaff scored three runs in the eighth inning and held the home club scoreless in the ninth to secure the victory. Apparently this was the second match between the two, the events of the first unreported in the newspaper. The railroad certainly benefitted from the new interest in baseball in both cities, as the rails would carry cranks from both towns back and forth for numerous games in the coming years. Baseball and the railroads made good business partners.

Feeling confident after their recent win over the Winslow club, the Flagstaff B.B.C. announced on August 6, 1887, that in a short time they would appear in uniform. Later that month, the *Weekly Champion* noted that "Flagstaff seems to be "spoiling" for a rematch"[27] with the Winslow club. With all of the baseball action going on in the region, there was a certain distaste that some of the more religious folk in Kingman took about the games being played on the Sabbath. In the *Mohave County Miner* on October 1, 1887, a local preacher, the Reverend Woolsack, discoursed on the ills of playing the national game on Sunday. In the printed sermon, the reverend pointed out,

> See that loafer with a bird cage on his head standing like a straddle bug behind the bat? He is not desecrating the Sabbath day by playing ball, because he isn't playing ball. He can't play. He imagines he can, of course, and goes through all the painful contortions of a real player, but in the devil's store book he is charged ten times over for any error he makes, and a nice record he will have when the season is over and the time for his eternal rest is at hand. It will be a sorry rest for him.[28]

The scathing rhetoric from the pastor was inflamed by the crowd in attendance cheering as one of their players made a long hit. The Reverend Woolsack—affectionately known in the *Mohave County Miner* as the "Deacon"—rose above the noise that his parishioners made, bellowing that the cheers should be in worship of the Lord, and that unless they did so they would not "reach the shining home plate of everlasting life."[29]

The communities of Kingman, Flagstaff and Winslow continued to support baseball despite the exhortations against such practices. Kingman staged regular games against a nine from nearby Peach Springs through the summer of 1888. The support grew to the point where the Kingman Base Ball Club made arrangements for a three-game series with a club from Needles, California, starting on November 4, 1888. The first game would be in Needles and the second in Kingman, with the location of the final match to be decided upon. The newspaper reported that an out-of-practice Kingman nine made the trip via railroad to Needles, playing in a rain-shortened game with no score reported. The other games never materialized, making us wonder why. Nevertheless, the games continued among these early towns. Finally, in 1890 a railroad line was established between Prescott and Flagstaff, and the first game between the towns took place on July 19, 1890. The *Arizona Champion* covered the game, noting the late start and "a big crowd" in attendance. Flagstaff won the toss, electing to take the field first, and the final tally of 14 to 6 stood in favor of Flagstaff.

By the time the Flagstaff nine took to the field in uniform in 1887, initially clad in long-sleeve fireman's shirts with shields, long pants, and pillbox caps, trying to make some kind of statement about who they were. Most clubs of the era wore simple uniforms, however the DeMund Lumber Company of Phoenix stood out for their garish uniforms. The "DeMunds," as they were known in the *Arizona Republican*, were sponsored by C. E. DeMund, owner of a lumber company in Phoenix. DeMund spared no expense in outfitting his club, gaining the attention of the *Republican*, which noted, in an article titled "Ball Men Bedecked Gaudily," that "In all the gorgeousness of bright red uniforms the DeMund baseball team blossomed out yesterday"[30] for the 1900 season. They took the field against their southside rivals, the Tempe Crimson Rims, in a well-contested Salt River Valley championship, only to lose in a three-game series. That year also saw a club from Williams take on a railroad nine out of Winslow in a game with a heavy wager of $500 per side. In the game report that arrived via telegraph, the *Tempe Daily News* related that the action was "one of the most exciting games of ball ever played in Arizona."[31] The article also noted that the Winslow nine was "principally railroad men." By 1900, the various railroads across the territory all had baseball clubs or employees playing for the local clubs. The related interests of baseball and the railroads was a long-continuing one.

The various fire or hose teams in Arizona didn't play much baseball. There have been scant findings of a club in Tombstone, aptly named the "Protectionists," organizing to play baseball in 1889 against a club from St. David. The proposal was issued by a scratch club of firemen from the various hose companies in Tombstone. Although the challenge was issued to play the "St. David's," the Tombstone B.B.C. accepted in their stead. The game occurred on the afternoon of August 13, 1889, on the ball grounds in Tombstone, with a large crowd in attendance. The Tombstone cranks witnessed their nine bested by a resounding tally of 23–3, with only six innings played. The *Daily Epitaph* noted that the firemen were "distinct from the Tombstone baseball club, and is composed entirely of members of the Protection Hose Company, No. 3."[32]

No other game reports exist of a fire company coming together to form a club until 1901, when Phoenix firemen organized a nine to challenge the Tempe Crimson Rims in a match to raise funds for new firefighting equipment. In a weather-shortened game during which the wind and blowing dust clearly interfered with the quality of play on the field, the Tempe Crimson Rims emerged victorious in front of a disappointing crowd at East Lake Park in Phoenix. The *Arizona Republican* paid tribute to the visitors, writing, "the Crimson Rims won it and are entitled to credit," noting the 7–3 score and adding, "If the Firemen could not do much business with the score keeper they were able to prevent the visitors from wearing out the score keeper's pencil."[33] From here, the games consisting of a fire company nine simply vanish. It seems that the everpresent danger of fire in towns constructed largely of wooden timbers was enough to keep any fire company completely occupied, making the notion of supporting a baseball club impractical at best.

Despite the short descriptions of games and surrounding histories, the importance of the mines, lumber companies and railroads in the development and spread of baseball during the territorial era cannot be downplayed. The mines utilized the game to temper rowdy employees, hoping that expending pent-up energy on the baseball diamond would be a productive pastime for the rugged and courageous men who worked underground. The mining companies also hoped that by sponsoring a baseball club or two, the employees would view this as a positive benefit from the company, as tempers usually ran short with mine workers who were usually overworked and underpaid. The lumber companies took a similar view, and in the case of the DeMund Lumber Company, the support offered verged on the extravagant. The motivations were similar—to gain attention in the press by supporting a winning club bedecked in new flashy uniforms was a great way to present a business. The railroads further expanded baseball by enabling residents of Phoenix, Tucson, Tombstone, Bisbee, Flagstaff, Winslow, Globe and Kingman to travel to other towns in Arizona and a few select destinations in New Mexico and California for games in better comfort and speed. The railroads enabled the first barnstorming clubs to visit Arizona. By 1900, the peak of company-sponsored clubs and railroad activity, baseball was firmly entrenched in the newspapers of the territory. Any town that didn't have a baseball nine was considered "out of touch" with the times. The coming era of barnstorming would push the attraction of baseball to another level of excitement. The clubs that visited Arizona, previously only read about in the newspapers, now could be watched on the diamond. More great games were on the horizon, all courtesy of the many miles of railroad track that had been laid many years before through the backbreaking labor of scores of Irish, Chinese, African American and Native American laborers.

CHAPTER 6

The Barnstormers

By the time baseball was established amongst the military posts, mining and frontier towns of the Arizona Territory during the 1870s and 1880s, the notion of baseball clubs traveling to other towns, states, territories and even other countries was a long-established practice in the eastern U.S. The earliest known tour of a pioneer-era baseball club was the Excelsiors of Philadelphia, who embarked on a long, multi-state journey through upstate New York and the upper South in 1860. After the Civil War and the phases of economic and physical reconstruction that followed, baseball would soon re-emerge into the national consciousness and in the pages of the largest newspapers in New York, Philadelphia and Chicago. The first club to embark on such a wide-ranging tour was the Nationals of Washington, D.C., in 1867. Their remarkable summer trip covered around 3,000 miles in three weeks. The Nationals took their regular nine, plus eight replacements and a few other interested parties, possibly notable cranks as well as journalist and later acclaimed "Father of Baseball" Henry Chadwick along on the grueling but historic trip to promote the growth of the emerging national pastime.

The party that left by train on July 11, 1867, numbered 40 in all. The club played in cities such as Columbus, Cincinnati (two games), Louisville, Indianapolis, St. Louis, and lastly Chicago, playing three games there during a week-long celebration of all things baseball. From the corresponding newspaper accounts, it is clear that the crowds in each city were enthralled, clamoring for more and more.

The most notable game came in Chicago, where the Nationals faced a resilient Forest City Club of Rockford, Illinois. The Forest City Club would itself travel nearly 100 miles to compete against the famed Nationals and featured a young hurler named Albert Goodwill Spalding.[1] The ballists from Rockford would be the only club to hand the mighty Nationals a defeat on their daring tour, leaving the Nationals to head home with a 9–1 record for the momentous expedition, despite many entreaties towards the Rockford Club for a rematch the following day to reclaim their lost honor and perhaps a few dollars in wagers. The Nationals wanted to erase the bitter 29–23 defeat which included two rain delays. The Rockford club knew better, knew that their luck had run out, thereby refusing all pleas for a rematch.

Other clubs would follow suit, such as the legendary 1869 Cincinnati Red Stockings, who took on all challengers across the nation, going undefeated for the entire season of 1869, even escaping in a few matches by the narrowest of margins.

A few years later, the first outside baseball club to visit the Arizona Territories was an impostor group representing the National League Champion Boston Red Stockings in 1876. As noted in Chapter 2, the original club was summoned at the request of the Champion B.B.C. of Prescott, Arizona Territory, to help them defeat their rivals, the Whipple B.B.C. from nearby Fort Whipple for the first known championship of the territory. While early transportation traveling west was difficult and dangerous, thus making the reality of the actual Red Stockings club making an appearance for the match all but impossible, the result was that the champions of Prescott would don the same suits worn by the famous Red Stockings, down to the smallest of detail, for the historic match on the plaza in the capitol city of the territory. The visual effect of having the Red Stockings visit Prescott helped spread the popularity of baseball immensely throughout the years and marked a first in the many contests between clubs from Arizona and other states, including professional clubs such as the Boston Red Sox, Chicago White Sox, New York Giants and Detroit Tigers.

Each of these professional nines would eventually make their way through the Arizona Territory as the railroad lines completed by the Southern Pacific, Santa Fe, Atlantic & Pacific and other railroad companies made travel to and through the arid land a distinct possibility. In 1880, the *Arizona Daily Citizen* printed an article regarding baseball in the far-removed tropical paradise of Cuba, noting that a club from Rochester, New York, had made the long journey to play the strong Havana club on December 21, 1879. The Havana club was a picked nine from four different clubs in town, who played valiantly but lost to the New Yorkers, 21–7, in "the presence of five thousand people,"[2] adding that the "Americans played with only two errors, winning rapturous applause." This entry notes the willingness of early baseball clubs to travel far distances for a good match, with early Arizona becoming a more frequent destination in the years to come.

As touched on in the previous chapter, the next reported match that occurred with clubs from outside the territory was on May 30, 1885, when a group of "excursionists" from Bangor, Maine, played the club from Winslow. Recalling the boastful remarks by the *Arizona Champion*, Winslow had a club that could "out bat, out catch, out run, out field and beat any club within 200 miles of them for any amount of shekels that can be put up—by outside parties of course." To answer such a bold claim, the group from Bangor picked their nine and took on the Winslow club. The visitors were enthusiastic at the start, but by the end of the final inning, when the tally stood 32–8 in favor of Winslow, the visitors had calmed down considerably from being humbled by the hometown lads.

It isn't known if any money was wagered or how much currency changed hands that afternoon. In 1886 there was talk of barnstorming "Bloomer Girls" visiting Benson on the way to the California coast. Despite initial interest, no ball game between this early women's team and a local club from Tombstone or Tucson was reported.

One year later, in the fall of 1887, the Flagstaff nine traveled by rail to the New Mexico Fair held in Albuquerque. The club from Flagstaff held a reputation amongst the territories of Arizona and New Mexico as a nine that didn't dispute or "kick" calls made by the umpire. This habit was frowned upon so much that a club's reputation hinged on it. If a club was perceived as too disagreeable for arguing every call, the news quickly spread and other clubs would simply refuse to play them.

On September 27, 1887, the *Albuquerque Morning Democrat* ran the headline "FLAGSTAFFS AHEAD" and reported a shortened game in which Flagstaff led, 8–7, until some unreported act by the umpire caused Flagstaff's captain, Haight, to pull his players from the field in protest. The *Morning Democrat* of Albuquerque gave credit to Haight's action of removing his players from the field in protest, noting that "the Flagstaff boys are not kickers and something must have been done or they would not have left the field."[3] Even the local newspaper had no idea exactly what transpired! While the boys from Flagstaff were busy competing in the New Mexico State Fair of 1887 for the crown and purse awarded to the winner, the Phoenix Base Ball Club was hectically working to arrange a series of matches between the St. Louis Browns and the "Chicagos." Both professional nines were heading to California on a post-season barnstorming tour.

The Phoenix B.B.C. quickly issued the challenge to both professional clubs for what the *Arizona Daily Citizen* termed the "Championship of Apache-land."[4] Three weeks later, a similarly worded article ran in the *Daily Citizen*, followed by a large-type advertisement placed by Tucson cigar merchant Samuel H. Drachman. The ad hailed both clubs and advertised a $6 round-trip fare to and from the games in Phoenix. Unfortunately, satisfactory arrangements were not made and the games between Phoenix and the traveling Browns and Chicagos didn't take place that year. Instead both clubs remained in California, for the Winter League Championship with the inaugural contest between the Chicagos and the St. Louis Browns on October 28 at Central Park in San Francisco, located at 8th & Market Streets. The *Daily Alta* estimated that 12,000 cranks packed the ball yard to witness the two professional nines play, adding that this was the "first time these clubs met on a San Francisco diamond, with the result of this game anxiously awaited."[5] The game marked the beginning of the Winter Series, lasting until February 18, 1888, and totaling 36 games. Interest was high, as the results were telegraphed out for coverage in the nationally circulated *St. Louis Globe-Democrat* and *The Sporting News*, reaching hundreds of thousands of readers nationwide.

The Browns won the inaugural match, 16 to 9, the game called "tightly contested" through the first seven innings. Interestingly enough, a year later a utility player named Fred Carroll, who played 91 games for the NL Pittsburgh Alleghenys, made a brief stop in Yuma on October 26, 1889, to take in the sights before continuing on to Tucson to visit an uncle who worked as a mechanic for the Southern Pacific Railroad. In 1889, Carroll batted .330 in 318 at-bats. Eventually, the locals hoped, the professional clubs would stop somewhere in Arizona to play a few games, based on the good word of Carroll.

In the Arizona Territory, the interested parties hoping to bring professional clubs would have to wait. The Chicagos and Browns skipped a stop in Phoenix because either gate receipts would be inadequate or the professional players and their wives who made the trip out west simply weren't interested. Either way, there was considerable angst felt by more than a few interested businesses and baseball cranks in Tucson and Phoenix after being slighted by the professionals. Considerable money had been spent in preparing and advertising the touring professional clubs' exhibition matches. Baseball was picking up momentum territory-wide and continued over the coming years as other clubs, professional or not, visited the baseball grounds of Arizona.

A few more years passed before another professional club from the National League proposed a stop in Phoenix. This time, in the fall of 1895,

6. The Barnstormers 157

it was two unnamed National League clubs on their way to California via the Union Pacific line who entertained the idea of making a detour through Arizona for a few games with the Phoenix Base Ball Club.

Mr. Dave Goldberg, notable local businessman and serious baseball fanatic, took the offer of the professional club seriously and set about making arrangements with local hotels and businesses to support a professional nine stopping in Phoenix. After challenging the strong Albuquerque Base Ball Club for a game during race week in mid–December, the manager of the Phoenix B.B.C. sent several telegraphic wires to both professional nines of the National League now in San Francisco, and boasted to the *Republican* that the clubs "will probably come"[6] to Arizona for a few games. Word of the pending arrangements reached as far as Tucson, where the *Arizona Daily Citizen* quickly took interest, following the developments of the proposed games. In November 1895, it appeared that the arrangements were set, and the games were scheduled for the week of November 18 as a result of a telegram received by manager Goldberg of the Phoenix nine. The *Arizona Republican* noted that even the "south siders will also have an opportunity to witness the games, for special trains will be run from Tempe and a large delegation is expected will attend."[7] The first game on Friday would be between the National Leaguers, and the next day the winner would face the Phoenix nine. The teams, with 30 men total between both clubs, were scheduled to arrive in Phoenix on the morning of November 22, with games that afternoon and the next day before a scheduled departure northward towards Prescott.

Much to the outrage of Dave Goldberg and the other businessmen, the unnamed National League clubs never bothered to show up or even send word via telegraph calling off the games. The snubbed Phoenicians read the next morning: "[In] what is locally termed a 'dirty trick,' they took the northern train at Colton without even advising the Phoenix management, and started on their return east by way of Ogden,"[8] moaned the angry *Arizona Republican*, which had spent considerable print space drumming up interest in the games. There was considerable disgust felt by many in Phoenix at the failure of the professional clubs to show up or even send notice that travel plans eastward had changed. Instead of calling the weekend a complete loss, Goldberg scrambled and quickly made arrangements with the Prescott B.B.C. for two games on Sunday and Monday, November 24–25.

While tempers were soothed by the medicine of passing time and good baseball between towns in the central and northern parts of the territory, a lesser-known nine would make an appearance in November of

1897, when the Boston Bloomer Girls, a semi-professional nine made up of mostly women ball players, paid a visit to Phoenix. As mentioned earlier, the novelty of a women's baseball club drew immense interest in Phoenix. The baseball cranks wanted to see if these girls could play as well as advertised against the Phoenix Base Ball Club, though many Phoenicians still felt it was improper for young ladies to participate in sports of any kind.

The game drew a large crowd, providing the Bloomer Girls with enough funds from gate receipts at East Lake Park to continue the eastward, home-bound leg of a long trip. The new century came and went with no notable barnstorming clubs coming westward. Years passed until 1905, when the El Paso Base Ball Club visited Tucson for games on October 14–15. The *Tucson Citizen* declared that the games "will practically decide the Championship of the Southwest,"[9] featuring a grey-clad hometown club that entered the contest with an 11–2 record and a .846 winning percentage. Despite large newspaper ads, the first game at Elysian Grove drew only 100 spectators who witnessed a clean game. Tucson's 6–5 victory featured the indefatigable Manny Drachman, who worked behind the plate for both games. The next afternoon was an entirely different affair. Word spread around Tucson that their boys had defeated the visiting El Paso nine, resulting in a packed house. The *Tucson Citizen* noted, "with the grandstand groaning under its human load, and with the right field shade trees sheltering more than a hundred,"[10] who needed a visit by professional clubs when baseball in the Southwest was this good? Certainly not the obsessed cranks in Tucson!

In the second game, on Sunday, October 15, El Paso scored a single run in the top of the second inning, but was held scoreless the rest of the way by a swift-fielding Tucson club. Tucson tied the game in the bottom of the second before adding two tallies in the fifth and a single run in the seventh inning to secure the 4–1 victory and title of "Champions of the Southwest" for 1905. The quick game lasted a mere hour and 25 minutes. The often critical editors of the *Tucson Citizen* had once remarked that baseball was dead in Tucson. In a column titled "Sunday Reflections" printed on Monday, October 16, the same critical writers declared "baseball is not dead here by any means when 400 paid admissions are taken in."

Tucson would face the ball club from Clifton to decide the "Championship of the Territory." The *Citizen* also noted that "Manny's arm was working nicely yesterday," high praise for the aging, but still stalwart Drachman. A decade prior, in 1894, Charles Comiskey had offered Drachman a contract to play professional baseball for the Cincinnati Reds. That season the Reds finished a dismal 35 games behind the National League pennant winner, the Baltimore Orioles, who went 89–39. Comiskey had heard about Drachman's versatility as a catcher, hurler and first baseman. Comiskey was the player-manager of the Reds, appearing in 61 games as a first baseman that season. Hearing of the success of the Tucson B.B.C. in 1894, especially the ability of Drachman in the field and at the plate, Comiskey got owner John T. Brush to offer Drachman a contract. Many years later, in a memoir of early Tucson penned by Manny's son, Roy P. Drachman recalled, "In his younger days he was a first-rate player who turned down repeated offers to turn pro{ellip}. Many old-timers told me that he could have easily made it to the big leagues if he had accepted the contracts offered him."[11] Manny's mother, fearing that her loyal and hardworking son would turn into a drunken, baseball hooligan, discouraged his ambitions to make the game of baseball a profession.

Manny Drachman is the first known baseball player from the Arizona Territory to be scouted by professional clubs. Several other players that would follow his example, some accepting contracts and making brief appearances in the big leagues while some never made it out of the minors.

The action in Tucson was always intense amongst city clubs vying for supremacy on the diamond at Elysian Grove. Located on the southwest corner of Main Street and McCormick Street just south of the downtown district in Tucson, Elysian Grove eventually showcased a successful "city league" in 1907, sponsored in part by the same Manuel Drachman who not only managed the Tucson club that season but also owned Elysian Grove. This successful entertainment venue featured an amphitheater and beer garden near the ball grounds that were very popular with early Tucsonans, providing a needed respite from the dry, dusty and tense reality of life in an early western town.

The copper camps of Clifton and Morenci contributed in their own way to the barnstorming story of baseball during this early, rough-and-tumble era. Those burghs, formed on the eastern San Francisco River, placed their collective hopes on the rise and fall of copper prices per pound. Established in the 1880s, they experienced a large boom in copper production with lucrative ore prices attracting thousands of miners, merchants, families and outcasts to the area. By 1901, Clifton had established a diamond complete with a rickety makeshift grandstand. As with other mining towns like Bisbee and Globe, the mines eventually sponsored baseball clubs as an alternative to drunken exploits usually favored by miners on paydays. As in metropolitan cousins in Tucson and Phoenix a decade and a half earlier, young men and boys who didn't root for the home club or play baseball themselves were "looked upon as decidedly behind the times."[12] Clifton and Morenci would make a mark on baseball history by having not one, but two future professional players spend time playing for the hometown nine.

John Tortes Meyers was born on July 29, 1880, as a member of the Cahuilla or Mission Indian tribe of southern California. He was left fatherless at the tender age of seven, and his mother would be an enormous influence in his life. For Meyers, baseball became an increasingly intense interest and a way for him to cope with early hardships. In the early book about professional baseball, *The Glory of Their Times*, the star catcher only briefly mentioned his time in southern Arizona. The only surviving newspaper of the area, the *Clifton Copper Era & Morenci Leader*, detailed how this young man set himself apart on the diamond and took a step towards eventual stardom in professional baseball. The young man from California got his start for the Phelps Dodge Company nine in Clifton during the summers of 1904–1905.

Little is known about his success or failure on the diamond with the mining company club. His performance and reputation was enough to gain the attention of a recruiter from Dartmouth College at a baseball tournament in Albuquerque, New Mexico, in 1907. He possessed a powerful arm and a sure bat to counter being slow-footed, and he was signed to an athletic scholarship for Dartmouth. The rest is history. Meyers went on to have a brilliant professional career finishing as one of the best hitters of the Deadball Era.

Another future star who followed Meyers in playing for the Morenci nine before embarking on a major league career was talented right-handed pitcher Robert Green Harmon. Later nicknamed "Hickory Bob" for his toughness on the field, the sure-handed ace gained experience as a hurler in the summer of 1907. The intense interest in local baseball had died down quite a bit by the time Hickory Bob made his first appearance for a joint Morenci/Clifton club on Labor Day, facing a talented nine from Albuquerque who had imported their own ace hurler for the match. Harmon was given a chance with a stern warning from his manager, who barked, "I'll jerk you when you run into trouble."[13] Harmon wouldn't need much help that afternoon as he put up a few scoreless innings to record a 4–3 victory, tying the Labor Day series with Albuquerque at one game each. He left Morenci for a short while to give semi-professional ball a try in Portland, Oregon, where he reported for practice on March 1, 1908. Although he was released after only one month on the club, he did manage to record a win, later joking that he finished that season with the highest win percentage of any pitcher in the league.

He returned to Morenci for the 1908 campaign on May 1 and recorded 146 strikeouts in his first 12 outings over 12 strike outs per game. Not bad for what the professional nines considered "sand lot" baseball! His outstanding performance that season earned him another shot at professional baseball, this time in Shreveport, Louisiana, when he pitched a no-hitter in June 1909. This initial success, combined with additional seasoning in Arizona, proved him good enough to be sent up to the major leagues, where he pitched for the St. Louis Cardinals and Pittsburgh Pirates.

With Arizona becoming more regularly traveled due to the dependable railroad service through most parts of the territory, future big league clubs were more certain that a stop in Yuma, Tucson, or Phoenix would be profitable while keeping a tight travel schedule for post-season games or early spring training. The first tour of a professional nine through the Arizona Territory came in 1909, by the Chicago White Sox, led by magnate Charles Comiskey. Their tour embarked from Chicago on February 28, as noted by the *Bisbee Daily Review*, aboard a special train that would carry the 30-man squad to California. After a few days of practice designed to eliminate the winter weight put on by ball players from inactivity and drinking, the squad was split into two squads who would each take a different route back to Chicago. Dubbed "the longest in point of traveling that has ever been taken by a professional ball team,"[14] the tour covered roughly 14,000 miles of railroad travel across the country.

One group headed to New Orleans and the Southern states, while the second squad toured the western United States, with special stops in Yuma, Tucson, Bisbee, Douglas and Phoenix, before embarking eastward to El Paso with a predicted arrival back in Chicago on April 13. Due to time constraints, and perhaps a lack of funds, only Yuma and Tucson saw baseball games between the White Sox and the best players each town could find. The baseball men of Tucson, notably Manny Drachman, were nervous about trying to lure Comiskey's professional players to Tucson, as the year prior similar arrangements had been offered but turned down due to no gate receipt guarantee being in place. In a letter to Manny Drachman, Charles Comiskey noted that he was "offered 85 percent of the gross gate receipts," but refused, wanting more."[15] It came as no surprise that the players appeared in Yuma and Tucson were mostly second-rate substitutes for the White Sox, who finished third in 1908 at 88–64, one-and-a-half games behind the American League champion Detroit Tigers.

The three games in Arizona figured into the 75 spring training games played by both White Sox squads during the spring 1909 tour. The *Arizona Daily Star* announced on March 13 that a celebration of the new Laguna Dam, spanning the Lower Colorado River, would be held in Yuma on March 30–31. Expected to be a state-wide event drawing scores of people from across Arizona, it included a grand parade, fireworks and baseball games to mark the completion of the construction project undertaken by the U.S. Reclamation Service to harness the power of the Colorado River, provide more available water for irrigation, and prevent destructive flooding that had plagued the area for decades. The *Daily Star* called the dam project "one of the finest engineering feats of modern times" while issuing the invitation to visit Yuma in order to "get acquainted with our country." Two weeks later, the *Arizona Sentinel* announced that the White Sox would indeed play in Yuma against a local nine as a part of the festivities planned for Tuesday, March 30, 1909.

Naturally, word of the White Sox visiting Arizona spread like wild fire. The Southern Pacific Railroad would carry interested parties on special trains running along the southwestern route from Los Angeles through Yuma and Tucson, and from as far eastbound as El Paso. The special fare from Phoenix was $7 per passenger for the round-trip, leaving at 8 a.m. "city time" in order to arrive before the ball game started at 2:30 that afternoon. Newspapers in Phoenix and Tucson advertised the first game in Yuma, while trying to lure the White Sox to their towns. Several offers were made by the Phoenix and Tucson clubs, with only Tucson being scheduled for games on March 31 at the grounds on Elysian Grove. The *Arizona Daily Star* reprinted the telegram received by Mr. Bicknell, traffic manager for the Tucson leg of the S & P Railroad line, from Charles Fredericks, Secretary of the White Sox. The telegram announced that the 25 players would arrive at the Tucson depot at 5:55 a.m. and asked for accommodations at a hotel with meal service for breakfast and lunch that day. The *Daily Star* called for "a few hours' holiday" when all stores in town would close from 2 to 5 p.m. to allow "fans and otherwise a chance to see the world's champions in action."[16] While the cranks in the Old Pueblo bubbled with anticipation of the arrival of Comiskey's White Sox, there was the matter of a ball game the day prior in Yuma.

The *Chicago Daily Tribune* announced on March 31, the morning after the game in Yuma, that it was a "Gala Day for Sox at Yuma," adding that there was joy in finishing the dam project, despite "Comiskey's Warriors" finding the locals to be easy picking. Transmitted by "H.E.K.," a special correspondent to the *Daily Tribune*, via telegraph to the editors, it described Yuma as "the Gate City of the Greater Southwest," citing the inscription on the arch spanning Main Street and heading eastward into Yuma. The article noted the lavish decorations for the celebration and a parade over one mile long, or as the article described it, "a quarter mile longer than the town." The "place was choked with miscellaneous people who came from hundreds of miles around to take part in it or look at it."

The game between a picked nine from Yuma and the formidable Sox was the featured event of the first day's festivities. Only four Yuma citizens took part in the game, as most of the locals were too frightened to compete against the professionals. The game came off without a hitch, as a reported 3,000 spectators crowded around the grounds for the exhibition game. Chicago won easily, with newly signed Jim Scott pitching the entire game, striking out four while holding the hometown nine to only one run and two hits. During the 1909 season, Scott went 12–12 with a 2.30 ERA in 36 appearances. The only Yuma player to record a run was Charley Parks, who was hit by a pitch and advanced all the way around the bases on errors and sacrifice hits. Parks played center field for the Yuma nine and pulled off a rare double play in the sixth inning. Despite the combined nine errors by both clubs, the game was considered a success. The White Sox won easily, 9–1, though the erroneous score of 8–1 was reported the next day by the *Arizona Daily Star*. With the ball game and day one of the dam festivities over, the White Sox boarded their train and departed for Tucson and the next challenge from a local nine.

The *Arizona Daily Star* trumpeted the excitement of the appearance of the White Sox on March 31, running several articles the day before and day of the scheduled game, in hopes of drawing an immense paying crowd at the ball park. The group of 25, including the ball players' wives and staff from the White Sox, took up residence at the Hotel Heidel. The new hotel, completed in 1907, offered a striking new triangular design and was made entirely from brick made by the Tucson Pressed Brick Company (TPBC). Located near the railroad depot on Toole Avenue in the eastern portion of downtown Tucson, it offered an easy trip after a long and tiring journey by rail into town, comfortable lodging and a hot meal. After years of operation, the hotel was remodeled and renamed the MacArthur Hotel in 1944. The hotel closed in 1979, sitting vacant until a public works project endorsed by the City of Tucson renovated the building for use as office space in 1985. After the White Sox arrived, they were met at the railroad depot and escorted to the hotel for breakfast, before a tour of the area. Later on came lunch before the baseball game, with the evening's entertainment arranged to take place at the Tucson Opera House.

Ah yes, the game! The game between the exhibition nine and a reported group from Tucson was indeed held at Elysian Grove. Both the *Arizona Daily Star* and *Tucson Citizen* covered the event, and the *Arizona Republican* of Phoenix, by way of special correspondent, printed several articles describing the action on the diamond. After the enormous crowd of 3,000 in Yuma, the game in Tucson drew only 400–500 interested spectators. The *Tucson Citizen* noted that "there was some dissatisfaction because the White Sox did not split up their team and loan Tucson some infielders instead of all pitchers." It was understandable that a manager of a professional club did not want to break up an infield owing to the need for practice as a complete unit. The *Citizen* also reprinted the article that was telegraphed back to Chicago by legendary sportswriter Charles Ambrose Hughes.

Though "most of the Tucson ball team had been mislaid through someone carelessness,"[17] the two clubs scoured Tucson to find willing participants for the game. Only four local Tucsonans took part in the game against the professionals. The *Arizona Daily Star* reported them to be "Sallinger, Wood, Knight and Hudson." Knight was from Albany, New York, and had spent the previous season pitching in the New York State League. The *Daily Star* also mentioned that Ed Walsh would "heave the pellets for the White Legs" and that the remaining Tucson team would be selected from left-over players amongst the visitors. The newspapers dubbed the affair as "When Sox met Sox," which was all too accurate. The result was a lopsided affair that saw the White Sox regulars crush the ball for 22 hits, driving in 17 runs. Masterful pitching by a young man known only as Miller held the other Sox and the four brave Tucsonans to seven hits, with four runs crossing the plate. The *Arizona Daily Star* labeled the game as "a picnic, as it were, without the fried chicken and boiled eggs."[18]

Despite the good nature of the visitors, the *Arizona Republican* took offense at the players loaned to the Tucson club, calling the affair "an act of duplicity which has but one counterpart in all of history—when the Greeks fed a wooden horse a belly full of fighting men to be smuggled inside the walls of Troy."[19] Citing this and the aid of swirling winds in the Yuma game as the real cause of the White Sox being undefeated in the 1909 tour of Arizona, such sour grapes on behalf of the *Republican* writer may have been an outward expression of frustration that the touring visitors failed to arrange a ball game in Phoenix. The White Sox took things in stride, making the two-hour, five-minute affair as much fun as possible. When the last out was recorded, the clubs retired to dinner at the Hotel Heidel, then enjoyed an evening of entertainment courtesy of the Local

6. The Barnstormers

Order Of Eagles at the Tucson Opera House. The Sox departed early the next morning, headed east to El Paso on their way home to begin the 1909 season.

The barnstorming tours weren't quite done for 1909. Later in the summer, the El Paso Browns visited Bisbee for the first games in the newly built ballpark in Warren. Still standing silent today, the historic and legendary Warren Ballpark has witnessed some truly great moments in baseball history. Originally built as a part of the "City Beautiful" project started on May 17, the park was finally finished on June 25, 1909, with the first official game played two days later due to a rainout. Originally costing $3,600 in 1909 (approximately $92,307.69 in 2013 dollars as adjusted for the current rate of inflation), the new park represented a new era of baseball in Arizona, one that encouraged clubs far and wide to come to Bisbee for games. When the weather finally cooperated enough to allow the first game at the newly built wooden park, the Bisbee club faced a good club from El Paso in front of an enthusiastic crowd, most of whom utilized the newly built trolley system serving Bisbee. The trolley line was a distinct feature of the new ball grounds operated by the Warren-Bisbee Railway, which charged a dime per passenger for the trip to the ball park. Over 500 fans packed their way onto the trolleys for the trip to the inaugural game on Sunday, June 27. While the Bisbee nine were victors on the field, 8 to 6, the real winner was the trolley line. The new park and trolley way proved a successful partnership in bringing baseball from far and wide into Bisbee. The park, which still stands today, would host the New York Giants World Tour of 1913, featuring the biggest stars of the sporting world, including John McGraw, Christy Mathewson, Tris Speaker and Jim Thorpe. The park would also stand to see disgraced players such as Chick Gandil, Buck Weaver and Hal Chase resume their baseball careers in the Outlaw Leagues of the 1920s.

In the meantime, Phoenix had to wait until the following spring before attracting a big league club to play an exhibition game against their beloved and storied Phoenix Base Ball Club. After the success of the White Sox tour of 1909 through Yuma and Tucson, arrangements were finally put in order by officers of both clubs for an exhibition game in March of 1910. Having completed another spring training trip to the California coast, the Sox were again returning home for the opening of the regular season. The *Arizona Republican* proudly announced on the front page of the March 23 edition, "White Sox to Play Game in Phoenix." The short article noted the players making the stop in Phoenix, most notably first baseman Chick Gandil. The game was scheduled for March 29 at the ball park in Eastlake Park. Anticipation ran high, prompting the *Republican* to declare, "The Best Game Ever Played in Arizona May Reasonably Be Expected" in a sub-headline, adding "there will be an immense crowd out to witness it."[20]

The following day, the headlines of newspapers across Arizona read "PHOENIX HITS WHITE SOX OVER DIAMOND"[21] and "WHITE SOX RAGGED GAME."[22] The game was error-filled and quite a disappointment to the baseball fans who packed the grounds of Eastlake Park in hopes of seeing professional-level baseball. Getting to the ball park in 1910 Phoenix was, by today's standards, an adventure in its own. Most early Phoenicians rode their own horses or drove a buggy or wagon to the game. The wealthy may have taken their own REO Speedwagon to Eastlake Park. For those who didn't have transportation, were traveling in large groups, or could afford the fare, the Phoenix Rail Way System was the answer. Opened in 1887, it would accommodate most Phoenicians eager to get to the ball park and all points in between on a rapidly advancing line that was first electrified in 1893. By 1909, horse-drawn trolleys were extinct, and by 1911 the entire line operated under electric power as Phoenix itself raced into the future. Telephone lines crossed downtown, while modern automobiles and early bicycle-like motorcycles made initial appearances as oddities on the cobbled streets and rutted roads of one of Arizona's emerging cities. The electric trolley cars offered more comfort to passengers and brought the owners bigger profits, charging a scant five cents for a one-way trip to the baseball grounds at Eastlake Park on 16th Street and Jefferson. For the cranks in attendance, a disappointing effort was shown by the visiting Chicagos, who lost to the home nine by a wide margin, 16–5. The Chicago club lent the Phoenix B.B.C. three players to make up their entire outfield, while veteran newspaper reporter Hugh S. Fullerton, who traveled with the White Sox, filled in at right field for the visiting Sox. It was an error-filled contest, certainly not what early Phoenicians paid to see. At one point the heckling of the crowd kept pace with the errors being made on the field of play, with one small boy loudly pleading with the players on the field, sarcastically calling for "five cents worth of baseball."[23] Adult spectators voiced their displeasure as well, in more vocal and vulgar terms deemed too strong for newsprint.

To the delight of the hometown crowd, they witnessed newspaperman Fullerton hit a sharp drive to right field in the seventh inning for a single. Hoping to take advantage of the hurler for Phoenix, he started to stroll innocently towards second base. "Smack!" rang out as the ball quickly hit the first baseman's mitt, catching Fullerton off the base for the out.

6. The Barnstormers 167

The crowd erupted in loud, rapturous cheering and applause. Just as the crowd settled down, Chick Gandil, later the infamous first baseman of the ill-fated Black Sox, drove a towering home run. Game time was a quick one hour and 15 minutes. The *Arizona Republican* noted that the game between the Tempe Normal School and Mesa High School was far more interesting than this one, and the game report confirmed it. No mention was made about the departure of the White Sox, and rightly so. Early Phoenicians could be a fickle bunch, especially when it came to good baseball. They always demanded a "square game" from their local nines and visiting challengers.

The following spring a split squad of Boston Red Sox paid a visit to Yuma for an exhibition match with local baseball enthusiasts. Traveling with the train carrying the American League stars was veteran baseball player and early *Boston Globe* sports writer, Timothy Murnane. Recalling his exploits as a ballist for the early Boston National League and later Union Association Clubs, he tagged along in 1911, filing game reports via telegraph or telephone for the *Globe.* The game played by the Red Sox was historic on at least one count. It was the first game the club ever played outside of the United States proper, as Arizona was still a territory in 1911. Statehood was mere months away. According to the excellent chronicle of the journey titled *The Great Red Sox Spring Training Tour of 1911*, by the resilient researcher and writer Bill Nowlin, the population of Yuma County was only 7,733 in 1910, and he expresses doubt about whether there may have been many "self-confident baseball players among them." While this may have been the case in 1911, Yuma had once been a regional powerhouse on the diamond with roots of the game stretching back to 1875.

The Red Sox players, their wives and the press corps that accompanied them were met on the morning of March 27 by Newt Parks, chief of the Yuma Fire Department. Acting as the head of the town booster club, Parks brought a crowd complete with marching band and automobiles for the honored guests to officially greet the Red Sox on behalf of the city of Yuma. Mr. Parks was charged with arranging entertainment for the players, including a small group who had arrived early, featuring outfielder George Edward "Duffy" Lewis. Though he came from Alameda, California, the *Yuma Morning Sun* declared, "Yuma claims Duffy as her own."[24] The group was chauffeured by automobile to sites of interest around the Yuma valley before the 2:30 start time. After lunch at the Gandolfo Hotel, the players from Boston and their four brave competitors from town assembled under sunny skies on the dry, rocky and sandy grounds of the

Red Sox of 1911 posed in front of the "Red Sox Special," heading east towards El Paso on a barnstorming tour originating from Point Loma, California. (Boston Public Library, Michael T. McGreevey Collection)

local baseball diamond at Athletic Park. Tim Murnane called it a "tropical sun working overtime"[25] in describing the intense desert heat felt by everyone in attendance that afternoon.

The crowd was small by comparison to most of the crowds the Red Sox contingent would see for the rest of the tour back to Boston. The cranks numbered 350, with some 300 of them being soldiers from Troop A, 5th Cavalry of the U.S. Army. The soldiers had set up camp adjacent to the ball grounds, being stationed in Yuma to defend U.S. soil from incursions by Mexican bandits led by revolutionary Pancho Villa. The playing field was substandard at worst and questionable at best to the professionals. Describing it as "a joke" was being kind. Red Sox trainer Doc Green said, "No sand lot ever held more sand; the grand stand was a bleacher, with a covering formed by palm leaves."[26] Another correspondent from Boston, Paul Shannon of the *Boston Post*, joked that the field resembled rough ground complete with "an army encampment for the left field boundary, a big horse corral in centre field, and an outfield composed of mostly cactus, sage brush, and glittering sand."[27] This field was the setting for another first. Later that October, aviator Robert Fowler would land his Wright Model B biplane there while on a cross-country flight from Santa Monica, California, to somewhere in Florida. In 2010, a monument was erected in Yuma to mark the event.

Adding insult to injury was the fact that only four men from Yuma volunteered to play against the big leaguers. The Red Sox would have to loan the other club players to make sure a game could be played. Counted as the "local boys" for the contest were Duffy Lewis, Dan Maddox, and fleet-footed "Chico" Morales who nearly hit a home run against Red Sox hurler Eddie Cicotte. The *Yuma Morning Sun* reported that the umpire was a member of the "military visitors" that were in town. He called the game with "the power of the United States army behind him, [and] he handed out decisions with the haughty scorn of the impotent vociferications [sic] of the populist."[28] To put it bluntly, he officiated the game despite the howling, cat-calls and heckling of the crowd which continually disagreed with his decisions.

As far as baseball games go, there wasn't much to see. The players from Yuma did their best, and the Red Sox, despite loaning out quite a few players, put a drubbing on the local nine, 17 to 5. After surviving the game and climate, the group boarded their train at 6 p.m. and departed for a brief stop in Tucson for dinner while a change of engines took place, before heading for another game in El Paso, Texas. Organizers from Tucson had missed the game and perhaps the opportunity to entice the barnstorming Sox to stop for a game as well against the finest ball tossers from the Old Pueblo.

The "barnstorming" era was far richer than what can be retold in these pages. Once connected to each other, towns inside and outside the territory would make bigger strides in traveling to compete against clubs far and wide. Moreover, even ball players like Bob Harmon and John Meyers saw the clubs in Arizona as a way to get experience while trying to catch on with the semi-professional nines in California, the Midwest and Eastern leagues. Barnstorming opened the territory to new visitors and brought publicity about Arizona to other parts of the country that there was more than gunfights, red-light ladies and mining development going on here. Eventually, the professional ball clubs would return—in 1913— as the New York Giants World Tour led by John McGraw stopped in Douglas and Bisbee for games on their way to the West Coast. In 1927, the Detroit Tigers established a spring training camp in Mesa. The Cactus

League blossomed much later, but that story is for another chapter or book perhaps. Barnstorming took baseball to another level of popularity in Arizona. By 1900 most newspapers were published on a daily basis and included some kind of dedicated "sports page" or column for baseball enthusiasts. In previous decades most newspapers were weekly publications with baseball reported on an inconsistent basis. Local clubs and players that traveled benefitted from the publicity. Towns in Arizona were still competing with each other for business development through outside investment and old fashioned civic pride. A ball club that could win at home and abroad helped foster the impression that living or doing business in that town was somehow more desirable.

Baseball helped convince Americans across the country that Arizona was keeping pace with the changing times. Along with increased tourism and commerce, the territory as a whole experienced continued population growth which spurred on the development of technology. In years to come, the game and those who played it would take Arizona from frontier territory to newly admitted state.

Summary

So, what have we learned through the previous six chapters? First and foremost, there is ample evidence in the preceding chapters that baseball, labeled as the "National Game," was brought to the Arizona Territory by the soldiers of the U.S. Army during the Indian Wars period. Although we do not know who specifically introduced baseball to the military posts from the 1870s through the end of the 19th century, we know it was brought westward by soldiers transferring to new duty stations in the untamed frontier of Arizona. The games played by the early military clubs provide a glimpse of a more simple time, when young soldiers used their free time constructively to engage in baseball games with each other and then, over time, with citizens of nearby towns such as Phoenix, Tucson, Tombstone, Bisbee and Yuma. Baseball equipment consisted of nothing more than a bat and a ball, also most likely handmade. Uniforms were simple, too, if a club chose to outfit themselves in one. A club might have a good seamstress on post, or would order uniforms from suppliers such as Spalding or Reach, who had retailers in Los Angeles and Denver, making sporting goods available by stage or rail from 1881 through the 1890s. Simply put, uniforms, bats, balls and later catcher's gear and gloves were uncommonly expensive. An early club required the support of the entire community to be outfitted properly. Most elected to play in their daily clothing and make their own bases and bats, and perhaps attempt a homemade ball.

We've also seen how inconsistently the results and details of early games were reported to the early Arizona newspapers like the *Arizona Sentinel*, *Arizona Daily Citizen*, *Arizona Weekly Star*, *Arizona Republican*, *Tombstone Epitaph* and *Arizona Journal-Miner*. The games were reported only when the copy space was available in a weekly or eventual daily edition. Often a box score, game account or even final score was omitted from a newspaper because the reporter either forgot to include it or found something more interesting to report. This doesn't mean the games did not happen, just that the details are lost in the mists of time. Eventually sports reporting was refined to include rudimentary box scores, line scores and a more complete game report. The early newspapers were rife with misspelled names, confusing readers of the day and modern researchers about the true identity of the men who played baseball on the rough and rocky grounds that were crudely, but effectively leveled and marked out for play.

When newspapers covering larger cities like Phoenix and Tucson gained recognition as professional journalistic efforts, the reporting of baseball and other sporting pastimes evolved into a more familiar form. Early on, mentions of baseball games and related activities of the home nine were mixed within columns appropriately labeled "Talk of the Town" or "Local Happenings." This tactic was employed by editors to keep a subscribed reader coming back for more. Separated "sports" sections wouldn't appear in the major newspapers of the territory until well after 1900. Baseball helped Arizona's early journalists fall in line with the reporting style of newspapers in large cities like San Francisco, Chicago and New York City.

We've also seen that the early town clubs from Tombstone, Tucson, Phoenix, Tempe, Mesa, Prescott, Bisbee, Flagstaff and Winslow were an immense source of civic pride. The three elements that marked a successful town were to have an opera, a good saloon or two, and a winning baseball nine. The success of a town's baseball club gave a resident something to boast about to associates in other towns in the territory as well as relatives living in other parts of the country. This view spurred on economic expansion, a key element in the growth and survival of early settlements in Arizona. As the territory grew with the introduction of the railroads in the early 1880s, clubs from across the state could travel farther than ever before to compete against other towns at Territorial Fairs and Fourth of July festivities. In many instances, these games fostered town rivalries which continue to this day.

We've even seen a bit of theatrical trickery. The first declared "championship" contest held in May of 1876 pitted the Prescott Champions versus the soldiers from nearby Fort Whipple. Most of the members of the Prescott Champions were also accomplished actors and singers, comprising the Prescott Minstrels group that regularly toured to other towns in the Arizona and New Mexico Territories. In addition to singing well, it's very possible that they followed the games and other happenings of the

National Association. During the winter meetings of 1875–1876, the Association was disbanded in favor of creating the new National League under direction of William A. Hulbert, who had been a financial backer of the Chicago White Stockings since the club's inception in 1871. Today, the same White Stockings of 19th-century lore are known as the Chicago Cubs. After the Great Chicago fire in October 1871, the club resumed play two years later with Hulbert serving as club president. Eventually he became the architect of the National League.

To the men of the Prescott Champions, following baseball in the newspapers from Chicago, St. Louis, New York and Boston served to ignite their imaginations, especially the game reports of the National Association champion Boston Red Stockings. In 1875, Boston won the championship by 15 games over the second-place club from Philadelphia. This feat marked four titles in a row for Boston. The Prescott Champions most likely followed the Red Stockings' on-field exploits in the *Boston Daily Globe.* They got the idea of impersonating their baseball idols for the big game against the soldiers, most likely as a feint designed to strike a bit of fear into their opponents to win the crown and the betting purse that was likely to have been negotiated. Whatever their true reasoning for the ruse was, it translated into very early baseball history, paving the way for many more games in Prescott and northern Arizona.

From there, we've waltzed through history while seeing evidence of baseball growing in relationship with the development of the railroad lines first introduced in Yuma in 1879, and in Tucson two years later. The early newspapers in Tucson had their own baseball clubs, even for just a brief season in the sun during the 1879 campaign that saw the *Arizona Weekly Citizen* and *Arizona Daily Star* compete for the Star Cup. The action was intense, but after a winner was declared, both clubs disbanded and were absorbed into a more permanent nine representing Tucson as a whole. From there, the rivalry between Tucson and Tombstone grew, with some very good games taking place for very large prize money. Soon town clubs were appearing all over the territory. Phoenix, Fort McDowell, and a rejuvenated club from Prescott joined the baseball scene in 1881.

Throughout the remainder of the 1880s, baseball action was sporadic. Due to uncertain economic conditions across the territory and rampant losses of life and property due to fire and flood, baseball at times seemed secondary, almost distant to the foremost concerns of pioneering Arizonans. For the most part, the more densely populated towns in the 1880s, like Tombstone and Tucson, staged more consistent baseball games, at least as reported in the newspapers. Once the "Gay Nineties" fell in, baseball took another step towards wide popularity. Sporting goods shops like Ezra W. Thayer opened in downtown Phoenix, soon offering baseball goods from Spalding, Reach and others for the consummate players and fans.

Notably, the development of widespread railroad lines did much to advance baseball across the territory and into other states like New Mexico, California and even Mexico. Ball clubs, with rooters in tow, could now play in faraway places that had once been unthought-of or too expensive to get to on a stage line. The railroads boosted industry and tourism. As more lines were added, ticket prices would fall. Railroads often ran "specials" on round-trip fares to baseball games for holidays or large tournaments. The national game found a friend in the railroads. Soon, the workers of the railroads had clubs of their own, playing when they had time away from the line work or repair shops. Quite a few of the early railroad clubs were comprised of blacksmiths and linemen. It wasn't long until the mines took notice, encouraging nines of their own as a way of controlling their often rowdy laborers, albeit in an enjoyable manner.

One of the things that stands out from today's perspective is the eventual blurring of the unspoken color line. The early newspapers often labeled black players with derogatory names. Early Hispanic and later African American baseball clubs helped advance equality first by demonstrating that they too could handle a bat, catch and throw as well as any white man could. The first inter-racial club, the Tempe Crimson Rims, also paved the way as the first club to have whites, Hispanics and one African American ballplayer on the same nine. They took on all comers from 1899–1906 with a record of resounding success in the early Salt River valley.

With Arizona growing by leaps and bounds in population and economically, and embracing new technology such as electricity, railroads, and later the telephone and early automobiles, the professional clubs of the National League took notice. By the early 1900s, most clubs were conducting an early form of "spring training" in California. There they enjoyed the moderate winter climate so they could boil, or sweat off unhealthy winter weight that ball players were known to pack on by way of copious amounts of alcohol and poor food. Arizona was simply "on the way home" for clubs from Chicago, New York and Boston. It took a few years for organizers in Tucson and Phoenix to agree on arrangements with the ownership of the White Sox, Red Sox and later Giants. The games were attended by large crowds showing enthusiastic zeal for the game and their home nine. By the time the professional clubs came through Arizona in successive tours every fall, Arizonans had come to expect a higher level of play or "a fast" game. Sometimes the professionals delivered, sometimes they fell on the diamond to a strong local club. Either way the White Sox, Red Sox and Giants were an enormous draw. This ensured large gate receipts, which pleased the club owners and local businessmen who had invested in the enclosed wooden grandstands of early parks like Eastlake Park in Phoenix.

Arizona was even treated to the sight of a group of women, all professionals, playing baseball. Despite losing games in Phoenix, they stirred the imaginations and piqued the curiosity of early Phoenicians. They did well enough to encourage local organizers to keep up efforts to persuade the regular professionals to add Phoenix and Tucson to their list of stops on the way home from winter training in California. Even early women's clubs, although barely reported in the pages of the *Arizona Republican*, caused quite a stir by stepping onto a local diamond to challenge a group of young men to a match. They caused even more of an uproar by winning the contest!

In writing this book, I hope I have dispelled a few myths about Arizona. Hopefully, I have shown here that there was far more going on than gunfights, cattle rustling or any other subject matter that serves as fodder for TV and movie Westerns. Early Arizonans wanted the same comforts relatives had in other parts of the nation. Baseball seemed to be a natural fit, as the game was sweeping the rest of the nation. Why not Arizona?

I also hope that the material presented has fascinated you, dear reader. I have labored to relate the goings-on in the pages of early newspapers in a way that would draw a reader in, and I hope I have accomplished such a large task. I also hope that in the years to come, more historical documents are found relating to this topic. I honestly believe that there is more material out there beyond the newspaper articles on microfilm, simply hiding in attics, untouched and underappreciated family collections of the men who played this glorious American game on Arizona's dry and rocky soil over 100 years ago. Finding those items is my one eternal and solitary wish. I hope to see it fulfilled in my lifetime.

In closing, I thank you. Thank you for reading. Thank you for taking a trip with me back through time when Arizona was far more wild, exuberant and interesting than it is today. I hope you've enjoyed reading about it as much as I enjoyed discovering the facts used in creating this work. Again, I thank you. I only have one last thing to add: PLAY BALL!! HURRAH!!

Appendix A: List of Active Arizona Territorial Newspapers, 1863 to 1912

The Arizona Champion (Peach Springs/Flagstaff, Mohave County) 1883–1891
The Arizona Daily Orb (Bisbee) 1898–1900
Arizona Daily Republican (Phoenix) 1890–1900.
The Arizona Daily Star (Tucson) 1879–present Day
Arizona Journal Miner (Prescott) 1864–1912
Arizona Miner (Prescott) 1868–1877
The Arizona Sentinel (Yuma) 1872–1911.
The Arizona Silver Belt (Globe City, Pinal County) 1878–1906
The Arizona Weekly Citizen (Tucson) 1881–1901.
Arizona Weekly Gazette (Phoenix) 1881–1887(?)
Arizona Weekly Republican (Phoenix) 1892–1899
The Arizona Weekly Star (Tucson) 1877–1907.
Bisbee Daily Review 1901–1971
The Clifton Clarion (Clifton, Graham County) 1883–1889.
The Coconino Weekly Sun (Flagstaff) 1891–1896.
Daily Arizona Silver Belt (Globe) 1906–1929.
The Daily Tombstone (Tombstone) 1885–1886.
The Douglas Daily Dispatch (Douglas) 1903–1961
The Graham County Bulletin (Safford, Thatcher, Pima) 1890–1897
Mohave County Miner (Mineral Park, Ariz. Terr.) 1882–1918.
Phoenix Herald 1879–1900.
Salt River Herald (Phoenix) 1878–1879
Tombstone Daily Epitaph (Tombstone) 1887–1890.
Tubac Arizonian, 1858 (published one year only).
The Valley Bulletin (Graham County) 1889–1891
The Weekly Orb (Bisbee, Cochise County) 1896–1900
The Yuma Weekly Sun (Yuma) 1896–1934

Appendix B: Chronological List of Base Ball Clubs During the Territorial Period

Independent B.B.C. of Camp Hualpai (1872)
Whipple Base Ball Club of Fort Whipple (1876; 1880–1902)
Champions BBC of Prescott (1876)
Lone Star BBC of Tucson (1877)
Worth BBC of Fort Lowell, a.k.a. the Lowells (1877)
Fort Verde Excelsiors (1879–1884)
Norvall Club of Fort McDowell (1881)
Tucson BBC (1881–1900)
Prescott B.B.C. (1880–1886; 1887–1895)
Grand Centrals of Tombstone: (1883–1885)
San Pedro Boys (1883)
Boston Mill Nine (1883)
Globe Base Ball Club (1884–1885)
Tombstone Reds (1884–1885)
Winslow Nine (1885–1888)
Phoenix BBC (1880–1883; 1887–1895)
Tombstone Tigers (1887–1888)
Young Americans BBC of Flagstaff (1889)
Stringtown Nine (1891–194)
Flagstaff Nine (1887–1896)
Tempe Crimson Rims (1899–1906)
The Mesa Diamond Club (1880; 1897–1904)
Arizona Apaches, of Phoenix Indian School (1899–1901)
The DeMunds (1899–1903)
True Blues (1899–1901)
Union Stars (1899–1901)
Cyclones (1899–1900)

Cracker Jacks (1899–1900)
The Yucatecs (1899–1900)
Shirley's Bully's (1899)
Bolton's Possumala's (1899)
The Congress B.B.C. (1899)
Bisbee Copper Kings (1899–1901)
Tempe O.K.'s (1906–1909)
Phoenix Colored Cubs (1908–1911)
Winslow Cardinals (1909–1911)

Chapter Notes

Chapter 1

1. George Kirsch, "Bats, Balls, Baseball during the Civil War," *The Civil War Times Illustrated* (May 1998), 34.
2. Harold Seymour, *Baseball: The People's Game* (New York: Oxford University Press, 1990), 298.
3. *Arizona Miner*, April 27, 1872, 3.
4. *Arizona Miner*, January 11, 1873.
5. Douglas McChristian, *Fort Bowie Arizona: Combat Post of the Southwest, 1858–1894* (Norman: University Press of Oklahoma, 2005), 221.
6. *Army and Navy Journal*, December 20, 1873. Vol. XI, No. 19, 293.
7. *Arizona Sentinel*, February 5, 1876.
8. *Arizona Sentinel*, March 18, 1876.
9. *Arizona Sentinel*, March 25, 1876.
10. *The Arizona Daily Star*, November 29, 1877.
11. *The Weekly Arizona Miner*, May 20, 1881, 3.
12. Alexander Family Letters, November 2, 1868, 2.
13. *Weekly Arizona Miner*, January 15, 1875.
14. *The Phoenix Herald*, January 2, 1880.
15. *The Phoenix Herald*, January 16, 1880.
16. *Ibid.*
17. *Ibid.*
18. *Phoenix Weekly Herald*, January 24, 1880.
19. *Arizona Weekly Herald*, January 3, 1881.
20. *Arizona Weekly Gazette*, January 17, 1881.
21. *The Tombstone*, March 23, 1885.
22. *The Daily Tombstone*, November 26, 1886.
23. *Tombstone Prospector*, May 31, 1893.
24. *The Oasis*, April 27, 1907.
25. *Arizona Silver Belt*, April 12, 1884.
26. *Arizona Silver Belt*, September 20, 1884.
27. *Arizona Silver Belt*, October 18, 1884.
28. Harold Seymour, *Baseball*, 294.
29. *Arizona Silver Belt*, November 8, 1884.
30. *The Arizona Silver Belt*, March 7, 1891.
31. *The Arizona Daily Star*, September 15, 1895.
32. *The Arizona Republican*, September 19, 1895.

Chapter 2

1. *Arizona Weekly Miner*, May 26, 1876.
2. *Arizona Weekly Miner*, March 16, 1877.
3. A "ballist" is the 19th-century term for a baseball player.
4. *Arizona Weekly Miner*, May 5, 1876.
5. *Ibid.*
6. *Bridgeport Banner*, "A Fitting Tribute for Orator Jim," June 17, 2009.
7. David Nemec, *The Great Encyclopedia of 19th-Century Major League Baseball* (Tuscaloosa: University of Alabama Press), 94.
8. Nemec, *Encyclopedia of 19th-Century Major League Baseball*, 197–199.
9. A "sack" is the 19th-century term for a base or bag. It also applies to a base-

man or base tender; a first-baseman was known as "first sack" or "first sacker."
10. "Left gardener" is the 19th century term for a left fielder.
11. *New York Clipper*, May 27, 1876.
12. *Arizona Weekly Miner*, January 26, 1877.
13. *Tombstone Epitaph*, October 13, 1895.

Chapter 3

1. *Phoenix Gazette*, November 1, 1887.
2. *Arizona Sentinel*, February 21, 1874.
3. *Arizona Sentinel*, December 1, 1888.
4. *Arizona Sentinel*, January 26, 1889.
5. *The Arizona Weekly Star*, November 29, 1877.
6. George O Hand, and Neil Carmony, *Whiskey, Six-Guns and Red Light Ladies: George Hand's Saloon Diary, Tucson 1875–1878*, edited by Neil Carmony, 2nd Edition (Silver City, NM: High-Lonesome Books, 1995).
7. *Arizona Weekly Star*, December 26, 1878.
8. *The Arizona Daily Citizen*, July 3, 1879.
9. *The Arizona Daily Citizen*, November 11, 1879.
10. *Arizona Daily Citizen*, November 24, 1879.
11. *Arizona Daily Citizen*, November 27, 1879.
12. *Arizona Daily Citizen*, December 12, 1879.
13. *Arizona Daily Citizen*, February 2, 1880.
14. *The Daily Nugget*, May 6, 1882.
15. *Arizona Daily Star*, May 12, 1882.
16. *Arizona Daily Star*, May 17, 1882.
17. *The Weekly Epitaph*, June 10, 1882.
18. *Arizona Daily Citizen*, June 5, 1889.
19. *Arizona Daily Citizen*, July 1, 1889.
20. *Arizona Daily Citizen*, August 19, 1889.
21. *Arizona Daily Citizen*, May 14, 1890.
22. *Arizona Daily Citizen*, June 16, 1890.
23. Roy P. Drachman, *This Is Not a Book: Just Memories* (R.P. Drachman, 1979), 29.
24. *The Arizona Daily Citizen*, August 11, 1890.
25. *The Arizona Daily Citizen*, September 5, 1890.
26. *The Arizona Daily Citizen*, May 23, 1893.
27. *The Phoenix Gazette*, June 23, 1893.
28. *The Tombstone Prospector*, July 12, 1893.
29. *The Arizona Daily Citizen*, July 31, 1893.
30. *The Salt River Herald*, May 18, 1878.
31. *The Salt River Herald*, June 1, 1878.
32. *The Salt River Herald*, February 12, 1879.
33. *The Phoenix Herald*, February 27, 1880.
34. *The Phoenix Herald*, January 3, 1881.
35. *The Arizona Gazette*, February 28, 1881.
36. *The Arizona Gazette*, May 15, 1882.
37. *The Arizona Gazette*, April 7, 1887.
38. *The Arizona Gazette*, April 12, 1887.
39. *The Arizona Republican*, June 1, 1890.
40. *The Arizona Republican*, July 5, 1890.
41. *The Arizona Republican*, December 1, 1899.
42. *The Arizona Republican*, January 1, 1900.
43. *The Arizona Gazette*, January 31, 1881.
44. S.J. Reidhead, *A Church for Helldorado* (Roswell, NM: Jinglebob Press, 2006), 24.
45. Journal Entry of Endicott Peabody, February 28, 1882, from Riedhead, *A Church for Helldorado*, 43.
46. *The Tombstone Weekly Republican*, July 7, 1883.
47. Katherine Bagg Hastings, Hastings Family Papers: 1882–1887.
48. *Daily Alta California*, October 19, 1886.
49. *The Arizona Democrat*, April 16, 1880.
50. *The Daily Arizona Miner*, May 8, 1880.
51. *The Arizona Daily Miner*, May 17, 1881.
52. *The Arizona Daily Miner*, April 23, 1881.
53. *The Phoenix Herald*, May 20, 1881.
54. *The Weekly Arizona Miner*, July 25, 1881.

55. *Phoenix Gazette*, October 15, 1887.
56. *The Arizona Weekly Miner*, October 26, 1887.
57. *The Arizona Daily Gazette*, October 18, 1889.
58. *The Arizona Daily Citizen*, September 24, 1890.
59. *The Arizona Gazette*, June 17, 1882.

Chapter 4

1. *The Arizona Weekly Star*, December 26, 1878.
2. *The Salt River Herald*, July 6, 1878.
3. *Arizona Sentinel*, April 3, 1886.
4. *The Arizona Daily Citizen*, August 8, 1893.
5. *The Arizona Republican*, November 3, 1890.
6. *The Weekly Arizona Republican*, February 23, 1890.
7. *The Arizona Republican*, May 3, 1891.
8. *The Arizona Republican*, November 19, 1891.
9. *The Arizona Republican*, August 17, 1899.
10. *The Arizona Republican*, September 7, 1899.
11. *The Arizona Republican*, September 11, 1899.
12. *The Phoenix Daily Herald*, September 11, 1899.
13. *Tempe Daily News*, August 21, 1899.
14. *The Arizona Republican*, September 25, 1899.
15. *The Tempe Daily News*, August 21, 1899.
16. *The Tempe Daily News*, September 1, 1899.
17. *The Arizona Republican*, September 24, 1899.
18. *The Arizona Republican*, March 6, 1899.
19. *The Tempe Daily News*, September 19, 1899.
20. *The Tempe Daily News*, August 29, 1900.
21. *The Tempe Daily News*, September 21, 1900.
22. Ibid.
23. *The Tempe Daily News*, October 26, 1900.
24. *The Daily Tombstone*, December 6, 1886.
25. *The Arizona Weekly Journal-Miner*, November 10, 1897.
26. *The Phoenix Daily Herald*, November 22, 1897.
27. *The Arizona Republican*, November 23, 1897.
28. *Mesa Free Press*, November 26, 1897.
29. *The Arizona Republican*, October 26, 1899.
30. *Bisbee Daily Review*, November 5, 1906.
31. *The Arizona Sentinel*, September 16, 1908.

Chapter 5

1. *The Arizona Daily Star*, November 11, 1879.
2. *Weekly Pinal Drill*, December 25, 1880.
3. *Weekly Pinal Drill*, July 9, 1881.
4. *The Arizona Silver Belt*, July 30, 1892.
5. *The Daily Arizona Silver Belt*, February 20, 1910.
6. *The Tombstone Epitaph*, June 19, 1892.
7. *The Weekly Orb*, April 10, 1898.
8. *The Arizona Daily Orb*, October 23, 1899.
9. *Sports Illustrated*, September 17, 1956.
10. David F. Myrick, *Railroads of Arizona: Volume 1: The Southern Roads* (Berkeley, CA: Howell-North Books, 1975), 22.
11. Ibid.
12. Myrick, *Railroads of Arizona*, 24.
13. *The Arizona Daily Citizen*, September 13, 1899.
14. Ibid.
15. *Arizona Daily Citizen*, October 7, 1889.
16. *Arizona Daily Citizen*, October 15, 1889.
17. Roy P. Drachman, *This Is Not a Book: Just Memories* (R.P. Drachman, 1979), 29.
18. *The Tucson Citizen*, July 13, 1907.
19. *The Tucson Citizen*, September 3, 1907.
20. Drachman, *This Is Not a Book*, 30.
21. *Arizona Sentinel*, March 9, 1889.
22. *Arizona Sentinel*, January 26, 1889.
23. *Arizona Sentinel*, July 4, 1906.
24. *Arizona Weekly Champion*, May 30, 1885.

25. *Ibid.*
26. *Arizona Weekly Champion*, July 30, 1887.
27. *Arizona Weekly Champion*, August 27, 1887.
28. *Mohave County Miner*, October 1, 1887.
29. *Ibid.*
30. *Arizona Republican*, September 3, 1900.
31. *Tempe Daily News*, July 20, 1900.
32. *Tombstone Daily Epitaph*, August 20, 1889.
33. *Arizona Republican*, October 24, 1901.

Chapter 6

1. William J. Ryczek, *When Johnny Came Sliding Home: The Post-Civil War Baseball Boom, 1865–1870* (Jefferson, NC: McFarland, 1998).
2. *Arizona Daily Citizen*, January 6, 1880.
3. *Albuquerque Morning Democrat*, September 27, 1887.
4. *Arizona Daily Citizen*, October 14, 1887.
5. *Daily Alta California*, November 28, 1887.
6. *Arizona Republican*, November 15, 1895.
7. *Arizona Republican*, November 20, 1895.
8. *Arizona Republican*, November 23, 1895.
9. *Tucson Citizen*, October 13, 1905.
10. *Tucson Citizen*, October 16, 1905.
11. Roy P. Drachman, *This Is Not a Book: Just Memories* (R.P. Drachman, 1979).
12. *Arizona Daily Citizen*, August 19, 1889.
13. Glenn Burgess, and William Ryder Ridgeway, *Mount Graham Profiles: Volume 2, Rider-Ridgeway Collection* (Safford, AZ: Graham County Historical Society, 1988), 2.
14. *The Washington Post*, January 2, 1909.
15. *Bisbee Daily Review*, February 26, 1908.
16. *Arizona Daily Star*, March 27, 1909.
17. *The Tucson Citizen*, April 1, 1909.
18. *The Arizona Daily Star*, April 1, 1909.
19. *The Arizona Republican*, April 1, 1909.
20. *The Arizona Republican*, March 29, 1910.
21. *Daily Arizona Silver Belt*, March 30, 1910.
22. *The Arizona Republican*, March 30, 1910.
23. *Ibid.*
24. *Yuma Morning Sun*, March 26, 1911.
25. *Daily Boston Globe*, March 28, 1911.
26. Bill Nowlin, *The Great Red Sox Spring Training Tour of 1911: Sixty Three Games, Coast to Coast* (Jefferson, NC: McFarland, 2010).
27. *Boston Post*, March 28, 1911.
28. *Yuma Daily Sun*, March 28, 1911.

Bibliography

Books and Periodicals

Army and Navy Journal 11, no. 19 (December 20, 1873).
Burgess, Glenn, ed. *Mount Graham Profiles, Vol. 2.* Rider-Ridgway Collection. Graham County, AZ: Graham County Historical Society, 1988.
Carmony, Neil, ed. *Whiskey, Six-Guns and Red Light Ladies: George Hand's Saloon Diary, Tucson 1875–1878.* Silver City, NM: High-Lonesome Books, 1994.
Drachman, Roy P. *This Is Not a Book: Just Memories.* Tucson, AZ: self-published, 1979.
Kirsch, George. "Bats, Balls, and Bullets." *Civil War Times Illustrated* 37, no. 2 (May 1998).
McChristian, Douglas C. *Fort Bowie, Arizona: Combat Post of the Southwest, 1858–1894.* Norman: University of Oklahoma Press, 2012.
Mills, Dorothy Seymour, and Harold Seymour. *Baseball: The People's Game.* New York: Oxford University Press, 1990.
Myrick, David F. *The Southern Roads.* Vol. 1, *Railroads of Arizona.* Berkeley, CA: Howell-North Books, 1975.
Nemec, David. *The Great Encyclopedia of 19th Century Major League Baseball.* New York: Donald I. Fine, 1997.
Nowlin, Bill. *The Great Red Sox Spring Training Tour of 1911: Sixty-Three Games, Coast to Coast.* Jefferson, NC: McFarland, 2010.
Reidhead, S.J., ed. *A Church for Helldorado.* Roswell, NM: Jinglebob Press, 2006.
Ryczek, William J. *When Johnny Came Sliding Home: The Post–Civil War Baseball Boom, 1865–1870.* Jefferson, NC: McFarland, 1998.
Sports Illustrated, September 17, 1956.

Archival Sources

Evy Alexander, letter to her mother, November 2, 1868, page 2. Alexander Family Letters. Arizona Historical Foundation, Tempe, Arizona.
Katherine Bagg Hastings journal, Hastings Family Papers: 1882–1887. Arizona Historical Society, Tucson, Arizona.

Newspapers

Arizona

Arizona Daily Citizen (Tucson)
Arizona Daily Orb (Bisbee)

Arizona Daily Star (Tucson)
Arizona Democrat (Prescott)
Arizona Gazette (Phoenix)
Arizona Journal-Miner (Prescott)
Arizona Republican (Phoenix)
Arizona Silver Belt (Globe)
Arizona Weekly Champion (Flagstaff)
Arizona Weekly Gazette (Phoenix)
Arizona Weekly Herald (Phoenix)
Arizona Weekly Star (Tucson)
Bisbee Daily Review
Bisbee Weekly Orb
Mesa Free Press
Mojave County Miner (Kingman)
Nogales Oasis
Phoenix Herald
Phoenix Weekly Herald
Salt River Herald (Phoenix)
Tempe Daily News
Tempe Weekly News
Tombstone
Tombstone Daily Nugget
Tombstone Epitaph
Tombstone Prospector
Weekly Arizona Miner (Prescott)
Weekly Arizona Republican (Phoenix)
Weekly Pinal Drill (Pinal City)
Weekly Tombstone Epitaph
Yuma Arizona Sentinel
Yuma Daily Sun
Yuma Morning Sun

Other States

Albuquerque (NM) *Morning Democrat*
Boston Post
Bridgeport (CT) *Banner*
Daily Alta California (San Francisco, CA)
Daily Boston Globe
New York Clipper
Washington Post

Index

Adams, J.C. (Hotelier) 96; see also Territorial Fair Grounds
The African American Experience in Tempe 111; see also Tempe Crimson Rims Base Ball Club
Agricultural Park (Phoenix, Arizona) 93
Albuquerque, New Mexico 62, 78, 88–90, 155, 157, 160
Albuquerque (New Mexico) Browns Base Ball Club 88
Albuquerque Morning Democrat (Albuquerque, New Mexico) 155
American Association, Cincinnati, Ohio 34, 100–101
Arizona Apaches Base Ball Club (Phoenix, Arizona) 111
Arizona Citizen (Tucson, Arizona) 16, 56–57, 64, 85
Arizona Daily Orb (Bisbee, Arizona) 136–137
Arizona Daily Star (Tucson, Arizona) 32, 59–61, 70, 103, 162–164, 173
Arizona Democrat (Prescott, Arizona) 52, 85
Arizona Gazette (Phoenix, Arizona) 17, 74–76, 89–90
Arizona Journal Miner (Prescott, Arizona) 11, 14, 49–50, 91
Arizona Miner (Prescott, Arizona) 11–12, 15, 18–19, 36, 73, 85–87, 90
Arizona Republican (Phoenix, Arizona) 34–36, 68–69, 77–80, 93–94, 104–108, 110–114, 119–121, 151–152, 157, 164–165, 167, 171, 175
Arizona Sentinel (Yuma, Arizona) 15, 52–54, 103, 123, 141, 146–147, 162, 171
Arizona Silver Belt (Globe, Arizona) 28–31, 36, 52, 129–131
Arizona Weekly Herald (Phoenix, Arizona) 20–21
Arizona Weekly Miner (Prescott, Arizona) 37, 39, 48, 50–52, 86, 89

Arizona Weekly Star (Tucson, Arizona) 17, 24, 56–57, 59, 62, 101, 171

barbers 107–108, 111, 131; see also Stearns, R.S.
Bare Knuckle Prize Fight 138, 145
Baseball: The People's Game 29
Benson, Arizona 68, 85, 117, 137, 155
Bernal, Augustin C. 109; see also True Blues (Phoenix)
Bernal, Gus 145; see also boxing
betting 59, 72, 89, 149, 173
bicycles 76–77, 88, 109–113, 166
Bisbee, Arizona 21, 26–27, 32, 85, 98, 117, 12–125, 132–138, 152, 159, 161, 165, 169, 171–172
Bisbee Base Ball Club 26, 133
Bisbee Daily Review (Bisbee, Arizona) 27, 122–124, 161
Bisbee Weekly Orb (Bisbee, Arizona) 135
Bisbee Youngsters Base Ball Club 134
Border Vidette (Nogales, Arizona) 28
Boston Bloomer Girls 117–119, 123–124, 158
Boston Globe (Boston, Massachusetts) 47, 167
Boston Mill (Tombstone, Arizona) 82, 129
Boston Post (Boston, Massachusetts) 168
Boston Red Caps 43–45, 47–48, 51
Boston Red Sox 154, 167–169; see also Boston Red Caps; Boston Red Stockings
Boston Red Stockings 39, 42, 52, 154, 173
boxing 70, 103, 138; see also Bare Knuckle Prize Fight
Bradley, Foghorn 44–45
Brown, Lew 44–45
Buehman, Henry (frontier photographer) 65

Calumet & Arizona Mining Company (Bisbee, Arizona) 134
Camp Goodwin, Arizona 31

Index

Camp Grant, Arizona 11–12; *see also* Fort Grant, Arizona
Camp Hualpai, Arizona 11–14, 17, 38
Camp Lowell, Arizona 16–17, *see also* Fort Lowell, Arizona
Camp San Carlos, Arizona 28–30, 129
Camp Verde, Arizona 18, 41 *see also* Fort Verde, Arizona
Cananea, Sonora, Mexico 27, 131, 138–139, 144–146; *see also* Gandil, Arthur "Chick"
Carr, Edward P. 112–114
Carrillo's Garden, Tucson, Arizona 64, 68, 70; *see also* Elysian Grove (Tucson, Arizona); Levin's Park (Tucson, Arizona)
Carroll, Fred 156
Central Hotel (Phoenix, Arizona) 93
Chaffee Base Ball Club (Fort McDowell, Arizona) 19–20
Champion Base Ball Club (Prescott, Arizona) 14, 37–40, 42–43, 49–51, 85, 154
cheating 89–91, 98, 104
Chicago White Sox 138, 154, 161–167, 174–175; *see also* Gandil, Arthur "Chick"
Christmas 20–21, 5–57, 73, 117, 126–127
Cicotte, Eddie 169
Citizen Base Ball Club (Tucson) 57–58, 125
Clifton, Arizona 158–160
Coconino Weekly Sun (Flagstaff, Arizona) 36
color line 115, 174; *see also* segregation
Colorado River 15, 36, 49, 56, 139–140, 162
Comiskey, Charles 158–159, 161–162; *see also* Chicago White Sox
Congress Mining Company (Congress, Arizona) 110, 117, 129
Copper King Mining Company (Bisbee, Arizona) 134
Copper Kings Base Ball Club (Bisbee, Arizona) 134–135
Copper Nine Base Ball Club (Bisbee, Arizona) 134
Copper Queen Mining Company (Bisbee, Arizona) 123, 134–137
Cracker Jack Base Ball Club (Phoenix, Arizona) 107
C.T. Rogers & Co. (Prescott, Arizona) 41, 47
curveball (use of) 33, 65, 67, 69, 78, 87, 106
Cyclones Base Ball Club (Phoenix, Arizona) 107–108

Daily Alta California (San Francisco, California) 12, 76
Decoration Day 26, 97
DeMund, C.E. (proprietor) 151–152
DeMund Lumber Company (Phoenix, Arizona) 151–152
Demund's Base Ball Club (Phoenix, Arizona) 107, 109–110, 114–116, 151
disease outbreak 31, 76, 115
Doling's Park, Tombstone, Arizona 62, 82–83
Don Luis, Arizona 122, 134–136; *see also* Bisbee, Arizona; Warren Ballpark (Warren, Arizona)
Douglas, Arizona 138, 161, 169
Drachman, Emmanuel "Manny" 32–33, 64–67, 69–70, 78, 106, 144–146, 158–159, 161
Drachman, Mose 65–66, 69
Drachman, Samuel H. 65

Earnest, C.A. (post trader, Yuma, Arizona) 15–16, 54
East Lake Park (Phoenix, Arizona) 34–35, 69, 79–80, 96, 108, 152, 158; *see also* Agricultural Park (Phoenix, Arizona); Patton's Park (Phoenix, Arizona)
8th Infantry, United States Army 19
El Paso, Texas 56, 67–68, 70, 78, 88, 111, 117, 130, 138, 140, 143, 158, 161–162, 165, 168–169
Elks Day 122
Elysian Grove (Tucson, Arizona) 64, 70, 117, 145, 158–159, 162, 164; *see also* Carrillo's Garden (Tucson, Arizona; Levin's Park (Tucson, Arizona)
enclosed ball park 82, 88, 97
Erwin, Lt. James Brailsford 24

Fashion Barber Shop (Phoenix, Arizona) 107–108
5th Cavalry, United States Army 11–12, 14, 19, 27–28, 169
fire 31, 59, 61, 76, 173
firemen 151–152
fireworks 78, 148–149, 162; *see also* Fourth of July
fist fight 32, 61, 64, 83, 134, 137–138, 146
Flagstaff, Arizona 36, 49, 88, 125, 138, 148–152, 155, 172
Flagstaff Base Ball Club 149, 151, 155
flood 31, 66, 96, 130, 162, 173
foreign substance 91; *see also* cheating
Fort Bowie, Arizona 14, 31, 36, 130
Fort Grant, Arizona 12–14, 19, 21, 23, 78–79, 135; *see also* Camp Grant, Arizona
Fort Huachuca, Arizona 21–28, 83–85, 90, 104, 133–134
Fort Lowell, Arizona 16–17, 23–24, 56–57, 63, 65–67, 74, 76
Fort McDowell, Arizona 18–21, 59, 70–71, 76, 173
Fort Thomas, Arizona 31–35, 106
Fort Verde, Arizona 14, 17–18, 75, 87
Fort Verde Excelsiors 17–18; *see also* The Verde Nine
Fort Whipple, Arizona 11, 13–14, 17, 35,

37–39, 41, 50–51, 79, 85–89, 91, 121, 154, 172
Fort Whipple Reds Base Ball Club 91
Fort Yuma, California 15–16, 54, 56, 141, 147
4th Cavalry, United States Army 22–25, 76
Fourth of July 26, 56, 65, 68, 77–78, 88, 97, 128, 133, 144, 147–149, 172
Fowler, John W. "Bud" 100
Frisch, Harry (business owner) 115; *see also* color line; segregation

Gandil, Arthur "Chick" 138–139, 165, 167; *see also* Cananea (Sonora, Mexico); Chicago White Sox; Humbolt Arizona
Gandolfo Hotel (Yuma, Arizona) 167
Gem City, Arizona 113; *see also* Mesa, Arizona
Gila River 16, 31, 147
Glendale, Arizona 80, 102, 104, 114
Glendale Base Ball Club 80, 104
Globe, Arizona 28–32, 50, 125, 129–134, 137, 152, 159
Globe Athletic Club 131
Globe Base Ball Club 28–32, 129
Goldberg, Dave 78–79, 93–96, 127
Grand Central Mining Company (Tombstone, Arizona) 129
Grand Hotel (Pinal City, Arizona) 126–127
Graveyard Kids Base Ball Club (Tombstone, Arizona) 134
Gray, Lee 78, 95–96, 106
The Great Red Sox Spring Training Tour of 1911 167

Hand, George O. (Frontier Diarist) 56–57
Harmon, Robert Green "Hickory Bob" 160, 169
Hastings, Katherine Bagg (Tombstone, Arizona, pioneer) 84
Herdic Coach Company (Tucson, Arizona) 60
Herdic coaches 59–60
hidden ball trick 67, 69
Hoover, Sgt. Ward C.R. 27–28
Hotel Heidel (Tucson, Arizona) 163–164
hotels 61, 105, 110, 157; *see also* color line
Hughes, L.C. (territorial governor) 70
Humboldt, Arizona 138; *see also* Gandil, Arthur "Chick"

ice cream 102, 149; *see also* Fourth of July
Independent Base Ball Club (Camp Hualpai, Prescott, Arizona) 11

Kingman, Arizona 148, 150, 152
Kingman Base Ball Club 150
knuckleball 114; *see also* curveball, use of

Lemon Hotel (Phoenix, Arizona) 78, 104
Leonard, Andy 44, 46

Levin's Park, Tucson, Arizona 63, 66; *see also* Carrillo's Garden (Tucson, Arizona); Elysian Grove (Tucson, Arizona)
Lewis, Bob 59, 83
Lewis, George Edward "Duffy" 167, 169
Lightfoot Base Ball Club (Fort McDowell, Arizona) 19
Lone Star Base Ball Club (Tucson) 17, 56

Manning, Jack 44, 46
Maricopa Rail Road (Phoenix, Arizona) 34, 75, 92
McGintler, Jerry (Tucson, Arizona) 63, 142–143
Merrimacers (Tombstone) Base Ball Club 81
Mesa, Arizona 72, 78, 96–97, 101, 105–106, 110, 112–113, 115–116, 120, 167, 169, 172
Mesa City Base Ball Club (Mesa, Arizona) 72
Mesa Diamond Club (Mesa, Arizona) 112, 115; *see also* Mesa City Base Ball Club
Mesa Free Press (Mesa, Arizona) 120
Meyers, John Tortes "Chief" 160, 169
Miami, Arizona 125, 131–132
Military Plaza (Tucson, Arizona) 57, 59, 63, 66, 102, 142–143
Mohawk Plungers Base Ball Club (Yuma, Arizona) 55, 146
Morenci, Arizona 135–137, 159–161
Morrill, "Honest" John 44, 47, 49
Murnane, Timothy (sports journalist) 44, 46–47, 49, 167–168

Naco, Arizona 137
National League (New York City, New York) 23, 34, 42–46, 49, 99–101, 145, 154, 156–157, 159, 167, 173, 175
Nelson, Maud 119–120; *see also* Boston Bloomer Girls
Neversink Base Ball Club (Fort Bowie, Arizona) 14
New Year's Day 19, 58–59, 80
New York Giants 9, 45, 92, 154, 165, 170
Nogales, Arizona 84–85
Norvall Base Ball Club (Fort McDowell, Arizona) 20–21, 71–73
Nowlin, Bill 167
The Oasis (Nogales, Arizona) 28

Old Dominion Copper Company (Globe, Arizona) 129–131
Old Pueblo (Tucson, Arizona) 17, 56–60, 62, 71, 74, 92, 126, 141, 145, 162, 169
Opera House 31, 53, 97, 122, 163, 165
O'Rourke, Jim "Orator" 44–45, 47

Palace Hotel (Tucson, Arizona) 60
Parsons, George Whitwell (frontier diarist) 23, 83

Index

Patton's Park, Phoenix, Arizona 77–79, 93–94, 96, 105–106; *see also* Agricultural Park; East Lake Park (Phoenix, Arizona); Phoenix Arizona
Pauly, Sgt. Emil H. 22
Peabody, Rev. Endicott 81
Pearce, Arizona 144
Phoenix, Arizona 9, 17, 19–21, 26, 32–35, 51–53, 55, 58–59, 63–64, 67–80, 89–91, 93, 95–98, 101–102, 104–105, 107–121, 125, 128, 136, 141, 151–152, 156–159, 161–162, 164–166, 171, 173–175
Phoenix Baptist Church (Phoenix, Arizona) 121
Phoenix Base Ball Club 19–21, 58, 67, 71–75, 78–79, 89–93, 95, 104–106, 108, 110, 128, 155, 166
Phoenix Herald (Phoenix, Arizona) 19–20, 52, 59, 71–72, 74–75, 85, 87, 102, 128
Phoenix Indian School (Phoenix, Arizona) 79, 111, 113–114
Phoenix Railway System 166; *see also* Valley Street Railway Company
Phoenix Weekly Herald (Phoenix, Arizona) 72, 86
Picket Post, Arizona 74, 126, 128
Picket Post Base Ball Club 126; *see also* Pinal Base Ball Club
Pinal Base Ball Club (Pinal City, Arizona) 127–128
Pinal Drill (Pinal City, Arizona) 52, 126–128
Pinney & Robinson (Phoenix, Arizona, sporting goods retailer) 110; *see also* sporting goods
Pioneer (Tombstone) Base Ball Club 134
Prescott, Arizona 11, 14, 17–19, 36–39, 41–44, 48–52, 56, 72–73, 75, 78–79, 85–91, 109, 115, 119, 121, 125, 148–150, 154, 157, 172–173

Red Shirts Base Ball Club (Yuma, Arizona) 15–16, 54
Rhodes, John P. (frontier photographer) 77–78
Rice, George S. 81
ringers (hiring of) 84, 91, 98; *see also* cheating
Rough Riders Base Ball Club (Phoenix, Arizona) 79–80, 104; *see also* Phoenix Base Ball Club

St. David, Arizona 151
St. Louis Browns 155–156
Salt River Herald (Phoenix, Arizona) 52, 70–71, 102
Salt River Valley Championship 112, 116, 151
Santa Fe Rail Road (Chicago, Illinois) 49, 97, 154
2nd Cavalry, United States Army 25–26, 31, 105

segregation 101, 115
Seymour, Harold 29
Shafer, Harry 44–46
Shamrock Base Ball Club (Fort McDowell, Arizona) 19
Sigala, Chris Cresencio 34, 116–17
Silver King, Arizona 75, 126, 128, 130
Silver King Base Ball Club 126–127
6th Cavalry, United States Army 16–17, 20–21
Smith, Jared 111
Solomonville Athletics Base Ball Club 131–132
Southern Pacific Rail Road (San Francisco, California) 31, 49, 65, 97, 111, 130, 140, 142–144, 146–147, 154, 156, 162
sporting goods 11, 23, 110, 171, 174
Star Base Ball Club (Tucson, Arizona) 57–58, 126
Star Cup 57–59, 125, 173
Stearns, R.S. (Phoenix, Arizona) 107–108
Sumner Base Ball Club (Fort Grant, Arizona) 14
Syracuse Bicycle Company (Syracuse, New York) 112

Tempe, Arizona 34, 68–69, 78–79, 96, 98, 101, 105–107, 109–117, 124, 151–152, 157, 167, 172, 174
Tempe Bicycle Store (Tempe, Arizona) 109, 112
Tempe Crimson Rims Base Ball Club 34, 105, 107, 109–117, 151–152, 174
Tempe Daily News (Tempe, Arizona) 105, 109–110, 112–116, 151
Tempe O.K.'s Base Ball Club 72
Tempe Weekly News (Tempe, Arizona) 109; *see also Tempe Daily News*
Territorial Championship 14, 17, 32–33, 35, 38–39, 51–52, 62, 67, 76, 82, 85, 90, 96, 96
Territorial Fair (Phoenix, Arizona) 89–97
Territorial Fair Association (Phoenix, Arizona) 90–91, 96
Territorial Fair Grounds (Phoenix, Arizona) 21
Thanksgiving 13–14, 56–57, 85, 96
Thayer, Ezra W. (Phoenix, Arizona, sporting goods retailer) 174; *see also* sporting goods
theatre 50, 101–102, 143
Thomas, Eugene 109, 111
Thomas, Maggie 111
Thomas, Theodore 111
Tombstone, Arizona 23–27, 36, 52, 59–68, 76, 80–85, 88, 90–93, 97–98, 104–105, 117, 129, 133–134, 151–152, 155, 171, 173
Tombstone Base Ball Club 62, 65, 80–84, 90–92, 151
Tombstone Baseball Association (Tomb-

Index

stone, Arizona) 81; *see also* Peabody, Rev. Endicott; Rice, George S.
Tombstone Epitaph (Tombstone, Arizona) 24, 36, 52, 80, 85, 133, 172
Tombstone Nugget (Tombstone, Arizona) 61
Tombstone Prospector (Tombstone, Arizona) 68, 104, 134
Tombstone Reds Base Ball Club 129
True Blues Base Ball Club (Phoenix, Arizona) 107–109, 111–113, 115–116
Tucson, Arizona 16–17, 21, 23–24, 26, 32–34, 50, 56–71, 73–76, 78, 80–82, 84, 88, 91–98, 101–106, 110, 117, 121, 125–126, 130, 136, 138, 141–146, 152, 155–159, 161–165, 169, 171–175
Tucson Base Ball Club 32–33, 58–71, 74, 78, 81, 92–94, 96, 143–145
Tucson Citizen (Tucson, Arizona) 59, 126, 145, 158, 164
12th Infantry, United States Army 15–17, 20
24th Infantry, United States Army 25, 104, 133

Union Stars Base Ball Club (Phoenix, Arizona) 107

Valley Street Railway Company (Phoenix, Arizona) 93
Verde Nine(Camp Verde, Arizona) 18, 86–87; *see also* Fort Verde Excelsiors

wagering 33, 35–36, 54, 60–61, 71, 84–85, 88, 106, 108, 129, 135, 151, 154–155; *see also* betting
Walker, Moses "Fleetwood" 100–101
Warren Ballpark, Warren, Arizona 165; *see also* Bisbee, Arizona
West Prescott 18, 86–87
Whipple Base Ball Club (Fort Whipple, Arizona) 14, 17, 37–42, 56, 87
Williams, Arizona 49, 78, 88, 115, 148, 151
Williscraft, W.H. (frontier photographer) 41, 43, 47, 50
Winslow, Arizona 78, 115, 148–152, 155, 172
Winslow Base Ball Club 148–149, 151
Women's Christian Temperance Union (WCTU) 121, 123
Worth Base Ball Club (Fort Lowell, Arizona) 15, 156

Young Americas Base Ball Club (Phoenix, Arizona) 72
Yuma, Arizona 15–16, 49, 52–56, 91–92, 103, 123, 125, 139–141, 146–148, 156, 161–169, 171, 173
Yuma Morning Sun (Yuma, Arizona) 167, 169

Zabriskie, B.J. 33, 64, 66–67, 93–95
Zabriskie, Walter 32–33, 63, 66–67, 93–94, 96
Zeckendorf, Louis (Tucson, Arizona) 63

www.ingramcontent.com/pod-product-compliance
Ingram Content Group UK Ltd.
Pitfield, Milton Keynes, MK11 3LW, UK
UKHW042012140426
5217IPUK00015B/1125